THE GOOD WAR'S
Greatest Hits

THE GOOD WAR'S

Greatest Hits

WORLD WAR II AND
AMERICAN REMEMBERING
BY PHILIP D. BEIDLER

The University of Georgia Press Athens & London

© 1998 by the
University of Georgia Press
Athens, Georgia 30602
All rights reserved
Designed by Richard Hendel
Set in Electra and Eagle types
by G & S Typesetters, Inc.
Printed and bound by Maple-Vail
The paper in this book meets the
guidelines for permanence and durability
of the Committee on Production Guidelines
for Book Longevity of the Council on
Library Resources.
Printed in the United States of America
02 01 00 99 98 C 5 4 3 2 1

Library of Congress
Cataloging in Publication Data

Beidler, Philip D.
The Good War's greatest hits : World War II
and American remembering / by Philip D.
Beidler.
p.   cm.
Includes bibliographical references (p.) and
index.
ISBN 0-8203-2001-3 (alk. paper)
1. World War, 1939–1945—Psychological
aspects.   2. World War, 1939–1945—Motion
pictures and the war.   3. World War, 1939–
1945—Literature and the war.   4. World
War, 1939–1945—Propaganda.   I. Title.
D744.55.B45   1998
791.43'658—dc21   97-51434

British Library Cataloging in
Publication Data available

To the Generation of the War

CONTENTS

Preface, ix

Acknowledgments, xi

1 The Good War's Greatest Hits, 1

2 Making a Production Out of It, 8

3 Big War, Big Book, Big Movie, 86

4 The Good War and the Great SNAFU, 150

Notes, 173

Bibliography, 209

Index, 215

PREFACE

Early readers of this study, while allowing that I had found a subject, also agreed that I was trying to write more than one book. They were correct. What I want to do here is honor their recognition of an implicit design with an avowal of explicit purpose. In the main narrative of *The Good War's Greatest Hits*, I write for an audience with a general interest in cultural myth. In the notes, mainly, I try to augment that narrative for readers with more specialized interests; and even here, I do not mean academic specialists, necessarily, but perhaps an audience interested at various points in fuller elaboration of theoretical issues or more detailed technical analysis. In all this, I hope I do not imply classes of readership so much as styles of readerly participation. I simply wanted to keep the main narrative free of certain kinds of in-depth reference and investigation that a general readership might find tedious and/or interruptive. Some of the notes are bibliographic; some are explanatory; some are argumentative to the degree that a certain interpretation of affairs is being advanced. As to overall argument, I do not propose some unitary cultural-studies thesis about the relationship between ideology and representation. As one reader suggested, it might have been nice to have come up with a marketing blurb about "how DeWitt Wallace, Henry Luce, and the Department of Defense rewon World War II." (Even then, I would have added Broadway, Hollywood, NBC, RCA, and the Book-of-the-Month Club.) But the conspiracy theory is just not there. The matter of the Good War's Greatest Hits and American Remembering must be allowed to work out its own complexities and indeterminacies as another peculiarly American case study, albeit a large and interesting one, in what Paul Fussell has called the curious reciprocity of art and life.

ACKNOWLEDGMENTS

I gratefully acknowledge the help of the following people: Garry Beidler, Malcolm Call, Kelly Caudle, Mary Corliss, Salli Davis, Dwight Eddins, Katherine Eddins, Marylou Gjernes, Ellen Harris, Gloria Jones, Brian Keene, Kristine Krueger, Karal Ann Marling, David Parker, Diane Roberts, Lawrence Suid, Gary Taylor, Bill Ulmer, Jack Weiser, Bob Willoughby, Ricky Yanaura, and Jim Yarbrough. Illustration credits are noted in the text. Acknowledgment is also due the editors of the *Journal of American Studies, Prospects,* and *Virginia Quarterly Review,* for publishing early portions of this book; the University of Alabama Academic Affairs Office for a research leave enabling me to write a first draft; and the staff of the Amelia Gayle Gorgas Library for countless instances of their unfailing helpfulness and courtesy.

Most of all, I would like to express my appreciation to Ellen Eddins Beidler and our daughter, Katherine.

THE GOOD WAR'S
Greatest Hits

CHAPTER I
THE GOOD WAR'S
GREATEST HITS

ost Americans who remember the Second World War think of themselves as agreeing with Studs Terkel. World War II, they say, without the hint of ambiguity supplied by Terkel's own quotation marks, was the Good War. Hitler and the Nazis were palpable evil, with revelations about the death camps and atrocities committed against conquered peoples serving as dread confirmation. In fact, even before the Germans declared war against the United States, they were already considered so malign that once they had turned to attack their quondam ally, the Soviet Union, even that dreaded totalitarian regime could be welcomed into the anti-Axis fold as brave, beleaguered Mother Russia. Around the Mediterranean and in Africa, the Fascist Italy of Hitler's confrere Mussolini was as bad as a bad joke with a big army and navy could be. Across the Pacific the Japanese, joining in Axis partnership, crowned their bloody adventurism in China with the villainy of Pearl Harbor. By the time the United States officially entered the war, the perceived malevolence of the enemy left no room for compromise in the American conviction about the goodness of the cause; and current opinion suggests that time has done little to convince anyone that this conviction was in error.[1]

To be sure, from 1945 onward various historical and literary interpreters have arrived at far less generous positions concerning the fundamental rightness of Allied goals and operational conduct. Indeed, at their most extreme some of them now counterclaim that World War II may have been any number of things besides the Good War. Geopolitically, they say, it was but a continuation of the old greeds and mendacities of World War I, further extended, especially in Africa and Asia, into ongoing colonialist power-mongering and robbery—and with all of it further allowed to fester through global economic depression into new ideological imperialisms.[2] And operationally, they now assert in markedly increasing numbers, it should be thought of as something like *Catch*-22 squared, the war they really ought to have called the Great SNAFU.[3]

Still, such attempts at historical critique have done little to change general American attitudes. The legend of the Good War has not only persisted, fostered by wartime propaganda and reinforced in the aftermath of victory, but has proven remarkably flexible in its capacity both to resist specific historical challenge and to restyle its more general mythological configurings so as to serve the needs of a series of changing social and geopolitical contexts. It has weathered out the immediate post-1945 Russian establishment of Iron-Curtain Europe and the ensuing Cold War; the 1948 Berlin Blockade; the 1949 "loss" of China and the bloody anti-Communist police action that resulted in Korea; late '40s and early '50s episodes of domestic political paranoia and fears of a global nuclear holocaust; '60s upheavals, including the civil rights struggle, the Vietnam War, assassinations of major public figures, and successive eruptions of domestic unrest; and ultimate '70s post-Vietnam and post-Watergate disillusionments and retrenchments. Indeed, especially after Reagan- and Bush-era neoconservative revisionisms of national myth, and now in the more recent wake of countless fiftieth-anniversary commemorations and retrospections, one finds the legend of the Good War, if anything, resolutely solidified, with *perdurable* perhaps the better word. With the end of the Cold War, the fall of the Iron Curtain, the vanishing of the Soviet menace, the normalization of trade and diplomatic relations with Communist Vietnam and China; with Germany reunited and Japan an economic powerhouse, in both cases still keeping militarism under stringent controls: at least a version of the dream of 1945 somehow, magically, really has seemed to come true. Half a century later, *everything* really has been somehow accommodated to the terms of the great victory; or perhaps the terms of ac-commodation at least have now made it possible to think that. Whatever the logic of history or memory, somehow World War II has shaken off all the challenges along the way and really has proven itself to have been what we have been calling it all along, "The Good War" — maybe, even, in Michael Adams's adroitly sardonic formulation, "The Best War Ever." To be sure, abroad there has been genocidal slaughter in the Balkans and in Africa. The former Soviet Union undergoes savage internecine fragmen-tation. The Middle East bloodily lurches toward an Israeli-Palestinian peace settlement. Continuing blows against Iraqi militarism seem to have little effect on a powerful dictator's aggressive designs on the region and its crucial oil resources. At home cities reel under the strain of poverty, vio-lence, drugs, and racial and class hatreds. American small towns and farms wither and die in the shadow of exurban malls and high-rise business cen-ters. A resurgent right attempts to dismantle the New Deal welfare state. An increasingly discredited liberalism threatens to vanish amid the hub-bub of a welter of often conflicting special-interest claims upon its own or-thodoxies. The judicial system collapses under the weight of caseloads and celebrity murder trials. But the glow of 1945 persists as a kind of beacon, a moment in which Americans' attitudes toward themselves and their rela-tion to the world at least once seem to have been filled with a clarity and purpose — and perhaps even more important, a generosity of purpose — no longer available, and exactly for all those reasons so worthy therefore of attempting to locate and possibly recapture.

My purpose here is to show how such attitudes were set in place, in the decades after the war, and continue even now to be perpetuated and rein-forced by a set of remarkably complex *and* durable popular-culture repre-sentations of the war. They are works frequently candid — in retrospect, even surprisingly so — about the war's hardships and follies; yet at the same time, they also keep faith with its truly heightened sense of collective moral enterprise. These productions, properties, cultural commodities — as they might be variously described — I have elected to call here "The Good War's Greatest Hits." What I specifically mean to identify is a set of postwar depictions of the conflict — in print, film, photography, and musi-cal recording, as well as on the stage and, eventually, in the emergent medium of television — that came to serve for the generation of the war and their immediate inheritors as a collocation of core texts, a canon, perhaps even a curriculum. They are works, I will propose, that, through their com-plex reifying and commodifying of wartime myth into popular-culture images of history and memory, would become enshrined themselves as forms of history and memory.

The titles of these texts are familiar, many of them perhaps even tiresomely so. They include *The Best Years of Our Lives, Mister Roberts, South Pacific, Sands of Iwo Jima, Life's Picture History of World War II,* and *Victory at Sea; The Naked and the Dead, The Young Lions, From Here to Eternity, The Caine Mutiny,* and *Battle Cry; The Longest Day* and *Catch-22.* On the other hand, as I have intentionally suggested by a simple listing, it is exactly in the titles themselves that we find the various and complicated ideas of "information," "entertainment," "production," and "commodification"[4] taking on their most concrete cultural relevance. To put it directly, what do I mean by a title? Do I mean in a particular instance the book, the play, the movie, or some composite notion of these? In another, do I mean a Broadway show or a long-playing record? A musical score or a TV presentation? A tape, a compact disc, or a videocassette? If I mean a book or a play, do I mean the original one or the one most people assume to be the original? A popular original or perhaps a lesser-known source? If a book, do I mean the hardbound or the paperback? If a play, do I mean the stage or the print version? If I claim to speak of the best-known or most popular version, to what set of production circumstances or contexts of reception do I refer? By *The Naked and the Dead,* for instance, do I mean a controversial, bestselling 1948 novel that propelled Norman Mailer to instant literary celebrity, or a garishly popular 1958 war movie starring Cliff Robertson, Aldo Ray, and Lily St. Cyr? By *Victory at Sea* do I mean a landmark thirteen-hour, twenty-six-part 1953 television documentary? The ubiquitous rebroadcasts of the installments as a series of syndicated half-hour programs? A 1954 theater film? A coffee-table book? A musical score? A series of popular long-playing records? A multivolume set of video recordings? By *Mister Roberts* do I mean a collection of stories by Thomas Heggen or a Broadway play and Hollywood movie, both of which led to permanent identification of Henry Fonda with the title role? By *The Caine Mutiny* do I mean a bestselling novel by Herman Wouk or a classic 1954 movie featuring Humphrey Bogart as Captain Queeg and José Ferrer as the lawyer Barney Greenwald? Or do I mean a Broadway play entitled *The Caine Mutiny Court-Martial* featuring Lloyd Nolan as Queeg and Henry Fonda as Greenwald? By *Catch-22* do I mean a 1961 novel by Joseph Heller that eventually achieved cult status among the literati or a widely publicized 1969 film starring Alan Arkin as Yossarian? And if the latter, what does one make of the fact that Major Major Major Major is played by the comedian Bob Newhart when one of the novel's great absurd jokes is that character's bewildering resemblance to Henry Fonda?

And then, to complicate matters further, there is that other phrase: American remembering. I choose a gerund intentionally, wishing to define an old American habit of remembering as an ongoing process, something that mediates between what we might call (very approximately) history — what happened — and memory — how it is retrospectively constructed in a certain cultural moment.[5] But mainly I do so to put a grammatically specific signature on what might be understood as triumph of that fluid, ad hoc, peculiarly American operationalism that, from the earliest days of the Republic, has frequently attempted to redefine not only the relationship between history and memory but often what we actually mean in a given moment by history or memory.

At the same time, I do not mean to imply that we have ever attempted to reject as strenuously as has been claimed the idea of a "past" conjoining history and memory in the forms of what is loosely called in most cultures tradition. In fact, if anything, by virtue of the knowledge of our being created as a nation by political-linguistic fiat, we have been from the outset the most history-hungry and memory-hungry of all peoples for a usable past. From the outset we have continued to define and redefine ourselves by the instituting of instant "traditions," the forming of innumerable "heritage" commissions, the garnishing of ubiquitous "attractions" and "sites." We are fuller than any Swiss canton of costume pageants and festivals. We consume historical fiction, film, and television with unbridled appetite. With regard to our military past, especially, on battlefields and at other historic sites across the nation we have become nearly obsessive weekend participants in the perverse ritual we call "reenactment."

Still, in our own century at least, as concerns the geopolitical implications of some properly meditated sense of relationship between history and memory, such is hardly our chief reputation. Rather, if anything here, we have been most often simultaneously accused, by ourselves and others, of being in the deep cultural habit of denying the very existence of history, or at the very least of clinging to a myth of historical exceptionalism that somehow makes us exempt from having to remember it, its mistakes, its lessons, its great geopolitical risings and fallings. That is, in terms of geopolitical policy at least, we have often continued to exercise forms of remembering by selectively alternating between history and memory and have frequently accorded them honored status at the expense of the very idea of "tradition" as itself possessed of ideological content. In both respects we have been relentlessly good at revising memory as to make things "history" — as in, well, yes, but that's history. "Redeemer nation," we have called ourselves, "the city on a hill." As the Vietnam War made clear, "amnesiac nation" would frequently have done as well.

My claim here is that American remembering so defined found itself abetted from 1945 onward by a new set of circumstances of production that the war had helped to put in place. Now the old habit of instant ideological invention had evolved its own industrial base in the fullest sense of that term: history and memory had finally intersected with commodity on a scale commensurate with the long national love affair with creative self-mythologizing. A vast set of wartime technologies of popular-culture representation would find themselves enlisted in one last victory drive; and the product would be the image of victory itself as an ongoing technology of remembering.

Never mind, of course, as to cultural particulars of class, race, ethnicity, and gender, that such postwar mythologizing would relentlessly construct itself with a host of old wartime avoidances and sanitizations in place. There would be virtually no black Americans represented, save accidentally, and then only in the menial roles to which they were actually confined for the most part in wartime: ammunition handlers blown to smithereens in *Tales of the South Pacific* or the mess boys aboard the USS *Caine*. In novels and films one might find the occasional Native American and Hispanic, along with the other members of the melting-pot platoon: the Irishman, the Pole, the Italian, the WASP intellectual, and nearly always somebody from Brooklyn. Jewish-American characters depicted at any length would be a function largely of the novels, with four of the five major postwar classics written by Jewish veterans. The Holocaust, however, is barely mentioned, with the exception of the lawyer Barney Greenwald's concluding philippic to the acquitted mutineers of the *Caine*. Brutal military anti-Semitism, on the other hand, is emphasized in *The Young Lions* in the plot sections involving Noah Ackerman, one of the three major characters. To a lesser degree, it is also at least suggested in the depiction of the Jewish boxer, Bloom, in *From Here to Eternity*, and in such marginalized Jews as Roth and Goldstein in *The Naked and the Dead*.

At the same time, as will be seen, one finds a form of curious heroic compensation by Wouk and Uris. For Wouk, the lawyer Barney Greenwald becomes a truly heroic Jewish figure in the novel, a decorated Marine aviator and the text's moral interlocutor, amid all the WASP and would-be intellectuals. For Uris, the Jewish hero is the wisecracking, unbelievably daring, combat-happy Two Gun Shapiro.

Women for the most part figure in interwoven romantic relationships or play other supporting roles. As will be seen, the relatively strong and independent female characters played by Myrna Loy and Teresa Wright in *The Best Years of Our Lives* — ironically, the first of the great postwar classics — do connect visibly with the images of empowered women in films of the '30s and the war years. But subsequent texts would generally come to image the retrograde state of affairs described by Betty Friedan in *The Feminine Mystique*, as women returned to more traditional roles as wives, mothers, and homemakers. Especially in the "love and war" genre, sexual typecasting of female characters became a given.

To be sure, on various cultural fronts an awareness of domestic inequities and mendacities would quickly catch up with the demoralizations of postwar geopolitical realities in the minds of Americans trying to hold on to the hopeful assumptions and attitudes of 1945. "Victory Culture," as recorded by Tom Engelhardt and others, enjoyed a kind of starburst evanescence from the outset. Its death would begin early and then go on to be painful and lingering.[6] But for nearly a quarter century at least, the Good War's greatest hits could help with the long denial. To use an appropriately industrial-strength figure, it was as if a massive wartime information and entertainment apparatus, finding itself no longer shackled by military restriction on either account, were allowed to recommit itself to one last great production achievement of war industry; and that achievement would be, of course, the ongoing production of the war itself.

CHAPTER 2
MAKING A PRODUCTION
OUT OF IT

rom the moment of official U.S. entry into World War II until final victory slightly less than four years later, making a production out of the American experience of the conflict as information *and* entertainment became a crucial component of war manufacture. All of the media of popular-culture representation — books, plays, movies, newspapers, and magazines; photographs and newsreels; posters, cartoons, illustrations, and advertisements; radio programs and phonograph records — were enlisted for the duration. Indeed, the wartime information and entertainmment industry became so integral to American attitudes and understandings at home and abroad that by the time of victory in 1945, short of actual combat or direct involvement of a family member, it could be said that such productions came to constitute for most Americans the primary dimension of their experience of the war.

This was obviously true for Americans on the home front. At the same time, however, one could also count within such a popular-culture constituency the relatively large proportion of American forces overseas not engaged in actual combat and spending their war chiefly in areas with ready access to most of these media. For these, too, such popular representations in much the same way constituted their experience of the war as well. Further, this could even be presumed to some degree of many combat-theater participants — sailors aboard ships, for instance, or airmen operating out of established bases, or army and marine ground forces pulled out of action to rear areas for rest and refitting. In fact, given the ubiquitousness of stateside information and entertainment productions, the incongruity of popular-media representations of the war with the actual conditions experienced by front-line consumers became for the latter a constant subject of humorous commentary. See, for instance, the classic Bill Mauldin cartoon of miserable, exhausted, rain-sodden German POWs being herded along by equally miserable, exhausted, and rain-sodden GIs. The caption is a newspaper quote, presumably garnered from the latest mail: "Fresh, spirited American troops, flushed with victory, are bringing in thousands of hungry, ragged, battle-weary prisoners" (Mauldin 21).[1]

To be sure, during the war years proper, popular-media representations of the conflict constituted almost without exception a very particular way of making a production out of it: a set of representations constituting a carefully defined political or ideological construction of experience as regards the shaping of attitudes and understandings. We might call it re-membering in wartime. A more common and serviceable term, of course, for all the sinister overtones it has generally come to carry, would be propaganda. Propaganda: one makes the customary associations of insignias, armbands, banners, posters; marches, rallies, speeches, slogans, communiqués; censored media; silenced opposition; total information control. Here, centralized powers of control over popular-culture media were quickly vested in an agency called the Office of War Information; and it did its job with a thoroughness and dispatch — not to mention a ready acquiescence of the information and entertainment industries themselves — that a post-Vietnam or post-Watergate society might continue to find unsettling in the extreme.[2] Certainly Americans were spared the mind-numbing indoctrination undergone by citizens of the great totalitarian states and various other conquered peoples. From first to last, it could be truly said that the nation endured the war with virtually no change in the basic configurations of the popular media we would now classify as the arts, information, and entertainment. But in every case, unprecedented central-government control became the order of the day: in newspaper, magazine, and radio reporting; film and photojournalism; visual art and advertising; and popular books, plays, and movies. Remembering in wartime became a function of propaganda as official policy at every level of operation.

The linkage had already begun to be made, of course, in quasi-official ways a good deal earlier. With few exceptions,[3] major American newspapers and magazines charted with alarm and a growing sense of interventionist urgency the early stages of the Fascist nightmare in Europe: the Spanish Civil War; formation of the Rome–Berlin Axis; Mussolini's conquest of Ethiopia. Likewise graphically chronicled were Hitler's ensuing moves in the Rhineland, the Sudetenland, Austria, and Czechoslovakia — albeit with such accounts frequently paralleled by stark views of Communist totalitarianism, including coverage of purges and show trials at home and Stalinist machinations among fellow dictators abroad. Meanwhile, Japanese barbarisms and predations in China were similarly reported in horrific detail in newsprint, magazine journalism, and film.[4]

Indeed, as events mounted from 1939 into 1940 and early 1941, it must have seemed to Americans, as yet officially uninvolved, that there was little else in the world besides war news — the defeat of the Spanish Loyalists by Franco; the German occupation of Czechoslovakia; the Italian invasion of Albania, the Russian attack on Finland, the continuing Japanese depradations in China; the German-Soviet nonaggression pact, the German blitzkrieg against Poland, followed by German-Russian partition; the declaration of war by Britain and France; German occupations of Denmark, Norway, Romania, Hungary, Yugoslavia, Greece; after new lightning war in the West, the fall of most of the remaining continent — Belgium, Holland, Luxembourg, France; submarine warfare in the Atlantic; desert campaigns in North Africa; the stunning German invasion of Russia; the actual possibility of a linkup of Axis forces in the Middle East and possibly across the great land bridge of Asia.

To augment the daily and weekly bad news, on bookstore shelves they also found topical volumes, of course: William Shirer's *Berlin Diary*, Jean Vautin's *Out of the Night*, and Alice Duer Miller's *The White Cliffs of Dover* all spent time on the best-seller lists. Theatergoers likewise bought tickets for Lillian Hellman's *Watch on the Rhine* and Robert Sherwood's *There Shall Be No Night*. In Hollywood, Charlie Chaplin and Jack Oakie made merry, if menacing, slapstick out of Hitler and Mussolini in *The Great Dictator*. Even in something so seemingly fanciful as the 1939 *Wizard of Oz*, a careful observer could catch the allegory of Axis totalitarianism and aggression: the chanting, goose-stepping, jack-booted myrmidons of the witch's castle were Nazis, if for the moment with their greatcoats and astrakhan hats keeping open movie options on the Soviets; the simian hordes darkening the skies, on the other hand, looked exactly as they were supposed to, flying monkeys gleefully intent on Jap-like rape and pillage.

On the other hand, as a kind of counterpoise to the constant deluge of disastrous war information issuing forth from newspapers, magazines, and radio, less news-anchored media, such as popular books, plays, and movies, also tried their best to offer some breathing distance; and Americans in general reciprocated by continuing to express Depression-era preferences for social uplift and escapism. As late as 1939, bestselling books included, for instance, John Steinbeck's *The Grapes of Wrath*, Marjorie Kinnan Rawlings's *The Yearling*, and Christopher Morley's *Kitty Foyle*;[5] popular plays included such mainly diverting fare as *Life with Father, The Philadelphia Story, The Man Who Came to Dinner*, and *DuBarry Was a Lady*. Hollywood enjoyed a banner entertainment year: in addition to *The Wizard of Oz*, viewers flocked to the long-awaited movie version of *Gone with the Wind* and other classics of screen romance including *Wuthering Heights, Dark Victory*, and *Intermezzo*. For sentimental humor, they preferred *Good-bye, Mr. Chips* and *Mr. Smith Goes to Washington*.

After the United States entered belligerent status, active propaganda production quickly began with the early wartime masterpiece *Casablanca*, based on an obscure, unproduced play entitled *Everyone Comes to Rick's*, rushed into production after Pearl Harbor, and given its debut in eerie congruence with actual events of Allied landings in North Africa. As such, it came to stand for the frequently composite, ad hoc genius of popular-culture invention at work in the propaganda enterprise, becoming the first in an avalanche of industrial-strength wartime classics.[6] And like *Casablanca* and its signature song, "As Time Goes By," many others of these would become familiar parts of the national mythology. Book titles included Marion Hargrove's *See Here, Private Hargrove*, William S. White's *They Were Expendable*, Ted Lawson's *Thirty Seconds over Tokyo*, Richard Tregaskis's *Guadalcanal Diary*, Bill Mauldin's *Up Front*, and Ernie Pyle's *Brave Men* and *Here Is Your War* — nearly all becoming the basis of equally well known movies; and lavishly staged musical reviews with uplifting military themes such as *This Is the Army* and *Winged Victory* likewise made the transition to film. Stirring combat movies included *Wake Island, Flying Tigers, In Which We Serve, Air Force, Five Graves to Cairo, So Proudly We Hail, Marine Raiders, Bataan, Bombardier, Objective Burma, Destination Tokyo*, and *The Purple Heart*. Analogous home-front depictions were typified by *Stage Door Canteen* and *Since You Went Away.* Even the USO got two freestanding films, *Follow the Boys* and *Four Jills in a Jeep.*

Important documentaries included the *Why We Fight* series and real-life productions commissioned from major directors — Leland Heyward's *Marines on Tarawa;* John Ford's *The Battle of Midway;* John Huston's *Report from the Aleutians* and *The Battle of San Pietro;* William Wyler's *Memphis Belle;* and Louis de Rochemont's *The Fighting Lady.*

Predictably, standard wartime stylizations predominated across the board. The good Chinese depicted, for instance, in Hollywood versions of *Dragon Seed* or *The Keys of the Kingdom,* were filtered out of already idealized depictions by Pearl S. Buck and A. J. Cronin into easy identification with the brave Chinese of Chiang Kai-shek by way of Henry Luce. The dark night of Europe under occupation likewise found its own style of cinematic melodrama in such stirring titles as *Commandos Strike at Dawn, Hangmen Also Die, Assignment in Brittany, Passage to Marseilles, The Pied Piper, Desperate Journey, The Cross of Lorraine.* (One more, *The Moon Is Down,* became the most controversial of the lot because of its depiction, as in the original John Steinbeck novel, of the Nazi occupiers in a Norwegian village as humanly troubled by their harsh duties.) Plucky, indomitable England showed up in *Mrs. Miniver, This Above All,* and *The White Cliffs of Dover.* And the Soviet contribution received due notice in *Days of Glory, Song of Russia, The North Star,* and *Mission to Moscow.*

The movie enemy likewise proved gratifyingly predictable: favored impersonations of villainous Japs included those of Richard Loo, Sen Yung, and Philip Ahn — all of them, as it turned out, Chinese- or Korean-American; Nazi counterparts included Eric Von Stroheim, Raymond Massey, Helmut Dantine, Conrad Veidt, Cedric Hardwicke, Martin Kosleck, and Peter Lorre.

To be sure, across the spectrum of popular-culture genre and mode, the worth of plenty of wartime production was measured by escape value. In romantic fiction Kathleen Winsor's *Forever Amber,* one of the great bodice-rippers of all time, was joined on best-seller lists by *The Captain from Castille* and *The Black Rose.* Similarly popular were novels of religious inspiration like *The Robe* and *Song of Bernadette.* The bestselling single book of the whole war turned out to be Wendell Willkie's utopian paean to a multiculturalist future, *One World.*

On the stage, after an early decline in theatergoing, Broadway returned to form with *The Skin of Our Teeth, One Touch of Venus, Harvey, Ten Little Indians, The Late George Apley,* and *I Remember Mama.* And Hollywood, rising brilliantly to the challenge, produced equally varied entertainment fare, including a remarkable number of enduring films that would have been classics of any era: *Woman of the Year, Random Harvest, The Pride of the Yankees, Holiday Inn, Yankee Doodle Dandy, The Road to Morocco, For Whom the Bell Tolls, The Human Comedy, Song of Bernadette, My Friend Flicka, Gaslight, Jane Eyre, Double Indemnity, National Velvet, Going My Way, Meet Me in St. Louis, The Corn Is Green, Laura, Saratoga Trunk, State Fair, The Bells of St. Mary's, A Song to Remember.*

Thus one makes a brief survey of remembering in wartime.[7] And thus one arrives at the essential model of the wartime information-entertainment classic that would in turn become the basis of the postwar genre of remembering called the Good War's greatest hits. Making a production out of it became truly corporate in the largest sense: in its complex intersections and distributions of creative genealogy and authority; and equally in its multiple configurings of genre and mode from across the full range of popular-culture media. Here was the commodification of the American role in World War II as at once felt experience and collective myth.[8] And it would be the same model — freed now of wartime information requirements *and* wartime material constraints — that would become the basis for channeling postwar creative commemoration through virtually unlimited production capabilities to the new task of shaping popular attitudes and understandings of the war for years, decades, even generations to come. Further, as the experience of the war itself receded, such would be the power of the model that it would continue to be formed as much in the relationship between audience and artifact as in any material actuality depicted. The product, that is, would increasingly become American remembering itself.

Making a production out of it in this new, postwar key began everywhere at full capacity as final victory was secured. With paper and binding materials now readily available in abundance, book publishing took off again, both in hardbound and in a newly flourishing paperback market; a reawakening of interest in the stage made Broadway the theater capital of the world. It became a venue for the work of postwar literary experimentalists; and it continued to produce distinguished comedy and new achievement in the American musical; movie production could return to spectacle, elaborate set construction, new color processing, casts of thousands. In the case of military subjects, frequently available now as well were large contributions of technical and material assistance from U.S. armed forces.

In this immediate post-1945 flourishing of popular-culture production, the first of the bona fide postwar classics turned out, not surprisingly, to be a Hollywood achievement, *The Best Years of Our Lives* — albeit in the form of an incongruously modest, understated, deeply human film partaking of wartime production values, achieving in the austerity of black and white its emphasis on romantic and family relationship.[9] Two more, *Mister Roberts* and *South Pacific*, grew out of two of the first popular books about the war to emerge in the immediate postwar era — both quickly produced, getting in ahead of the "big" novels that everyone assumed to be forthcoming, in the form of connected short stories, sketches, and humorous vignettes of the sort that had been so much a part of wartime journalism. In both literary cases here, however, the real avenue to popular-classic status came through the reawakening Broadway stage, now getting itself ready for one last great postwar, pre-TV flourishing as a popular-culture art form. And such success would in turn lead, as Hollywood likewise turned to face the new competition, to even more widely popular movie versions.

Two others came about as extensions of wartime documentary, in both cases essentially making new mileage out of existing, materially abundant media resources. The first, *Life's Picture History of World War II*, yoked a spare journalistic style of popular history to the boundless riches of wartime photojournalism. The second, of similar origin but far more creative in its approach to new media technologies and commercial venues, was *Victory at Sea*, which attempted to merge wartime film documentary with narration and an original musical score. Most important, it was devised from the beginning for the altogether new medium of network television.[10]

At the same time, trying to make mileage out of wartime models, Hollywood attempted its own classic reprise of the military guts-and-glory saga, with John Wayne starring in *Sands of Iwo Jima*. Yet here too, producers were at pains to piggyback the project onto a highly visible popular-culture iconography connecting the photograph of the 1945 Suribachi flag raising, surely the most famous journalistic image to come out of the war, with the much publicized erection at Arlington Cemetery of a massive statue reproducing the scene as the new Marine Corps memorial.

Meanwhile, one could also witness the conjunction of all these efforts, especially once postwar literary production got back into full stride, with the stream of major bestselling novels finally beginning to be produced by writers from the generation of the war; and the result would be a model sufficiently visible and influential, as will be shown in the second half of this book, to warrant discussion as a popular-culture genre in its own right.

Indeed a succession of classics, itself roughly equal in number to the texts described above, would be so produced: *The Naked and the Dead, The Young Lions, From Here to Eternity, The Caine Mutiny, Battle Cry*. And in turn, through a set of complex evolutions, a new production genealogy would emerge as the industry standard: big war, big book, big movie.[11]

Not that any of this, of course, would be unattended by ongoing changes both in the technologies of popular-culture production and in the demographics of consumption. In the model just discussed, for instance, the literary form would eventually be almost totally eclipsed by the cinematic; and the latter would in turn become more and more of an anachronism eventually struggling for *its* own life against such ascendant popular-culture media as television and videocassette recording. So, generally, print would be displaced by film; film would be replaced by television. With the demise of the great popular magazines and newspapers would come the relegation of classic reporting and photojournalism to collections and coffee-table volumes. So, too, would follow the arts of cartooning and illustration. A decline of film documentary would be accompanied by the extinction of newsreel. Live drama would become increasingly an isolated, esoteric pursuit, urban, intellectual, elite, enjoying but a short reprieve on television, which would quickly turn to more marketable materials. The Broadway musical would enjoy a postwar flourishing, temporarily boosted by advances in phonograph recording; and the advent of the long-playing record would provide an additional popular outlet for classic musical scores. But again, in drama as in fiction, film would shortly triumph, only to be eclipsed by television. And in popular recording, by the late '40s and early '50s, middle-of-the-road music such as show tunes and popular standards, many of them of wartime origin, would go the way of the victory ship and the B-25, displaced by rock and roll.

At the same time, in the face of such change, one of the hallmarks of the World War II classic would be its capacity to found much of its enduring appeal as a popular-culture genre in resistance to such change — or, to be more direct, in its audience-pleasing tendency to reproduce the presentational look and feel of wartime and immediate postwar genres. It would summon up, that is, the spirit of a time itself remembered as the era of the golden-age popular classic — of the literary bestseller, the Broadway hit, the big Hollywood movie, the film documentary, and the photojournalistic volume; and it would also avail itself of a broader nostalgia of media atmospherics. It would recall a music, for instance, that was still deeply a function of radio, stage, and film, not to mention of single-play wax recording and, as is often forgotten, of widely purchased sheet music. As important, it would also evoke the intensely visual dimension of World War II print information media — books, newspapers, and magazines — albeit in ways with which we are no longer familiar or even conversant. This was the last war, for instance, to generate major combat art and a large cartoon literature. It was also the last great poster war. Themselves in their heyday, prominent photographic magazines such as *Life* and *Look* were mainly pictorial with text confined to captions and narrative sidebars. More heavily print-oriented magazines such as the *Saturday Evening Post, Collier's, Time, Newsweek,* and *Reader's Digest* were still intensely visual in the same key. (The pictorial dimension of all of them was further accentuated by the omnipresence of wartime artwork connected with advertising.) And even such predominantly print magazines as the *New Yorker, Atlantic,* or *Saturday Review* interspersed text with both "serious" artwork — sketches and line-drawings, for instance — and humorous cartoons.[12]

All of this, to be sure, would eventually play itself out as part of a last great general-culture holding action. The big literary best-sellers, the hit plays, the classic movies, the standard songs, and the flagship magazines would all shortly go the way of the times. And soon to be gone as well would be all the other familiar hybridizations: the picture-history volume, for instance, and the romantic musical of stage and film; the classic documentary, part newsreel, part feature film, frequently attended by literary-quality text and professional narration; in books, newspapers, and magazines, the photojournalistic essay, combining photography or other visual illustration with artful caption and text.

Hastening the process was the new media giant on the scene: television. To be sure, it provided certain small avenues of assimilation. Film found a niche in the late-night and weekend movie; World War II combat drama had a few brief runs in the network series; the big novel eventually found new life in the made-for-TV miniepic; documentary survived in the multi-installment television history. Still, as will be seen, the general effect remained an abiding sense somehow of the unsuitability of the Big War for the small screen. Ironically, even the great exception, the classic World War II sitcom, such as *Hogan's Heroes* or *McHale's Navy,* seemed to achieve its prominence mainly because of a coincidental hospitality — as will be noted, even down to the formulaic titles — of the TV genre to the great anecdotally humorous representational products of the war — the cartoon, the comic strip, the service comedy, and other models of the genre that might be called humor in uniform. Further, even here, the marriage of the models itself partook of no great originality. Of the two best known TV classics, described above, the format of the first was stolen directly from *Stalag 17*, itself a classic postwar play and movie, and that of the second from the bizarre subgenre — running from *Francis the Talking Mule* through *Operation Petticoat* or *The Wackiest Ship in the Army* — one might call the funny war in the Pacific.

Even here, then, to put a historicist turn on the McLuhan commonplace, if the medium was the message, for the Good War's greatest hits the message would always remain integral to a unique collocation of wartime and immediate postwar production media as themselves dimensions of history and memory. As a cultural genre, the World War II classic would become the last of the Good War's great production efforts; and the secret of its production success would lie in large part in its reliance on forms of representation that themselves would continue to constitute the forms of remembering.

The Best Years of Our Lives

Fifty years after the making of the Samuel Goldwyn–William Wyler film *The Best Years of Our Lives*, it remains worthy of our remembering for its remarkably honest depiction of returning World War II veterans, and of the impact of their return on the veterans, their families, friends, and loved ones, and postwar society at large. In all these respects, it continues to strike us as an extraordinary production for its historical moment — risking its candor of cultural critique on Americans still proud of a unified national war effort and in the same moment already hearkening to the repressive overtures of the Cold War Right. Indeed, in the calm realism of the movie's concentration on problems likely to be encountered by a cross section of convincingly representative figures, one might contend that three major American wars and a number of overseas adventures later, we have yet to see its equal.

Moreover, intertwined with this story of the film's unusual success is also a production history perhaps as curious as any recorded for an American popular classic: a process that actually began, as will be more fully shown, with more than a year of bitter combat ahead for Americans, in the producer Samuel Goldwyn's enthusiastic reading of an August 1944 *Time* magazine article on returning veterans; and that concluded, just before the film's late 1946 release, with the titling of the as yet unnamed project by popular vote from a number of choices offered to test audiences. In between — to give but a sketch of events also more fully detailed below —

Goldwyn would commission the historical novelist McKinlay Kantor to write a film treatment based on the article. The assignment so conceived would result instead in *Glory for Me*, a novel in the form of a narrative poem. That strange artifact would then be converted into a screenplay by the prospective director, William Wyler, with the playwright and former Roosevelt advisor-speechwriter Robert Sherwood. In turn, with further changes by Goldwyn and others, it would be filmed by Wyler with an ensemble including Fredric March, Myrna Loy, Dana Andrews, Teresa Wright, Virginia Mayo, Hoagy Carmichael, and, in the role of a maimed veteran, a military amputee named Harold Russell. And after that, the rest would become, as they say, movie legend. The film in its first release would earn eight million dollars. It would receive a total of seven Academy Awards. Two of these would go to the nonactor Russell — the only time to date when a performer has been thus honored.

Attempting to assimilate this complicated set of cultural and commercial vectors, what follows is a history of that production, a particular act of remembering. As is invariably the case with the World War II popular classic, however, the real product ultimately at issue will be American remembering itself.

To begin with a number of converging accounts involving various principals in the project, the basic idea for *The Best Years of Our Lives* truly does seem to have originated as it is said: in a reading — suggested by his wife, some sources claim, during a quiet evening at home — by the immigrant-patriot Samuel Goldwyn of an article on the problems of returning combat veterans in Henry Luce's *Time* magazine. Featuring the piece as the lead item in its opening "U.S. at War" section, the issue can easily be identified as that of August 7, 1944 — although one also suspects Goldwyn's interest in a follow-up editor's column of the next week, elaborating various points in the previous story line.[13] On the other hand, if the *Time* report can be described as focusing on the transition of returning veterans back to what Vietnam successors would call, simply, "The World," it did so, especially in comparison with the figures depicted in the eventual movie, in an extremely limited way. To begin with, the veterans in question were not discharged servicemen but a trainload of furloughed members of the First Marine Division — veterans of bitter combat with commensurate homecoming anxieties, certainly, but still active-duty soldiers coming back only for thirty days of leave. Further, although the story detailed a nostalgic journey eastward across the continent, often describing stops in the small towns of America (including one where, as noted angrily by a sergeant, the price of a second beer quickly jumped from twenty-five cents to forty), the passengers aboard were all scheduled for East Coast destinations near Philadelphia and New York. And even among these, not one scene of homecoming with family, hometown friends, or loved ones was actually recorded. The single station-platform reunion shown, in fact, was that of a heroic lieutenant with his machine gunner.

What the text of the article does make poignantly clear about the veterans' feelings, nonetheless, is the degree to which they comprised a distinct mixture of joy and trepidation, with much emphasis on the latter. "I'm a little worried about how I'll look to them," reads a first, unattributed quote, "about how much I've changed" (15). To be sure, also recorded was some predictable chatter about ball games, free beers, first dates. One marine from Hartford, Connecticut, happily admitted that he had had no sleep on the last leg. "I just lay there all night grinning," he said (16). But on arrival in New York, most seemed to have had stomachs like that of "Lieut. Camille Tamucci, the tough guy in charge, who had been dreaming of mounds of spaghetti." "'It's all tied in knots,' he said" (16).

Alternatively one wonders if there may have been anything in the text, however, that struck Goldwyn nearly as movingly, given the filmmaker's visual imagination, as the accompanying photograph of a Pullman car with marines in new stateside khakis hanging out every available window. Most immediately notable there is the phrase "HOME AGAIN!!" chalked in large letters on the side of the car. Most indelible in impression, however, are the faces of the marines. To a man, they have a look of upbeat anticipation. Yet none of them is really grinning, or even visibly smiling. Perhaps they are just jaded with pulling into stations somewhere in the middle of America. More likely, they have simply settled down to being anxious, unable somehow to stop going to the windows in each new place, wondering how home will look to them, how much they have changed and how much home has changed. There, one sees already, the picture may have said it all.

Whatever the total effect of the article on Goldwyn, surely the idea of the visual artifact must have been deeply assumed *and* implied in his instructions to the writer McKinlay Kantor for a direct development from article to screen treatment in what was clearly identified from the outset as a film project. That is, after all — even if they are hiring writers at that stage to produce a print text — what moviemakers do. Moreover, in dealing with the popular historical novelist McKinlay Kantor, Goldwyn also must have assumed that Kantor, who had turned at least two of his own earlier works into successful film versions, had the screen-treatment idea in mind as well. And even if Kantor seems not to have been Goldwyn's real top choice for the project — those being Lillian Hellman, with whom, unfortunately, he was no longer speaking, or Sidney Howard, who had died — on the other hand, the producer also saw distinct positives in Kantor's background as a writer skilled in treating history and military life and also more recently experienced as an army air forces war correspondent.

Nonetheless, what Goldwyn shortly got from Kantor seemed so eccentric a text for his purposes that he gave up on it at once as unfilmable and prepared to write off the whole business as a bad $12,500 self-indulgence. For instead of a scenario or treatment, Kantor had given him a middlebrow verse epic in the vein of such popular classics as Stephen Vincent Benet's *John Brown's Body* and such venerable predecessors as Longfellow's *Song of Hiawatha. Glory for Me*, this one was called, with the source of its title noted in an epigraph from the devotional verse of one Charles H. Gabriel. And it, too, was poetry of a sort — to be precise, a book-length narrative centered on the homecoming of three discharged veterans. It is sometimes described as being in quasi-Shakespearean "blank verse." To be more accurate, it should be seen as a kind of homey conflation of verse modes — narrative, lyric, and dramatic — in an unrhymed iambic meter of varying line lengths, combining a formal stateliness with a vernacular flexibility.[14]

To give Kantor appropriate credit, his long poem does suggest the eventual movie not only in outline but also, at times quite movingly, in what might be called its essential spirit. The major characters are all there. In Kantor's version Al Stephenson, the middle-aged banker, has walked across Europe as an infantry sergeant so he can return to his wife, Milly, and his two nearly grown children. Lieutenant Fred Derry, the drugstore clerk of shabby origins, cast suddenly in the role of officer and having survived high-risk flying in the bombing campaigns of the Eighth Air Force against Germany, comes home to his contrastingly unfaithful spouse, a tawdry opportunist whom he has joined in a spur-of-the-moment wartime marriage and who has spent the duration (and most of Derry's pay allotments, apparently) in nonstop revelry. Homer Wermels, the navy enlisted man, torpedoed off Oran, returns a drooling, twitching spastic to his simple, hardworking middle-class family, and Wilma, the quiet girlfriend from next door. Similarly, the setting — called, as it will be in the movie, Boone City[15] — captures the quality of life in the midsized American metropolis, the state capital, the commercial center, yet on shaded streets and alleys, in bank lobbies, drugstores, and neighborhood bars, still a small town.

Likewise the plot, with a few small changes, will be transferred intact. Al will come back to banking only to grow quickly impatient with rules and regulations and find refuge in drink. Fred will get back his old drugstore job but lose it for quarreling with his officious supervisors. Homer will settle into a long encounter with his family's shock and uncomprehending pity. The three will have been united by chance in a bar on a spectacular drunk during their first night back. Then, with that scene as a focus, they will continue to pass in and out of one another's lives. Al, progressively unhappy with the balance-sheet coldness of banking, will note the growing attraction of his daughter Peggy to the already married Derry. The latter, facing divorce, fired from the drugstore job, and now desperate and unemployed, will make an abortive attempt at bank robbery, to be stopped short of the crime by Al's spontaneous intervention. Eventually at Homer's and Wilma's wedding, he will be reunited with Peggy after he has tried honorably to give her up. By then, Al will have quit the bank and invested in a garden and nursery business, where he will take Fred on as a partner and eventual son-in-law. At the end, all the principals are thus gathered in a momentary peace, though facing an uncertain future, a "sunset glare" where "the wild-west winds were galloping again" (268).

On the other hand, if the poem does suggest the combination of psychological insight and dramatic focus that will distinguish the film, one looks in vain at the print artifact for a lost classic. Indeed, not surprisingly, given the strangely hybrid nature of the medium, it winds up being — as Geoffrey Crayon describes Knickerbocker's *History* — not a bit better than it ought to be. In moments when thoughts or feelings are internalized by its carefully drawn characters, to be sure, it can strike a poignant lyricism. "Now, I will tell you all about the war," Al reflects, for instance. "It only has one sad consistency: / It's made of youth, it's made of boys" (113). By contrast, in others, where stylized narration jars against vernacular dialogue, for instance, or elaborate scene-setting lingers over homey atmospherics, it bespeaks all the trumperies of the popular genre in its long American provenance: melodrama, sentimentality, poetic "effect."

Reviews were split basically along these lines. Kantor was observed as joining a number of writers then responding to the war in ambitious forms of free verse. He was praised for a moving story told with craftsmanlike concentration. On the other hand, a newspaper review rightly described what must have been many readers' sense of overall effect. "Much of what perforce is termed 'free verse,'" observed the reviewer, "is merely rhetorical exhortation" combined with "a linear, broken-field, hardboiled prose."[16]

In any event, things might have ended there — with Kantor possessed of another moderately successful book and Goldwyn on to more promising possibilities, had not circumstances shortly intervened so as to bring in the other two most crucial figures in getting the project before the cameras. The first of these was the director William Wyler — himself just back from overseas service as a military filmmaker with the rank of lieutenant colonel — who had become available under prior contract, but with no particular assignment specified, as "owing" Goldwyn a film. The second was the Pulitzer Prize–winning dramatist Robert Sherwood — who also had spent a wartime hiatus from art in government, as a Roosevelt speechwriter and director of the Office of War Information — whom Goldwyn already had working for him on the treatment of a proposed film biography of Eisenhower.

On his part, Goldwyn acquainted Wyler with both the Eisenhower project and a comedy, eventually made with David Niven, Loretta Young, and Cary Grant, entitled *The Bishop's Wife*. In these the director showed no interest. As a fallback, presumably, Goldwyn next showed him the Kantor text, which by then had appeared independently in print as a January 1945 book. In this, by contrast, Wyler took immediate interest. Further, he also enlisted Sherwood, with whom he would have been scheduled to work had he accepted the Eisenhower assignment. By August or September the two began work on a script which would lead to a completed film within a year.[17]

What, we might ask, made Wyler see a script in Goldwyn's unfilmable Kantor property and, presumably, persuade Sherwood to that view as well? As detailed by Wyler and his biographers, immediate answers lay in the director's own recent experience of the war as a veteran of combat-zone moviemaking. To begin with the obvious, he surely knew the air war — he had made two acclaimed documentaries about it, *Thunderbolt* and *Memphis Belle*. He had also come home totally deaf in one ear as a result, and thus with a certain understanding of disability. But most important was his sense of having come back to a postwar America as changed somehow as he was changed. Wyler put it succinctly. "The war was an escape to reality," he said. "The only thing that mattered were human relationships; not money, not position, not even family." He went on: "Only relationships with people who might be dead tomorrow were important. It is a sort of wonderful state of mind. It's too bad it takes a war to create such a condition among men" (Madsen 258). Homecoming, in turn, put the perceptual twist so described into even fuller relief. As a result, for both himself and Sherwood, the film waiting in Kantor's book, he suggested, nearly created itself. "The picture was the result of social forces at work when the war ended," he said. "In a sense, it was written by events and imposed a responsibility on us to be true to these events and refrain from distorting them to our own ends" (Madsen 257–58).

Rewriting was careful. Sherwood, for instance, was dissuaded from enlarging the film's view of veterans' problems to include a housing riot, which Goldwyn insisted would be too Hollywood-like a mob scene in a film he wanted to keep "simple and believable" (Epstein 152). The latter also cannily adjusted the triangle relationship involving Fred Derry, his faithless wife, Marie, and the smitten Peggy Stephenson by making Derry's recognition of his wife's extramarital activities gradual as opposed to instant. For thereby was induced a sexual *and* moral tension into Fred's awareness of his growing attraction to Peggy that is mirrored in the reactions of the young woman and her parents, Al and Milly, to her interest in a still married man. Perhaps the most important change, however, was the refiguring of the disabled character, Homer Wermels, into the movie's Homer Parrish. Wyler especially feared that the spasticity resulting from his injuries, described in terrible detail in the book, might prove inadvertently humorous in the visual dimension. Parrish was made an amputee instead. And thereby was made possible, as described more fully below, the casting of Harold Russell in a role still celebrated for its candid and sensitive depiction of physical handicap, prosthesis, and related problems of social and psychological adjustment.

One other major alteration proved a happy combination of intent and chance. Wyler, while working on the project, had come upon an airplane graveyard in Ontario, California, just outside Los Angeles, filled with endless rows of castoff war machines, and he had determined instantly that he would somehow find a way to use it as a setting in the film (Epstein 263). The opportunity presented itself in allowing a way out of the book's retirement of Al Stephenson from his increasingly loathsome banking responsibilities to start a garden and nursery business *and* his eventual enlistment of Fred, after the latter's aborted attempt at bank robbery, as partner. Instead, the film allowed a celebrated flashback sequence involving the unemployed Derry sitting in a gutted cockpit, a used-up navigator reliving it all in a field of used-up bombers and fighters. This in turn leads to a confrontation with a yard manager who eventually helps him get a job on his construction crew, engaged in salvaging materials for the erection of new homes.

Some other changes that may have seemed smaller in detail made large differences in totality of effect. Al Stephenson, described in the book as having served in Europe as an infantry sergeant, kept his branch and rank but was given the combat patch of the Twenty-fifth "Tropic Lightning" Division, well known for its island campaigning in the Pacific. This distributed more representatively the experiences of the three veterans, with Fred representing the Air Corps in Europe, Homer the far-flung navy, and Al the island war against the Japanese. (They have also been described as distributing class relationships into upper [Al], middle [Homer], and lower [Fred]. This is accurate as a description neither of classes nor of the characters' positionings. Al is decidedly upper-middle. Homer could be best described as simple, hard-working, lower-middle. Fred just comes from a broken home.) Most important, it is also the memory of the savage Pacific war that puts the heart into Al's drunken reflections at his black-tie welcome-home dinner about the cost exacted on return upon those who have often borne the battle abroad. Once it was "kill Japs," as he has said elsewhere. Now it's "make money." Now, he tells his horrified audience, when there is a hill to be taken or a wound to be bandaged, there is always time for a discussion first about collateral.

One other significant change from book to film was an enlarging of the Milly part as a way of attracting Myrna Loy to it. That succeeded, but it also posed problems with Teresa Wright's playing her daughter, because Wright was obviously not a generation younger. Yet even now if these remain apparent to the viewer, they are more than compensated by Loy's capturing of Milly's full, mature, distinctly sexual beauty. A single early scene, taken down a long hallway, truly says it all. There she stands: gazing for the first time upon her returned soldier-husband, the banker who has come home an old, hardbitten infantry sergeant — the vibrant, sustaining, faithful wife who has been waiting for him, looking as magnificent as only Myrna Loy in those days could have looked, saying in a surprised whisper, "I look awful."

Casting was accomplished somewhat in reverse. The first player hired was the nonactor, Russell, whom Wyler and Sherwood, while visiting veterans' hospitals in search of a candidate, remembered from a short army film in which the serviceman — actually an airborne sergeant who had lost his hands in a dynamite explosion during training — demonstrated the proficiency he had acquired in using mechanical hooks. Next came Dana Andrews as Fred Derry and Fredric March as Al Stephenson, with the latter persuaded to take the aging sergeant's role, it is said, after losing out to

William Powell for the lead in *Life with Father*. As for Loy, the only real trepidation she felt concerning the Milly role, it turned out, involved the director's legendarily heartless perfectionism. "I hear Wyler's a sadist," she told Goldwyn. Not comfortingly, he is said to have replied with a vintage Goldwynism. "That isn't true," said the producer; "he's just a very mean fellow."[18] Loy took the role anyway, having liked its possibilities even in the unexpanded version contained in a scenario she had seen. And the core ensemble was then joined by the rest of the final cast, most notably with Virginia Mayo as Fred Derry's estranged wife, Marie; Cathy O'Donnell as Wilma Cameron, Homer's fiancée; and Hoagy Carmichael as Butch Engle, the piano-playing saloon owner.

The result, as no one who looks at it again must be persuaded to see, is for any time and set of production circumstances a great movie, full of great scenes. Some have already been mentioned: the voices-over flashback sequence with Derry in the cockpit at the airplane graveyard; the moment of Al Stephenson's homecoming; his drunken speech at the welcome-home dinner. Others include the three veterans' bombardier's-eye first glimpse of their hometown; Al's interview with a decent, honest fellow veteran seeking a farm loan; Homer's first reunion with his parents and with Wilma; and later his smashing out the garage windows with his hooks in rage at his kid sister and other neighborhood children who have been spying on him.

Many of the film's most powerful scenes are also distinguished, within the constraints of the time, by an oddly omnipresent and pervasive sexual candor that often translates the peculiar *human* and *emotional* intensity of relationships between returning veterans and their families and loved ones. During the homecoming drunk shared by the three male principals, for instance, alone at last on the dance floor, Al, playing the lonely soldier, and Milly, playing the lonely wife, literally seduce each other. The next morning, after the Stephensons have dragged Fred home to spend the night, their daughter, Peggy, appears alone and supportively wifelike with him during a flashback-nightmare scene in the spare room. Meanwhile, in the master suite Al and Milly play out their return to old connubial rhythms in a dance of comedic gesture. Al finally awakens in bed in the throes of a blistering hangover to find Milly gone. Stumbling to the bathroom, he goes out one door as she sneakily comes in the other. Once there, he contemplates the face in the mirror. Matted curls stand up on either side of his forehead — they are, perhaps, lovelocks, a satyr's horns, the wreath of a returned Caesar, or maybe just Al's thinning hair. Silk pajamas now clothe the body we have seen only in uniform. When he falls gasping out of the shower stall, he is still wearing them.

But the riskiest bedroom scene in the film is yet to come. That will be one with Homer and Wilma, upstairs in his house, where she helps him remove his hooks and prepare for sleep. It has been carefully prepared for, to be sure, with a parallel one between Homer and his father when the latter has put him to bed drunk. Yet nothing can deflect its sexual power. Today we are likely to regard it as somewhere between kinky and macabre. In its context then, we continue to feel its physical immediacy and risk as a quiet affirmation of love.

As to classic film aesthetics, two other scenes have come invariably to be praised for what is deemed their innovative syntheses of dramatic design and advanced camera technique. The first is a famous one set in Butch Engle's bar, a reunion of the three male protagonists during which Fred, still struggling to break off with his wife, is persuaded to end an incipient romantic relationship with Peggy. The second is the film's final gathering of all the principals for Homer's and Wilma's wedding, at which Fred, at last free of his unhappy marriage, will be reunited with Peggy.

Although both scenes are frequently cited for similar forms of multiple focus technique, the first is most often commented on as a major innovation allowing the camera to deal, without conventional cutting and jumping, with a number of intersecting dramas and problems of character as discrete, yet keep them simultaneously within a coherent larger frame. Again the scene is Engle's Bar, owned by Homer's cousin Butch, site of the three protagonists' unexpected meeting on their drunken first night home; and now it becomes the place of reuniting all three for the first time after each has experienced major problems of return — and with two of them, moreover, Homer and Al, now beginning to have pronounced and visible problems with alcohol. As the scene opens, Al confronts Fred with his and Milly's displeasure over the developing likelihood of an illicit relationship between Fred and their daughter. Fred then retires to a phone booth in the rear to make a call in which he will break it off. Meanwhile, Homer enters the bar and draws Al, listening over his shoulder to the sound of Fred's nickel dropping in the phone, to the piano, where Homer and Butch, played by Hoagy Carmichael, show off proudly a series of popular duets on which Butch has taught Homer to play a kind of obbligato accompaniment with his hooks. Apace, the camera creates its own crucial moment: Fred sits in the background inside the phone booth, making the call, while Al, having moved toward the center of the scene, now leans forward trying to look interested in Butch's and Homer's foreground antics at the piano. Yet by virtue of "deep" rather than a conventional "shallow" focus, *both* major actions, foreground and background, continue to be seen simultaneously, with Al's dramatic and cinematic involvement providing a link between the two centers of interest, and at the same time obviating the need of conventional cutting back and forth between them. Or, as the French critic Andre Bazin has suggested, *everything* thus going on in the scene, the presence of three main characters, the development of two main centers of dramatic interest, seems somehow to be kept in focus at once, with the viewer "democratically" allowed to participate in the scene, and in fact actually asked to make a choice in a given moment about which part of the drama to concentrate on (Anderegg 141–42).

From a technical standpoint, the wedding scene, often comparably celebrated, follows basically the same plan. Again the three male protagonists come together, this time for a formal reunion; and this time further, as Michael Anderegg has written, they join each other no longer in their first "shared isolation" or that of the ensuing bar scenes and various incidental meetings, but now in "the context of a public, socially hopeful event." Now, in the homely precincts of the bride's parents' living room, amid contributed cakes and refreshments, family and neighbors wait nervously, as Homer is helped by Fred, his best man, and Al, the self-appointed punch checker, to fortify himself for the ceremony, which will include the giving of a ring. Meanwhile, in a tense exchange of non sequitur, Fred has also just met Peggy for the first time since their breakup. Soon the ceremony begins, and again, through deep focus technique, we quickly realize that while we are watching the official union at hand, we are also watching a second soon to be consummated. As part of the first, Homer, seemingly the only person in the gathering *not* painfully nervous about his ability to get through the ceremony, including the placing of the ring on Wilma's finger, carries everything off well. As part of the second, Fred and Peggy also, through eye contact and facial expression, carry out their corresponding drama of recognition and reconciliation which will crown the ceremony with their own final embrace. And the point is again, of course, that all the while we have not been looking at one or the other but at both, dual celebrations of love and faith for the film's two youthful couples occurring separately but with a happy and convincing dramatic *and* social simultaneity: a closing of the ranks of the tribe, so to speak; a getting beyond the pain and tumult of the past and a jittery present in commitment to the vision of a happier future.

Yet as far as placing camera technique in the moral dimension is concerned, there is also something that importantly separates the wedding scene from the bar scene and makes it especially memorable as a conclusion. And that something is a sense of human spontaneousness, almost a home-movie quality that cuts against the sophistication of the camera work that in many ways is trying to imitate it. For everyone involved, the effect is democratic familiarity, for actor and viewer alike now, the family event captured once and for all on family film. We see the last-minute preparations, people coming and going with treats and refreshments. We feel, in the close quarters of the small, modest parlor, with the bride about to come down the stairs, preceded by the kid sister, the nervousness, the jostle, the unfeigned petty worrying. For Homer and Wilma, we wonder the usual things: Will the bride and groom be scared? Will the best man have remembered the ring? Will the groom manage to get the ring from the best man and then get it on the bride's finger (the right finger? the right hand?) without dropping it? With everyone else now, we wonder all these things — and probably berate ourselves for being here so *obsessively* thus preoccupied because the groom's hands are prosthetic steel hooks. Meanwhile, for Fred and Peggy, we smart with their embarrassment at the dangle of small talk; and for Al and Milly we wonder if Al's joking about the serious responsibilities of testing the punch means that he is going to get drunk again. Then, afterward, we all feel the relief, the nervous joy of the group portrait, a family picture in every sense of the term. For them, for us, it is one we know somehow will always seem to say "the best years of our lives" in ways that we will always seem to understand, albeit perhaps without being quite able to explain.

From start to finish, the project had grown out of a disparate, if not downright serendipitous, collection of experiments and circumstances. The product, almost magically, as just described, was really something close to a people's picture. And even here, as we discuss cultural results, we must remain content simply to mention a host of other unusual but inspired production features — some large and others small, some individual matters of craft and others major issues of corporate risk — each oddly destined somehow to come together happily with all the others. To emphasize, for instance, the close-to-home domestic seriousness of the film's psychological concerns, it was shot in black and white; and to further the effect, all principals had been provided with ready-made clothing, which they were instructed to wear in advance of filming to give it an everyday, lived-in look (Epstein 154). (Meanwhile, not above hedging his bets, Goldwyn also allayed his unease over Hollywood gossip about possibly unfavorable audience response to the strong material by taking the then unprecedented step, before a frame had been shot, of engaging a marketing firm, the Audience Research Institute, to make sure Americans had not tired of the domestic problems involved in dealing with the returned veteran.) At the same time, despite the heavy emotional demands it might thus make upon an audience, it was also allowed to run extraordinarily long — twice as long, in fact, as most conventional films, with its more than two hours and forty minutes comparing only to *Gone with the Wind*. As noted earlier, test audiences actually selected by popular vote the title. And it was also the response of yet another set of trial viewers that led to its early release, in late 1946, after it had been officially slated for 1947. The success, however, of an East Coast preview prompted Goldwyn to rush it into a November release to compete for that year's Oscars (Epstein 153–55; Freedland 194).

As noted earlier, the rush was a good bet, with the payoff resulting in an unprecedented seven Oscars. As important, most reviews were also favorable *and* discerning, devoted to particular praise for directing and various individual performances and overall for the film's critical realism. (An oddly dissenting voice, on the other hand, was James Agee, who, with a kind of obsessive fascination, picked his way through various objections in a review extending over several weeks in his *Nation* column that wound up being favorable in spite of itself.) Indeed, if anything, as Ivan Butler has remarked, various aspects of the film ranging all the way from its production merits to its social relevance came in for so much laudatory attention that later response almost naturally mounted a reaction (Anderegg 143; Langman and Borg 80). And so it happened, with film criticism growing technically more self-conscious as film aesthetics became more experimentally sophisticated, that *The Best Years of Our Lives* took its predictable downslide as the artifact of what was simply *assumed* a less critical, more innocent time.

Now, fifty years and a number of American wars later, particularly in the aftermath of Vietnam, we have sat through waves of astringent depictions of the returned veteran — *The Deer Hunter, Coming Home, First Blood, In Country, Born on the Fourth of July* — invariably troubled albeit necessary exercises in national self-examination. Yet perhaps if we have learned through our difficult passage out of the Vietnam era that there actually is more than one kind of national experience of war, so perhaps we may now see that there is also more than one way to make a film that bravely confronts the problems of return, especially to an America once flushed with victory and not without reason deeming itself the geopolitical hope of a new order of history. To put this another way, even as we may newly measure the achievement of *The Best Years of Our Lives* in its political contexts now — and especially in its relation to comparable Vietnam films — we also need to remember the nature of its achievement in its particular political contexts then, the sense of critical difference provided exactly by the courage of its complex critical realism. Here, the title continues to say it all, itself a kind of ultimate Goldwynism — with the legendarily obtuse but sentimental immigrant characteristically having left the matter to test audiences in a democratic vote. ("I want every man, woman, and child in America to see this film," he is also said to have averred as to its promotion, "even if I don't make a cent" [Freedland 194]). In its strange quality of non sequitur, indeed, that title would always supply at once the signature and the gloss. Somehow the Americans of the generation of World War II — military participants and civilians alike — knew they had gone through an experience that had at once taken the best years of their lives and in some strange way also given the best years of their lives. Moreover, this strange ambiguity itself, they seemed to realize even at the time, would continue to configure their basic structure of remembering. Sometimes it had been the Good War; and sometimes it had been the Great SNAFU. By any assessment, it had been the right war, even a necessary war. And, like the mythical infantryman at the end of James Jones's *WWII*, looking back over his shoulder into the setting sun of history, the whole generation of the war could agree on one thing at least about this important and magnificent thing that had happened to them: "None of them would ever really get over it" (256).

At the same time, however, *it* was finally over; and now someone also had to show them honestly to themselves as they tried getting on with the rest of their lives as well. Appearing first among the great post-1945 production classics, *The Best Years of Our Lives* did that by candidly confronting a postwar present and future; but it did that best by bravely projecting these against a past already mythologizing itself into legend and — like the question Goldwyn seems to have read in the faces of those *Time* magazine marines — deeply in need of its own complex structures of critical remembering.

Mister Roberts

Although the idea may be hard for us to imagine fifty years later, especially given the historical weight of the subject, the first of the great postwar entertainment classics to come out of the American experience of World War II took shape initially as a set of comic short stories by Thomas Heggen about the backwater Pacific navy.[19] Gathered into a slim 1946 novel, they became the basis of a hit Broadway play of 1948; and that play in turn became the basis of an extraordinarily popular 1955 movie. The classic so described, of course, was *Mister Roberts*, with the titular hero eventually so thoroughly identified with the actor playing him on stage and screen that by the end of the decade in question, a *New York Times* reviewer would observe of the actor, Henry Fonda, "It now appears he *is* Mr. Roberts" (Weiler 14).

As with a host of other postwar classics to come, *Mister Roberts* thus becomes an early case study in which the forms and processes of cultural mythmaking find themselves simultaneously reified into a quintessentially American history of production. The particular production at hand will be a text and a cultural commodity called *Mister Roberts*. But the ultimate product, as is invariably the case with the World War II popular classic, will be American remembering itself.

Actually, if literary anecdote is to be believed, the history of the Henry Fonda business in *Mister Roberts* seems to have involved its own bizarre logic of resemblance from birth. Thomas Heggen, having achieved overnight success for his 1946 short novel, which centered on his wartime service aboard a navy cargo vessel assigned to Pacific support duty, had undertaken a first, failed attempt at dramatizing it with a college friend, Max Shulman. Then, shortly, he had been recruited by Leland Hayward to join Joshua Logan for a new attempt. This time, in marathon composition sessions conducted at Logan's country house in Connecticut, the book quickly began to take the familiar shape of the Broadway play. The stages by which this occurred, detailed by Logan in his memoirs, became a staple of entertainment legend. Among them, no single exchange must have proved as important as the one recorded by Logan about casting:

> Then Tom said, "Josh, I know it's crazy, but when I was writing *Roberts*, I was always thinking of Henry Fonda."
> "That's a terrible idea," I said. "I ought to know, because I've had the same terrible idea for a long time." (207)

Thus, both authorial figures attested to the degree to which the processes of creation, narrative *and* dramatic, seemed from the outset to have involved the identification of a character named Mr. Roberts with an actor named Henry Fonda. (To complicate matters further, by the time the conversation occurred the two may also have discussed parallels between the experiences and motives ascribed to the Mr. Roberts character and actual details, elaborated more fully below, of Fonda's own naval service — a series of attempts, in spite of the navy bureaucracy, to get into combat, culminating in his near-miss in a kamikaze incident like that which kills Roberts.)[20] Literary archetype and entertainment image seemed already to have been merged in seamless conflation.

Major features of evolution in the original narrative, as recorded by John Leggett, further suggest the degree to which the story found its hero through a kind of strange consensus politics of art — authorial, editorial, entrepreneurial — whereby an imaginary Roberts, as a projection of both private wish-fulfillment *and* collective imagings of popular desire, somehow inevitably emerged into congruence with the actual Fonda as the prototype of the wartime American.

Heggen, a young midwesterner, had found himself shortly after college a reserve naval officer serving aboard the attack transport USS *Virgo* (Leggett 282–83). There, serving in basically noncombat duties like those portrayed on the *Reluctant* of the novel, he found the culmination of the writing impulse he had sensed throughout his youth and early adulthood — in college journalism as a columnist, editorialist, and feature writer, and afterward in a short, unhappy stint at *Reader's Digest.* Like his contemporary James Jones, he had found his call to be a writer. And like Jones, in military service he also found his material. To be precise, on the *Virgo* he surely found the model for the tyrannical captain — Lieutenant Commander Herbert Ezra Randall, whom he referred to familiarly as "Old Stupid" (284–85). He had also found himself much in the role of the novel's Ensign Frank Pulver, with his own bunk copy of *God's Little Acre* (285), a seriously bad attitude, and a talent for petty insubordination. A first story, however, about home, Minnesota, college life, proved a false lead. As important, though, a quietly admired fellow officer to whom he showed it, Alfred Jones, had the courage to tell him so. Such writing was frivolous, Jones told Heggen, when his real subject was all around him.[21]

Accordingly, Heggen turned to a first story about an episode at Pearl Harbor, involving a binocular-cleaning detail of enlisted men and their

observation of shower activities at some new beachside nurses' quarters —
a project shortly dashed by a junior officer's inviting aboard ship one of the
subjects of surveillance, who is put wise by an argument she overhears
about the placement of a birthmark. It was entitled, simply, "The Nurse's
Story" (286). Then, after a return voyage to San Francisco, where the captain had capriciously not allowed liberty, he wrote a more pensive story entitled "Night Watch" (288). The officer of the deck in the story he named
for his friends Doug Whipple and Chuck Roberts: Lieutenant Doug
Roberts. Meanwhile, in reprisal for the San Francisco episode, Heggen
himself had thrown overboard the captain's pet palm tree as well as two
replacements, cleverly diverting attention from his feat by having engineered the awarding of a special decoration — the Order of the Palm Tree —
to an unsuspecting fellow officer (290). Then, shortly, off Okinawa, there
had occurred a more serious episode of insubordination involving Alfred
Jones, whom the captain had ordered off the bridge after Jones, to the former's embarrassment, had saved the ship by a timely maneuver. When
Jones refused, the captain had threatened to put him in hack — in house
arrest, that is, relief from duty and confinement to his quarters. To the delight of Heggen and the rest of the crew, Jones, in need of relaxation, had
responded by insisting on just such a punishment.

By now, Heggen had mailed "Night Watch" to his cousin Wallace Stegner, at Harvard (290). He sent "The Nurse's Story" to Carol Lynn, his wife.
The idea meanwhile began to unfold in his mind about a book of stories,
prospectively entitled *The Iron-Bottomed Bucket* (292). At home, Stegner
on his part proposed to recommend "Night Watch" to his friend Edward
Weeks, editor of the *Atlantic,* and to propose to Dorothy Hillyer at Houghton Mifflin just such a book of stories. After V-J Day, Heggen returned to
meet with Stegner, now at Stanford, who told him that "Night Watch" was
likely to be published in the *Atlantic* and that Hillyer at Houghton Mifflin
was definitely interested in a collection. Heggen, as it turned out, already
had some new stories. Stegner quickly rejected one about Solomon, a
"steward's mate" (295–96). On the other hand, he felt that with modest
cutting, another about a spectacular liberty on "Elysium" should remain.
His strongest suggestion, however, was absolutely pivotal. According to
Leggett, he felt "it would be a mistake to let the stories go simply as a collection when there was a chance of tying them together and giving them
some aspect of a novel. He saw just such a possibility in the character of
Lieutenant Roberts. He was Tom's own reflection and a superb figure,

Wallace told him, and with very little rewriting he could be made to dominate the book, even the episodes, such as the nurse's story, in which he did not appear. Let the book begin and end with Roberts, he proposed" (296).

Out of one crucial idea seemed to grow another, this time arrived at independently by Heggen. "As he turned over Wallace's idea of making Roberts dominate the book from the start and tie it up some way at the end, it occurred to Tom that Roberts might leave the ship just as he had, with warm wishes of good luck. Then, instead of coming home, he would have his combat duty at last, and it followed that he would be killed by it — fulfillment and apotheosis in a stroke."

Leggett went on: "Never mind if a tragic end was at odds with the rest, it was appropriate. . . . In one final, tragic episode Roberts's hero death could give the book a wholeness and dimension he had never anticipated" (297).

Accordingly, when Heggen began sending Dorothy Hillyer the stories that would flesh out the book, she confirmed his instincts. She too was certain, she said, "that the book must end with Lieutenant Roberts' death, which made me water my desk with tears. It is very rare for a series of stories [or a war constituting one's experience of a lifetime] to achieve an emotional climax like this and we don't want to lose such an opportunity" (305). Then, with a final decision nearing on the book, Houghton's editor-in-chief, Paul Brooks, seemed to seal the bargain. He suggested that the book's title in fact be changed from *The Iron-Bottomed Bucket* to simply *Mister Roberts* (313).

Within the same week, Heggen was informed that the *Atlantic* would publish "not one, but three sections." The April issue would contain

> the "Night Watch" chapter preceded by the introduction. In May they would use a story involving the episode about the captain and his palm trees, preceded by the news of V-E Day and Roberts's discussion about the war with the ship's doctor. In June they would conclude with "So Long, Mister Roberts," which would include Ensign Pulver's ongoing pranks on the captain, the farewell party with its firing of the five-inch gun, Roberts's departure for combat duty and the subsequent news of his death. (313–14)

With the forthcoming novel already designated an "*Atlantic* First," Heggen "would receive their top story fees." As important, he would also "be a candidate for a Metro Goldwyn Mayer award of fifteen hundred dollars" (314).

Shortly, in February, Heggen received official acceptance and an advance from Houghton Mifflin and also news that the *Reader's Digest* was publishing an excerpt from "The Nurse's Story." For the book, about to go into production, in March he duly settled on a final arrangement —

> the "Nurse's Story" and "Flare-up on the Gun Watch" (the taunting of Red Stevens for trusting in his wife's fidelity), should be separated by a "sexless" story. He wanted the "Nurse's Story," now up front, made the seventh of the fourteen episodes. He wanted to put the Ensign Keith story up to the number two position because "it is in itself prefatory and because it introduces at some length a character, Dowdy, who becomes quite important to the book." Finally, he proposed moving the episode about Roberts trying to get a change of duty to the eighth position. Paul Brooks liked Tom's reordering, and that is the way he sent the manuscript to press. (314)

Meanwhile, the *Atlantic* stories had gained much favorable attention, and "Night Watch" was selected for the annual O. Henry collection. On the other hand, there was disappointment in the book's not being selected in advance by either the Book-of-the-Month Club or Literary Guild. (In the former case, especially, the main consideration seemed to be excessive profanity, which had already generated two pages of readers' letters, pro and con, in the *Atlantic*. Likewise, the *Digest* had already seen fit to bowdlerize the climax of "The Nurse's Story," where "birthmark on her ass" was changed to "birthmark on her fanny" [328].)

The book itself was published to extraordinary reviews (326). Perhaps the key tone was struck by an anonymous *New Yorker* critic, who noted the degree to which Heggen had captured the "real war" of the noncombatants who made up the vast bulk of the American forces. Here, he wrote, was "a quiet, credible story of the corroding effects of apathy and boredom on men who, in battle, might have been heroes" (70).[22] It was a story, in short, that an incredible number of war-era Americans could identify with.

Morever, *as a production item*, the text captured a wartime feel. It was a slim, fast-paced book, cut into interesting installments, resembling the popular *See Here, Private Hargrove* or *A Bell for Adano* — both of which also addressed the plight of American good Joes, one an enlisted man and the other an officer, in a world of GI regulation and the officious martinets who delight in its enforcement. Also, much in the vein of the *Reader's Digest*, where Heggen had served his publishing apprenticeship, as the "serious" plot evolved, short, lively chapters managed to strike a lighter tone,

combining colorful character and vignette with a spirit of humorous anecdote. (Indeed the general effect, one sees in retrospect, actually mimics the
rhythms of the magazine, alternating between melodrama and laughter,
with breaks in "serious" or "deep" writing punctuated by the equivalent of
sections such as "Humor in Uniform," "My Most Memorable Character,"
"Laughter, the Best Medicine.")

This was abetted, moreover, by visual design. The dust jacket scene, of
a solitary sailor looking out from above the enormously high, imprisoning
gunwale of a ship riding at anchor, recalls the wartime illustrations — at
once heartwarming and melancholy — of pictorialists such as Norman
Rockwell and Fletcher Martin. Inside, the text featured illustrations by
Samuel Hanks Bryant; and again, the wartime pictorial connection seems
prominent. The title page, for instance, with facial caricatures of navy
"types," actually looks like signature *Digest* artwork. Each chapter is then
introduced by a cartoonlike drawing of a key scene in the narrative to follow. Again, even when the chapter plot in question is severe, the general
effect is humorous or at the very least bittersweet. It is artwork, the style
seems to tell us, fit for a book for people whose war had been fought often
somewhere between the stark line drawings of Howard Brodie and Kerr
Eby and the more laugh-provoking, albeit frequently astringent cartoons of
Bill Mauldin and George Baker.[23]

Most important for the development of the text to the next stage of production, drama, was the fact that one of the Americans so identifying with
the work was the extraordinarily influential Broadway playwright and producer Joshua Logan. Or, as Logan himself put it, echoing the *New Yorker*
reviewer cited above, "although it was concerned with the Navy in the
Pacific, it was talking to me about my war, the boredom and idiocy of it,
and I felt it was written with a poetic lucidity seldom found anymore"
(194–95). Accordingly, the collaboration that shortly resulted, as suggested
by the exchange noted earlier, might more properly be called a symbiosis.[24] The marathon composition sessions confirmed to Logan that his instincts were all there, that in his creative relationship with the younger
author they had captured the rhythms of a drama comprising in large measure the average person's story of the war. This was especially the case, he
felt, with Roberts's epiphany, just before his death, even as he is at last
allowed to do brave work aboard a fighting ship, about the steadfastness of
his noncombatant comrades aboard "the bucket." Logan realized that
the play had plumbed the great, common wisdom of the average veteran.
Roberts "knows now," Logan wrote, "there is another, an even tougher

bravery — that of men who do not succumb to the most terrible enemy of this war — boredom" (201). And he thus shortly seemed not at all surprised, for instance, when for the Broadway production alone, nine hundred ex-servicemen showed up for general casting call (362). "Since it was shortly after the war, there were still many veterans who had read the novel and had felt as I did that it was their own story" (206).[25]

It was also, as it turned out, in the particular experience of the title character, almost uncannily Fonda's story of Fonda's war. "Fonda was out of the Navy by then," Logan began (207). What he might have added was that Fonda's own navy experience had been not simply parallel with that of the figure he was about to be selected to play but, save for the offstage hero's death at the end, nearly congruent. It would be one thing for critics to say, as noted earlier, at various after-the-fact stages in the evolution of the text and the production, that Fonda was Mr. Roberts. What they may or may not have known was that *literally* Fonda's own *real* military career had already been Roberts's — a set of frustrating, boring, pointless noncombat assignments, finally concluded with combat service on the intelligence staff of an admiral.

In fact, it had begun with Fonda the civilian struggling even to get into the navy, let alone finding a combat role. After acting in *The Ox-Bow Incident*, he attempted to enlist. Instead he found himself prevented from boarding the basic training bus to San Diego by Darryl Zanuck, who arranged to have him deferred long enough to play in *The Immortal Sergeant*. (Fonda was said later to have described himself as "never so mad in his life" [Roberts and Goldstein 76].) On the next try he actually managed to get in. After basic training he applied to serve as a gunner's mate. Instead he was assigned as a quartermaster third class. On the other hand, at least he had been assigned to a destroyer, the *Satterlee*, in the process of combat deployment — albeit with a captain, he later remarked, who made him instantly understand the source of crisis in *The Caine Mutiny*, in the dramatic version of which he eventually played the navy lawyer Barney Greenwald. Before departure from San Diego, however, he was abruptly informed of his transfer to the decidedly nonmaritime billet of service headquarters at 90 Church Street in New York City. (To compound the frustration, he continued to get actual destroyer service on the vessel while it served as transportation to the East Coast, from which it proceeded to duty with the British in the Atlantic [Fonda and Teichmann 151–52].) Upon arrival in New York, Major Major Major Major–like, he was instantly promoted to the somewhat advanced officer rank of lieutenant, junior grade.

Next came orders to Washington, where he would be assigned to make training films. Finally, however, a protest got him somewhere. He actually underwent officer candidate school, received training in air combat intelligence, and was assigned to duty in the Marianas on staff of Vice Admiral John H. Hoover, one of the chief deputies to Admiral Chester W. Nimitz, U.S. Navy commander in the Pacific. And there, his biographer records, Fonda was to get a first look at the "fighting navy." "It was an awesome sight," he recalled. "The lagoon was enormous and it was filled with battleships and carriers and cruisers and destroyers. That lagoon stretched so far out I couldn't see all the ships" (Fonda and Teichmann 156–57).

So, in almost uncannily Doug Roberts–like fashion, he arrived at the war. And so apparently, for the most part, he served, largely carrying messages between Hoover and Halsey, writing home fond, rueful letters about his general boredom and his itchings to get into the war. Off Saipan and Iwo Jima, he also finally found his own kamikazes, one missing his ship, the destroyer *Curtis*, by twenty-five feet. Then, while he took liberty on Guam, another hit the *Curtis*. When it returned, the location and extent of the damage persuaded him that he would himself likely have been killed. But it was just one last close call. While on Guam, Fonda heard the announcement of V-E Day. Shortly, he was out of the navy. The next call would be a casting call, for the starring role in *Mister Roberts*.

Thus within and without, so to speak, the Fonda-Roberts identification seemed to have found its own dynamic. Fonda was duly invited by Logan to a meeting in New York to listen to a reading. Also present was David Wayne, who struck the producer at least as a possibility for Roberts somewhat closer in image to Heggen himself. But after the reading, according to Logan, Wayne ran hurriedly from the room, leaving him with Fonda who, to his surprise, announced his unequivocal intention to play the part. Shortly, the phone rang. It was Wayne. "Hank Fonda should play Roberts," he insisted, "not me. I want to play Pulver. In fact, I've got to!" (208). It was, Logan observes, "the shortest casting session I ever went through" (208).

To fill the other major roles, Robert Keith became the doc; William Harrigan became the captain. As noted earlier, nearly a thousand veterans showed up for general casting. The tryout performance took place in New Haven, to an enthusiastic audience similarly heavy with veterans (368). Even more happily communitarian was the tumultuous New York opening, February 18, 1948. The new symbiosis, now involving authors, actors, and audience, was complete. There was cheering, weeping, a long series of curtain calls, concluded only when Fonda came out offering lamely to start over, since "this is all Tom and Josh wrote for us" (374).

Thus in a great theatrical moment was consummated the literary and dramatic chemistry whereby the memory of the war and the figure of Fonda as Mr. Roberts achieved permanent cultural fusion — in many ways became each other. The projection of that moment into the status of cultural institution took place shortly in a new, equally spectacular history of production. On Broadway alone, the play enjoyed one of the longest runs in American theater history. It also then went directly on the road, notably with Fonda himself remaining a fixture in the title part. It was estimated that he had appeared in seventeen hundred performances by 1950 (Thomas 231–32; Roberts and Goldstein 101).

By 1955 Logan and others had decided that the time had come for *Mister Roberts* the movie; and for the first time, the essential continuity among versions of the textual artifact that had grown out of the original Heggen-Logan-Fonda symbiosis looked as if it might be radically disrupted. Heggen, in any event, was dead, a 1949 suicide.[26] Logan too had moved on to other projects, most notably the even more successful and spectacular production of a new World War II classic, the musical *South Pacific*. And finally, as noted above, after playing Roberts for several years nearly everywhere in America, Fonda had gone on to other stage productions such as *Point of No Return* and *The Caine Mutiny Court-Martial*.

Most of the new developments involved in the movie project would derive from Hollywood production issues. Some of these, such as ideas of casting and direction, would eventually resolve themselves in attempts to connect (or, in some cases, reconnect) the film version with its narrative and dramatic antecedents. But others — especially those related to major new directions taken by the industry in its own depiction of the war in film — would play a tremendous part in producing the movie that most Americans would come to know as the "real" *Mister Roberts*.

The first questions, casting and direction, turned out to be intimately related. There was by now, for instance, the age of the character to consider. Roberts was supposed to be in his mid to late twenties; Fonda, if he was again to play the role — for which he had already, despite his professional boyishness, been slightly "old" on Broadway — was near fifty. (According to one biography, at least, Fonda was seriously thinking this time about asking to play the doc [Roberts and Goldstein 104].) There was also Hollywood pressure to showcase a rising star. Initial casting ideas for

Roberts ran from Marlon Brando to William Holden. That problem, however, was quickly resolved when the first choice of directors, John Ford, insisted on Fonda again as Roberts. And with the lead matter settled, there could now occur a constellation of other canny casting decisions, at once complementing and setting off Fonda's virtuoso lead. The David Wayne role of Pulver went to Jack Lemmon in the Academy Award–winning performance that would make him a star. William Powell was brought out of retirement to play late William Powell as the mannered, urbane, cynical doc. And in a curious but brilliant stroke, the versatile James Cagney — once everybody's baby-faced hoodlum but later flourishing in roles as diverse as the beloved George M. Cohan of *Yankee Doodle Dandy* and Flagg, the strutting, bantam *miles gloriosus* of *What Price Glory?* — became the captain, "Old Stupid," in a new key, his fulminating anger masking a stark loneliness. More conventionally, Ward Bond got to play the Ward Bond–Dan Dailey part of the faithful senior chief petty officer (in army films, the faithful senior sergeant). And as other principals, Betsy Palmer became the chief nurse and Phil Carey the tough-guy irritant in the enlisted crew to carry over a Broadway effect.

The directing, to be sure, at least initially promised to be signature work. And that might have been so with another property with a different production history. Here, *Mister Roberts* according to the director, John Ford, quickly clashed with *Mr. Roberts* according to Mr. Roberts himself, Ford's old friend Henry Fonda. Once, with Logan, the latter had quarreled over a road production which he had insisted on making his own, down to the mannerisms of the attendant players. In the process he had become so angry that he had vowed never to make the movie if Logan was chosen to direct. Now, against the formidable Ford, there was another battle over what Fonda considered distractions in focus from the spirit of the play. This time, the upshot was a fistfight, allegedly provoked by Ford, after which the latter shortly took to drink and retired to his yacht, never to return to the film.[27] The most important result of the quarrel, however, was that a far blander director, Mervyn LeRoy, was brought in to finish things up in a way that seemed to suggest no particular directorial tone at all.[28]

But the key ingredient remained, of course, Fonda again; and this time, as noted, he was getting both the role and the final word on the role in the *only* version of the artifact most Americans would ever be likely to know. The *Times* reviewer cited earlier had proven right beyond his own imaginings. As truly as Henry Fonda now *was* Mr. Roberts, so Mr. Roberts had now culminated his resemblance from birth to Henry Fonda.

Accordingly, the *production* artifact at large also made the final transition to a *Mister Roberts* dictated by Hollywood values now becoming dominant in the process of shaping World War II and the course of American remembering to a degree far beyond any single project or case of origin. Chief of these was that its July 1955 release could not have come more centrally in the great age of the big World War II movie — including *From Here to Eternity* (1953), *The Caine Mutiny* (1954), *Battle Cry* (1955), *To Hell and Back* (1955), *Bridge on the River Kwai* (1957), *The Young Lions* (1958), and *The Naked and the Dead* (1958).[29] And added correspondingly, as in many of the above — were flashy new lens and color technologies and advanced cinematography. Moreover, even as with those films that remained in black and white, the public was deluged with news of all-star casts and other forms of large-scale promotion. *Mister Roberts* now figured clearly as one of these "big" pictures.

A related and, as marked by *Mister Roberts* in particular, pivotal Hollywood development, would also turn out to be its benchmark role in the accrediting of a major new subgenre — what might be called, most simply, the funny World War II in the Pacific movie. This had been rehearsed, at least briefly, by the 1950 *Francis* with Donald O'Connor, the first in a "talking mule" series which, in early combat scenes, had parlayed into slapstick the humorous caricature of the feckless, jabbering little Japanese ("Wha' hoppen?") often a part of more serious films as well. *Mister Roberts* made definitive the strategy involved on a broader scale: exploit the "humor in uniform" possibilities of the Pacific war in particular by depicting the Japanese at a distance or, if possible, not at all. And as a result, it was recapitulated in a wave of comparable films such as *Don't Go Near the Water* (1957), with Glenn Ford, Gia Scala, and Eva Gabor — itself from a *Mister Roberts*–like humorous novel of 1951; *Operation Mad Ball* (1957), with Jack Lemmon, Mickey Rooney, and Ernie Kovacs; *South Pacific* (1958), with Mitzi Gaynor, Rossano Brazzi, Ray Walston, and Juanita Hall; *Operation Petticoat* (1960), with Cary Grant and Tony Curtis; *The Wackiest Ship in the Army* (1960), again with Jack Lemmon; and *Ensign Pulver* (1964), itself a *Mister Roberts* spinoff with Robert Walker Jr., Burl Ives, and Walter Matthau.[30]

Anticipating all this — and further, now drawing overtly, as would many of the successors named, on the provenance of the old South Seas adventure-cruise movie, complete with natives, outriggers, and so forth (Roberts and Goldstein 106) — the resulting film bears heavily the weight of its hybrid production values. Even in its peculiar genre, the mutiny drama,[31] the film is mainly distinguished by an intense visual beauty that quickly subordinates plot to setting. The atmosphere is the main character. Pacific dawns, sunsets, ocean vistas, brilliant blue skies, puffy clouds, gleaming white beaches, sleepy backwater ports on island paradises, palm trees, tropical nights, brilliantly sunlit days: all these tell us, from the first scene onward, with the ship riding at anchor near daybreak, a voice-over yielding to shipboard wakeup sounds, shouts of "hit the deck" from petty officers, grumbles and complaints from sleepy sailors, that we already know now it is going to be *that* kind of movie. What kind of movie? One with officers in suntans, sailors in dungarees, nurses, islanders, perhaps the odd castaway. Which one will it be? *Don't Go Near the Water? Away All Boats? Donovan's Reef? P.T. 109?*[32] Perhaps we cannot yet be sure of the seriousness quotient. What we can be sure of is that it will be *all in technicolor*, even when the dawn breezes lift and the sweat begins. As in the early scenes of the play, the doc and Roberts have their conversation about the task force that Roberts, on night watch, has seen passing in the darkness,[33] and the men are shortly reprimanded for working without their shirts. But it's sunlight now, and the sunlight is in living color: it's the Pacific, a slow-boat-to-somewhere, with a bunch of unruly sailors, and somehow even the sweat is just not real. Indeed, one gets the sense that were there any blood, save offscreen, it would look *exactly the same way.*[34]

To be sure, the drama, as it unfolds, remains essentially parallel to that of the Broadway classic. Indeed, if anything, in the way it is played — something Fonda himself is said to have made sure of — the vein is that of nostalgic reprise. Yet here, too, everything also is now in a movie of the genre, of the era, of the current technology. In the play, for instance, as noted earlier, after an early scene in which the restless crew, set to polishing binoculars, discover their view of the new nurses' quarters ashore, comes the visit of one of the latter, whom Pulver hopes to seduce with the help of a fifth of scotch but who instead finds out about their voyeuristic secret. In the movie, the one enlarges to six, direct from some don't-whistle-at-the-WACS/WAVES comedy, complete with tight khakis, curves, plenty of leg, and a bumbling parody of close-order drill.[35] Similarly, the explosion of Pulver's laundry becomes a Hollywood orgy of soapsuds and slip-and-falls. So the return of the drunken crew from liberty becomes a series of raucous visual gags culminating in the stunt-riding of a motorcycle off the end of a pier and into the drink. Even the conclusion — the transfiguring moment in which Lemmon-Pulver, informed of the death of his idol, Roberts, marches Roberts-like up the stairs, pounds defiantly on the captain's door, and with a triumphant shout announces that he, too, has just thrown the captain's "damn palm tree overboard" — is itself transfigured. One's sense of the Hollywood self-caricature — now Lemmon doing Lemmon — is indelibly that of a Daffy Duck cartoon.

But all this, too, was by now well on its way to becoming its own version of history. Released in July 1955, *Mister Roberts* the movie grossed $5.8 million in its first year; Lemmon got an Oscar and made a career (Roberts and Goldstein 112). Henry Fonda got his chance to play for all time the archetype of the archetype, so to speak, the old American story that even he somehow knew — as if in anticipation of Joseph Heller's celebrated parody of it in *Catch-22* — seemed to be his by resemblance from birth. It was all, he suggested "because of my skinny frame I inherited from my ancestors — because of an honest face I was born with — because of a Midwestern voice I've never tried to lose" that he could always be at the same time both Mr. Roberts and Mr. Fonda (or young Mr. Lincoln, for that matter, or young Mr. Joad) and vice versa — "the honest man with integrity" (Roberts and Goldstein 2).

Out of America's Good War, Henry Fonda thus became a key image of American remembering that could persist even as that remembering, like the image of James Jones's mythical infantryman in *WWII*, grew into a lengthening shadow of itself. Through Henry Fonda as Mr. Roberts, World War II–era Americans and their children after them could always picture themselves as the good Joe in a bad situation: too much a lover of freedom to cooperate with a dictator or a martinet; yet also too responsible a citizen to become an outright insurgent. And so contrived, that image would make possible the remembering of a war in which Mr. Roberts–like (or was it Henry Fonda–like?) people found it possible to grow larger than themselves at a time when it was required. Moreover — and this was the real genius of the unfolding versions of the artifact — they would also be allowed by casting fiat to grow gracefully older as Fonda grew gracefully older, the ones who, remembering themselves in their late twenties, liked to imagine they were perhaps Doug Roberts and who, moving on into their thirties, forties, and fifties like Fonda, found in him an ongoing way of identifying with the role. Like the part of them they called their youth, to be sure, Roberts would die in the war in the movie. But he would also, in the movie that was the war, live on in nostalgic myth *and* eternally escape, for good measure, coming home and going back to work at *Reader's*

Digest or just being a middle manager somewhere until it was really time to die. To put this simply, Doug Roberts as played by Henry Fonda would never have to come home from World War II and get over it. Neither he nor the good American of the Good War he seemed to embody by resemblance from birth would ever get old.

South Pacific

As with *Mister Roberts*, for many post-1945 Americans the theater and film title *South Pacific* does not describe a text so much as a process of remembering. For the cultural historian, it offers accordingly a parallel account of production. Again, it is the relationship of these that will be my subject.

As before, the pattern of the remembering will largely depend on the rememberer. It will be something of the book perhaps, the play, the movie, one song, another song. The manner of its production, on the other hand, albeit complicated, is traceable. The text has its literary provenance in a 1947 collection of fictional narratives by James A. Michener entitled *Tales of the South Pacific*, variously described as short stories or a novel, but always noted as winner of the Pulitzer Prize. In translation to Rodgers and Hammerstein's 1949 Broadway classic, it added another Pulitzer and a paperback fortune for the original honoree (Davis 133; Michener, *World* 329) to one of the most celebrated runs in the golden era of the American musical. It parlayed that success into one of the first widely popular 33⅓ RPM long-playing records, memorialized in its dramatic connection by a cover photograph of Mary Martin and Ezio Pinza in the lead roles of a U.S. Navy nurse named Nellie Forbush and a French planter, Emile DeBecque. It then reappears as a 1958 movie musical spectacular, leading to another joyride of the Michener narrative on the best-seller lists (Davis 213), and to yet another best-selling LP, now in stereo, with the cover photo of the lovers, here Mitzi Gaynor and Rossano Brazzi, resituated against a Hollywood backdrop of wide-screen tropical splendors. Along the way, it proliferates into endless road productions and revivals; TV showings and VCR rentals; re-recordings and new recordings on LP, tape, and compact disc.

My purpose here is to inquire into the process of production so described — the movement from "history" through "literature" into various forms of "classic" entertainment. I wish to make such an inquiry a case study in the conjoined forms *and* economics of cultural mythmaking. My specific approach will be to ask what made possible, in a certain set of cultural contexts, such a series of artifacts with regard to this particular history. Accordingly, my inquiry will begin with some proximate responses, having to do with the history of this particular war, the American war of 1941–45 in the Pacific, against this particular enemy, the empire of Japan. But it will shortly turn to the various "entertainment" commodifications of history described above as *themselves a form of history*. Finally, it will also attempt to locate such commodifications within a national poetics of history that has long achieved honored status — and often at the expense, I will propose, of the very idea of history as possessed of ideological content — as a kind of ultimate entertainment technology *itself* called American remembering.

The specific question that generates my inquiry, centered on the focal artifact, Rodgers and Hammerstein's *South Pacific*, is fairly simple: What kind of people, slightly more than seven years after Pearl Harbor and three years after Hiroshima and Nagasaki, could possibly make World War II against the Japanese into a Broadway musical?[36] The proximate idea I will advance involves a deeply American politics of constructing the racial other. Or, as regards the Japanese, that it was exactly Pearl Harbor first — the surprise attack on Paradise — and Hiroshima and Nagasaki last, the grand visitation of avenging wrath — with a host of other death orgies such as Bataan, Guadalcanal, Tarawa, Iwo Jima, and Okinawa sandwiched bloodily in between — that made such a grotesque transmission possible. But further, it also required precisely the ease of cultural erasure enabled by the figure of the Jap: the rat, the louse, the cockroach, the savage simian fanatic little yellow bastard, the garden keeper's nightmare, the exterminator's delight. This war musical, I would insist, could only have come, really, of what must to date remain the most American of all great American wars, the great Pacific war, compounded of its most virulent racisms, East and West: in John Dower's exact formulation, the "war without mercy."

At the same time, however, I will also suggest that a number of coexisting, high-investment media of popular entertainment — print, stage, sound recording, film — quickly operated to render that subtext of horror largely irrelevant within an autonomous genealogy of production *itself*, a conflation of tastes and technologies become self-reifying forms of cultural statement, entertainment visions of the world taken to be fundamental ways of experiencing the world. The result, I will suggest finally, would be a new version of the artifact known as the American popular classic. And to re-create the history of events whereby such a classic is produced, I believe, is thus to know something about a national habit of remembering that even today, and often in ways largely *un*remembered, remains part of the fabric *and* the business of our daily lives.

To begin by looking at the 1947 text in which the enterprise originates is to undertake in itself a work of curious recovery. Here is a preindustrial James Michener, an author in his debut having much in common with other up-and-coming "literary" chroniclers of the just-finished Pacific war — Thomas Heggen in *Mister Roberts*, Herman Wouk in *The Caine Mutiny*, Norman Mailer in *The Naked and the Dead*, Leon Uris in *Battle Cry*. To be sure, one hardly finds a neglected classic, a latter-day *Red Badge of Courage* or a prophetic *Catch-22*. Yet as to the Pacific conflict, Michener's book speaks with a terse authority. There is the feel of the naval war, professionals and opportunistic martinets mixed with average men and women called to roles in which they must somehow become bigger than themselves. There is the enormous military-logistical sprawl, island after island, as the bases multiply, bringing the line navy, the PT daredevils, the aviators, the marines, the nurses, the supply, maintenance, and paperwork types, with war-exotics and fast operators abounding, American and indigenous. There is the drama of interminable waiting, punctuated by violence almost beyond belief. An ammunition ship, lying at harbor in a rear-area depot, is literally disintegrated with all aboard in an inexplicable accident. An entire unit, various members of which have become individualized to us, is annihilated by a single artillery hit on a landing craft.

Emerging in major roles, through complex narrative involvements, are six characters who will become the central figures of the Rodgers and Hammerstein play. The navy ensign-nurse Nellie Forbush, from Arkansas, U.S.A.; her eventual husband, the handsome, mysterious French planter Emile DeBecque; the bawdy, jovial Tonkinese black-marketeer, Bloody Mary; the young Princeton lieutenant of marines, Joseph Cable; Liat, Bloody Mary's virginal daughter, soon to become the latter's tragic beloved; and, finally, the all-purpose scavenger and rapscallion, Seabee Luther Billis. These are joined by others: a shadowy American intelligence operative, Tony Fry; the rakish pilot Bus Adams; the enigmatic narrator, a "paperwork sailor" (Michener, *Tales* 3), as he calls himself, dispatched hither and yon through the combat theater; the exotic "Frenchman's Daughter," or, more properly, Madame Latouche DeBecque Barzan, daughter of the Gaullist renegade DeBecque, ex-wife of the Petainist traitor Achille Barzan, lover of Bus Adams, eventually wife of the doomed Tony Fry, exotic hostess at her island villa to the officers of all nations who come bearing the plunder of war; the Japanese lieutenant colonel, Hyaichi, a Cal Tech–educated engineer who, despite the blundering of his superiors, manages to turn the massively prepared-for expedition against Kuralei, the focal action of the book, into a near disaster for the American forces making the attack.

Yet as one reads along toward the climactic battle through a seemingly endless proliferation of characters and texts — indeed, the extent is barely sketched out above — one has the distinct sense of having somehow been there before. Then the realization takes shape. If we are seeing all this in a war, we understand that we are also seeing it within rather a familiar kind of book. It is a South Seas travel-adventure book, as Melville's *Typee* and *Omoo*, or the Pacific sections of Twain's *Roughing It* and *Following the Equator* are travel books. Most especially, it is such a book as Nordhoff and Hall's mid-1930s trilogy — *Mutiny on the Bounty, Pitcairn's Island,* and *Men Against the Sea* — are South Seas travel-adventure books. (Early chapters, in fact, under the pretext of building an airstrip, enable a long visit on Norfolk Island with the descendants of the old mutineers.) Similarly, its renegades, castaways, burnt-out cases, and sundry other *isolatos* seem often to owe less to contemporary historical action than they do to R. L. Stevenson, Joseph Conrad, or Somerset Maugham. In the matter of war reporting, even down to the paper, the print, the no-waste layout, the sections that begin and end in midpage, the locus classicus is the journalist Ernie Pyle. In the depiction of non-Western women, it is the painter Gauguin. And then, just there, the sensation of familiarity really hits. Often it is not really a book. Rather, it is a movie, a South Seas adventure movie. Or, to use a suitable figure, it is the accumulated flotsam of a 1930s tidal wave of them: "A" and "B," silent and sound, dramatic and musical, legendary and forgotten. In a recent memoir, amid reflections on his return to the islands, Michener himself drops the names of a few — *Mutiny on the Bounty, The Hurricane, South of Pago Pago, Tabu.* To these might be added, by conservative count, at least sixty others, ranging from *The Love Trader* (1930) through the Dorothy Lamour sarong classics *Jungle Princess* (1936) and *Jungle Love* (1938) to the immediately prewar Hedy Lamarr–Robert Taylor vehicle, *Lady of the Tropics* (1939), set, of all places, in the harbor at Saigon. Thus we come to see why we feel so much of the time that the text at hand has seemed a familiar precinct to the degree that the war often falls somewhere between local adventure and romantic backdrop. The real terrain at hand turns out to be a mythic geography firmly in possession of its real owners, the American audience.[37]

Recent evidence would suggest also how thoroughly the author re-garded the very project of the book as a basically literary "property." The ubiquity of the narrator, he reveals, turns out to have derived from a set of faked orders he managed to acquire allowing him unlimited travel to gather experience, a kind of passport to material. The experience of the war years spent in the Pacific, he freely admits, became mainly the experi-ence of producing the text that was to comprise the account of these years.

Yet such attitudes of authorial commodification seem almost innocent compared with those shortly evinced by heavy production types such as Kenneth McKenna, Jo Mielzener, Joshua Logan, Leland Hayward, Rich-ard Rodgers, and Oscar Hammerstein, to name just a few. Whatever the real story of Michener's version of the war without mercy, it now becomes wholly subsumed in the story of how it became the newest version of the Broadway–Tin Pan Alley–Hollywood Sure Thing.

How sure a thing is verified by accounts of the deal from the various principals. According to Michener, for instance, McKenna, head of a Holly-wood "literary department" disappointed by the negative response of his superiors to the book's film possibilities, recommended it to his half-brother Mielzener, a New York stage designer. Mielzener says that he ex-citedly got in touch with Richard Rodgers, who in turn talked to Oscar Hammerstein, and that shortly he found them leagued, in his words, "with two outstanding talents, Josh Logan, the director, and Leland Hayward, the charismatic producer" (Michener, World 290). Rodgers, on his part, sug-gests that the "property" was suggested to him by Logan during what seemed a fruitless period of seeking "an idea for a musical that excited me" (258). Logan, in turn, remembers a dinner with Mielzener and McKenna at which the latter recommended the book as possibly helpful in providing "some color" for a current Logan project, *Mister Roberts*. Logan took the book to Miami over a weekend with Hayward and their wives. Hayward borrowed it while Logan took a nap. Shortly, he exclaimed, "Josh, we're go-ing to buy this son of a bitch!"

"What are we going to do with the son of a bitch?", Logan replied.

"We'll make some son-of-a-bitching movies, some musical shows, maybe a couple of straight plays," said Logan, "— how the hell do I know? We'll just buy it quick, before somebody else does, and then make up our minds." (209–10)

Whatever the handling of the property, all accounts agree on one thing: the focal item for the new project was a relatively incidental story among the nineteen fictions making up the original, entitled "Fo'Dolla'," in which East meets West through a Tonkinese black-marketeer's sale to an upper-crust American lieutenant of her virginal daughter. Yet, as Rodgers recalls, there were obvious problems. First, they all wanted to avoid "just another variation of *Madame Butterfly*." More important, he goes on, "though we liked the story, we became convinced that it was not substantial or original enough to make a full evening's entertainment." It was thence, he says, that they turned to a second, parallel narrative found in "Our Heroine," a section containing the outlines of the love plot involving Emile DeBecque, a middle-aged planter possessed of two mysterious mixed-race children, and a young, ingenuous, provincial American nurse named Nellie Forbush. "This, we decided, had to be the main story." Yet here, too, were new problems. "All this was against the rules of musical-play construction," which insisted that "if the main love story is serious, the secondary romance is usually employed to provide comic relief." The difficulty then was "two serious themes, with the second becoming a tragedy." However, in a good cause, he concludes, "breaking the rules didn't bother us, but we did think the show needed comic leavening, so we went to still a third story for an affable wheeler-dealer named Luther Billis and added him to the cast" (259).[38]

Thus the transformation, or rather, as it is called in the business, the development. And it is against this backdrop of textual construction, rather than any one of putative history or ideology, that we must view perhaps the most cherished legend concerning the work's status as an American classic: and that is the legend of Rodgers and Hammerstein's attempt to use the Broadway theater to make a courageous statement against racial bigotry in general and institutional racism in the postwar United States in particular. After all, the story goes, central to both of the twinned romantic plots were complex issues of multicultural and interracial relationship. These, moreover, culminated memorably, the legend continues, in the "message" contained in the plea for racial understanding sung toward the end by Cable, shortly before his death, under the title "You've Got to Be Taught." And there is some happy, incidental truth to this. The touring play, we know for instance, as well as the 1958 movie, provoked anxiety among critics and certain active resistance in the American South. On the other hand, to arrive here we have to work through a truly inspired layering of racial substitutions. To put it simply, although the "Jap" problem in the text has been dispensed with, we now face two others. Both stem from that old American favorite, miscegenation. The first is focused in the main, Forbush-DeBecque love plot, the "family" plot as it were. It is, to use Nellie's own phrasing, a "nigger" problem. Ingeniously, *it* gets resolved by her acceptance of DeBecque and with him the children he has fathered by a Polynesian. She may be from Arkansas, but she is also an ingenue, a nurse, and a nurturing adoptive parent "in love with a wonderful guy." (When we see her last, she is serving soup.) DeBecque has gone Asiatic, but, because he is an occidental, he can come back across the line. (Curiously, the fact that he has committed in his youth what would now be called second-degree murder is far more easily dealt with than the fact of the children.) The offending wife is dead. The cute mixed-race children, like puppies or kittens, are eminently adoptable.

The second problem, focused in the parallel relationship of Cable with Liat, engineered by her black-marketeer mother, Bloody Mary, proves not so easy to work out. To borrow a phrasing that other Americans would eventually find for it, it is a "gook" problem.[39] Accordingly, as if in expiation for the other, it must be allowed to find its eventuation in tragedy. Here, to be sure, in matters oriental, the Puccini kill-the-courtesan model — a lesson not lost on the makers of the recent Broadway blockbuster *Miss Saigon* — does not even have to be sold. All that is required additionally for moral punctuation is that the lieutenant, for his sins, undertake a secret mission and be killed. And thus the racial calculus is complete, with the "nigger" problem resolved in ways having, as usual, nothing to do with American realities past or present and the "gook" problem drawn in the long, prophetic shadow of future "Tonkinese" realities still to be reckoned.[40]

Yet none of this in either case makes the basic cultural legend untrue. It simply locates the truth elsewhere in cultural remembering, so to speak, as a truth not so much of history as of popular desire. That is, if love and war were the themes, and racial understanding the received moral, the business was entertainment; and particularly, for the moment at least, the business at hand was that classic entertainment called the Broadway musical. For here, such bizarre hybridizations of "concept" had long seemed the norm rather than the oddity. In a single work there could be grandeur of opera, the seriousness of "legitimate" theater, the comedic possibilities of the variety show and vaudeville, the emotionality of melodrama.[41]

Here, then, seems to have been serious creative business and the business of popular entertainment, meeting in some common discourse of public interest and appreciation. Accordingly, critical response to *South Pacific* was lavish. One commentator praised the setting out of sensitive human drama — and remember, this is the play, not even the book —

against "the callous misery, boredom, and slaughter of war" (Coffin 312). Others noted the aesthetic uniqueness of something not really a musical so much as a structurally focused, thematically coherent interweaving of plots with musical score and libretto *creating* the drama at levels of extraordinarily high quality (312, 313). Many, not having had the benefits of a half century of shopping-mall and elevator music, teased out the compositional excellences of solos such as "Some Enchanted Evening," "Bali Ha'i," "I'm Gonna Wash That Man Right Out of My Hair," "Love with a Wonderful Guy," "Younger Than Springtime," "This Nearly Was Mine"; showstopping chorus numbers such as "Bloody Mary" and "There Is Nothing like a Dame"; atmospheric framings such as the charming "Dites Moi." And in all these respects, it does seem to have been a tremendously innovative and well-integrated production that had an appealing theatricality (including, for instance, instead of extraneously gaudy production and dance numbers, a razzle-dazzle show-within-a-show surely invoking nostalgic remembrances of wartime special services productions) and united song and plot with unprecedented ease of staging and movement. Indeed, as one commentator accurately points out, here may have been the index of a real technical leap forward, the creation of as much a stage movie as a stage play for audiences increasingly accustomed to the fluidity of the newer medium (Laufe 130).

As noted above, equally in circulation, moreover, was generalized public discussion of a sort now largely lost to us, a kind of "Talk of Broadway" discourse that once seems truly to have been something of the talk of the country. There was, in a phrase, the serious matter of popular pride in the production itself as a major cultural artifact, whether one could go to it or not, either on Broadway or at one of the stops of a national touring company. Here was one last something of New York, of American theatrical excitement, of the hubbub and bustle of a place where the biggest variety show on television, in the innocence of a time before Elvis or the Beatles, billed itself quite unironically as the "Toast of the Town."[42] One could catch, for instance, some of the energy by reading — in a city newspaper, perhaps, or in a big photographic layout in *Life* magazine, about the assemblage of an extraordinary cast. Mary Martin, the new heroine of Broadway, one would know as having been rediscovered, after being written off as the kitteness of "My Heart Belongs to Daddy," through her brassy replacement of Ethel Merman in the touring company of *Annie Get Your Gun*. Ezio Pinza, the most prominent bass in the Metropolitan Opera, would be described (amid accounts of his heroine's trepidations about measuring up to his grandeur) as Don Giovanni himself translated in full glory to the Great White Way. One would hear of two exciting "finds": Juanita Hall as Bloody Mary and Myron McCormick as Luther Billis. During its run, one would read about the play's eventually breaking the record for the longest-running Broadway show. (Today it still sits at a comfortable fifth.) In a novel media experiment, one could even look in through the fledgling medium of television at a live broadcast of a Sunday matinee. One could enjoy the fruits of an actual South Pacific production company offering various souvenir merchandise. Apace, one could partake in the media *and* in the marketplace of the fashion excitement generated by a novelty number, sung by Mary Martin in a makeshift shower stall, entitled "I'm Gonna Wash That Man Right Out of My Hair." Huge numbers of women, apparently, wanted to know what happened to the hair. Did it get washed that often — that is, once every day and twice with matinees? If so, how could it be done? The result would be, of course, on the marketing end, the "concept" of once-a-day home hair-care products, and on the purchasing, a highly manageable, easily dryable, cropped hairstyle that became instantly fashionable.[43]

It was, moreover, exactly this combination of serious cultural interest with popular appeal that facilitated the further, relatively novel, and instantly successful packaging of the property in toto into one quite attractive new form of commodity just appearing on the entertainment horizon, the 33⅓ RPM long-playing record. Indeed here it seemed that, almost by divine conjunction of technological accident with promotional opportunity, a new medium had appeared, and that further, in its own blend of popular appeal with minor cultural cachet, it had been designed exactly to endow *South Pacific* with yet a new configuration of popular "classic" status. This latest had appeared amidst the cumbersome and expensive multidisc 78 RPM collections required for opera and classical performances and the more common 78 middle-of-the-road single. Soon, it would be joined by the mass-production 45, the vehicle of an insurgent rock and roll. Shortly would begin what one historian of the market has called the battle of the speeds, with the main results being that the 78 would disappear, the 33⅓ would for the moment take over the "longhair" niche, and the 45 would begin a new evolution toward the pop single (Sanjak 39). In the meantime, however, a major crossover market remained; and a good portion of its needs proved to be quite successfully filled by that new phenomenon, the 33⅓ musical original-cast album that would seem for one last moment to capitalize precisely on the marriage of its audience demographics with demographics of the soon-to-be-eclipsed Broadway form, elevated but not highbrow, popular but not plebeian. A groundbreaking experiment in the medium, actually, had been Rodgers and Hammerstein's own *Oklahoma!*, which was the first original-cast album to enjoy large sales. *South Pacific* exploited a newly proven market and repaid handsomely. Occupying the number 1 sale position for sixty-nine weeks in all, by 1958, when displaced by the soundtrack of the movie, the Broadway album had sold one million copies. Not surprisingly, the movie version began its own run. Number 1 for fifty-four weeks, including two years in the U.S. top ten, it became the biggest soundtrack of the decade, with sales of five million copies.[44]

So, to the ongoing sound of success, our account of ongoing production comes at last to the text of *South Pacific* probably now most remembered by Americans: *South Pacific*, the 1958 film. In terms of how it is remembered, moreover, it also seems historically the easiest to situate, especially as to how its issues of racial relationship were being contextualized by national events. The year 1954 brought the U.S. Supreme Court decision in *Brown* v. *Board of Education*, declaring unconstitutional legally mandated school segregation. Nineteen fifty-five was the year of the Montgomery, Alabama, bus boycott. In 1956 pictures were blazoned across the world of police dogs attacking demonstrators in Birmingham, Alabama. By 1957 similar images of hate recorded the attempt to integrate Central High School in Little Rock, Arkansas. America had found its race problem. Since 1949 an Arkansas hick had been singing about the same race problem in America's favorite Broadway show. (In the show and movie, she got to be from Little Rock; in the book it had been Otolousa.) The Little Rock integration crisis was about children and education. The *South Pacific* song was entitled "You've Got to Be Taught." New pieties were ventilated regarding the film's topicality and timeliness. In at least one state legislature, a resolution was offered in condemnation of such political meddling.

Yet here again, I would now propose, in any attempt to compound remembering out of such impressions of historicality, one must take care not to confuse the general productions of history with a particular history of production. For, if anything, the film production seems to have taken place when and in the way it did largely exclusive of anyone's notions of topical concern. The chronological movement from stage to film, for instance, as in all Rodgers and Hammerstein properties, depended on length of dramatic run. *South Pacific* was a monster, closing on Broadway in 1954. It lasted on the road well into the decade. It may make us feel virtuous to suggest that it was the film for the time. We would be more accurate if we just said that it was time for the film.

Equally important, as to film possibilities, was that it was also technologically the right time. For, whatever the message, *South Pacific* the film proved a case of the medium triumphant. It made film history. Cinematic splendors unimagined by the fondest South Seas devotee or musical fancier emerged through stunning advances in lens capability, color and sound reproduction, and projection technique. The film, for instance, remains notable today for being one of the first filmed in both Todd-AO and Cinemascope. Widely remarked on at the time were the color filters used to enhance (and in some cases render quite bizarre) the atmospherics of various musical numbers. Dubbing techniques were perfected that allowed flights of song to be floated at will. Mitzi Gaynor and Ray Walston, experienced troupers, were allowed to go it on their own. The male lead, Rossano Brazzi, on the other hand, preserving the Pinza tradition of operatic grandeur, was endowed with the voice-over talents of a singing compatriot, Giorgio Tozzi.[45] On the receiving end of these effects, the film also benefited from settings and modes of presentation as close as the local theater. Rapidly vanishing were the days of "A" movies at theaters with names like the Majestic and "B" movies at picture halls with names like the Strand. As television began to crowd the visual market, the theater industry reconcentrated its own infrastructure on what it could do best: the popular classic as wide-screen spectacular. The new emphasis would set in as quasi-biblical — *The Robe, The Ten Commandments, Ben Hur.* Eventually it would lead to *Dances with Wolves.* But along the way, it would also provide the American musical with its own, last, spectacular flowering: *South Pacific, West Side Story, The Sound of Music, My Fair Lady,* and, perhaps writing the final nostalgia script of remembering for a country that somehow couldn't get over thinking of itself as a Broadway show with a noble message and a bittersweet ending, *Camelot.*

In addition, there were other new demographics of entertainment that *South Pacific* the movie also seemed uniquely to address. Chief among these was tourism. World War II had turned Americans into globetrotters scrawling "Kilroy was here" on everything from cathedral walls to coconuts. In the prosperous decades succeeding the event, they avidly pursued the habit. Given the political upheavals of post–World War II Europe, tourism turned them Pacific-ward in particular. (Besides, having been fought over so violently and exclusively by us, it certainly must have seemed ours to enjoy.) In 1959 Hawaii became a state. Shortly, in the entertainment market, there ensued a spate of films: *Blue Hawaii, Hawaii, Gidget Goes Hawaiian;* then of course came the inevitable sequence of television spinoffs: *Hawaiian Eye, Hawaii Five-o, Magnum P.I.* [46]

South Pacific made sure it got into the boom on the front end. Besides one song excised from the play, "My Girl Back Home," reintegrated for length and dramatic continuity, there was, the viewer would note, one decidedly major new addition to the film, the interminable, highly choreographed boar-tusk ceremony. It is, of course, the torchlight spectacle luau from the standard vacation package, itself largely come from the pagan fire dance in the big screen epic. (Not surprisingly, the one they used actually came from Michener, who already had it as part of the dramatic development in *his* South Seas spectacle.) Now it could also be fixed indelibly in the expectation or the memory of any vacationer in the islands. Indeed, to this day, in any place with hotels it is almost impossible to take an evening walk without running into one. The *South Pacific* profit symbiosis, moreover, seems far from playing itself out. Also to this day, any tourist to Kauai sold on the spectacular helicopter tour will come home with a memory of having seen, just out to sea off the pristine west coast, the *actual Bali Ha'i.* [47]

Meanwhile, a half century after Pearl Harbor, four decades after Hiroshima and Nagasaki, the Japanese own most of Kauai and a good part of the American entertainment business. Still, the musical comedy that is our subject trundles along, trailing the old subtexts and agendas. And one cannot leave the trail of evolving technologies and productions without at least mentioning a recent recording — a London-based studio recording, in fact, designed for the cassette-tape and compact-disc market — that keeps the old story going and pretty much sums it up. It is a strange hybrid, not the movie, not the play, not the book, but an aural "staging," several features of which become newly instructive. Most telling, as to the latest conflation of the history business with the entertainment business, is surely the listing of the cast. The male leads: first, as DeBecque — in the operatic lineage of Pinza, the cinematic one of Brazzi, Italians who make good Frenchmen — a Spaniard, a renowned opera singer, Jose Carreras; second, as Cable, a mainstay star of the American musical stage, Mandy Patinkin, whose achieved persona, in the long tradition of Broadway, has been a celebration of his ethnicity. No Liat, of course, in this aural setting, is mentioned. Her part is silence. Her "Tonkinese" mother, on the other hand, here *does* achieve a kind of breathtaking final evolution, portrayed by the venerable American jazz singer Sarah Vaughan. Finally, there is the gemstone role in the spectacle, that of Nellie Forbush; and now the whole business truly does come back to meet itself. It is sung by the operatic soprano Dame Kiri Te Kanawa, a New Zealander herself of mixed-race Anglo-European and Maori descent. Out of this, of course, some may take heart in such a presentation of this American classic with such a multiracial, multicultural cast, tease out some old lesson about the universality of music. That is certainly the "sell" implicit in the latest production described here, some misty moral that awaits every time the book is read, the show or movie seen, the sound track or recording heard.[48]

I, on the other hand, must reserve such judgments, especially having noted above the current run on Broadway of an analogous American classic entitled *Miss Saigon*. Of this newest *South Pacific* clone, in its packaging of Vietnam-era American myth as self-congratulatory folk opera, Michael Feingold, waxing apocalyptic, if somewhat ungrammatical, in the *Village Voice*, says, "Every civilization gets the theater it deserves, and we get *Miss Saigon*, which means we can now say definitively that our civilization is over" (91). Robert Stone's comment in the *New York Times* is closer to the mark when he says that "with the New York opening of *Miss Saigon*, the Vietnam experience begins its final slide into the past, into history, make-believe, and melodrama" (30). My point would be that we have been doing this for a long time, and pretty much in the terms Stone acutely triangulates: history, make-believe, melodrama. Many, indeed, will recognize here a common version of the official "literary" narrative of our historical culture: history *as* make-believe melodrama, the old serio-amusement, neither tragic nor comic, not even tragicomic, but rather, somehow, at once deadly earnest and deadly escapist; and for certain not ironic, for that would truly be to admit to the historicity of history. In the complex evolution of the American entertainment classic entitled *South Pacific*, the production of a history moves on apace with the history of a production, of a series of productions, in fact, constituting something called American remembering.

Sands of Iwo Jima

In the standard war-movie genre, none of the great production-entertainment classics to come out of World War II in the immediate postwar era is probably better known than the 1949 John Wayne film *Sands of Iwo Jima*. Nor does any trademark classic of any postwar genre blazon more overtly from start to finish its connection with a master iconography of national heroism, in this case the classic World War II image summoned up by its title: the Joseph Rosenthal photo of the marine flag-raising on Mount Suribachi, itself surely the most famous combat photograph of World War II; and at the same time, as is now well known, itself *also* an elaborate restaging of heroic image and event. Advertising campaigns and publicity for the film had the advantage of playing into already widespread institutional and popular representations — on postage stamps and recruitment posters, as part of late wartime bond-drive promotions and highly publicized postwar monument campaigns; and they also partook of new public-relations fanfare about the marines' elaborate participation in and endorsement of the Hollywood project. Meanwhile, from within the production process eventuating in the film artifact, the whole mythic genealogy would also be ingeniously brought full circle in a final scene of climactic reenactment, complete with three actual Iwo Jima participants.

Accordingly, in so complex an interweaving of symbologies, an account of production and commodification here becomes an account of the especially complex relationship of history and memory so created at every point: a process of remembering launched, it turns out, even before the frozen moment of glory itself, and extending far beyond into forms of popular mythmaking and institutional policy still making themselves felt fifty years later.

Indeed, as a classic instance of the interpenetration of American myth and American reality, of imaginative fiat and actualized event, the whole business now reads from start to finish like its own astonishing metanarrative.[49] At any single point, it seems to have been a legend looking for a historical reification, an idea or image that, even before it happened, seemed to construct and eventually contain the act.

Here, one actually begins even before the beginning, so to speak, of the project at hand, with the tactical concept of an Iwo Jima flag raising itself as its own kind of presentational spectacle. This seems to have suggested itself more or less autonomously on February 23, 1945, aboard Admiral Richmond Kelly Turner's flagship as a distinctly pragmatic, even cynical military option, quickly endorsed by Major General Holland M. Smith of the marines, commander of the invasion force, and Secretary of the Navy James Forrestal, also in attendance. Why? Four days into the event, the invasion was threatening to stall, bogging down in its own American carnage. Operationally, they decided, some sort of highly visible morale booster was called for, not only for marines on the island, but also for an American public getting restless with the slow going and the slaughter

(Marling and Wetenhall 27–28). A flag would therefore go up on Suribachi. Never mind that the whole invasion would then turn north into the real defenses of the island, the heavily fortified Kuribayashi line.

A more immediate problem of operational fact of course was that troops from some U.S. fighting unit would have to make their way posthaste to the top of Suribachi. That unit was the Twenty-eighth Marine Regiment, whose commander was ordered to the task with the notation that "the fate of the whole operation turns on the balance." And a patrol of E Company, Second Battalion, Twenty-eighth Marines was duly sent to do the job.

Fulfillment of the mission occurred with astonishing dispatch. By 10:35 the same day, the patrol, trailed by a photographer, Lou Lowery from *Leatherneck* magazine, had actually walked unopposed to the summit. Just in case, Lowery had also been taking pictures all the way up with the flag they carried in prominent evidence. When they got on top, someone found a twenty-foot length of drainpipe. As quickly, the flag itself went up. Participants were Lieutenant Harold Schrier, the patrol leader, and three enlisted marines, Ivy Thomas, Henry Hansen, and Chuck Lindberg, with another, Jim Michaels, keeping guard. Lowery took an official photograph.

Thus came into being the first photographic image of an Iwo Jima flag raising; but even in the relative excitement of an important mission's being completed, it was an undramatic and, in many respects, rather staged and phony affair. One of the party was actually wearing a soft hat. They all had to wait one last moment for Lowery to reload with film.

Nevertheless, it turned out to be a crucial event historically in every sense. As far as marines on the island were concerned, a large number actually seem to have seen this version: a small, tattered flag raised on the end of a long piece of steel pipe. According to some accounts the whole island seemed to stop fighting for a moment to send up a cheer. Horns blared from ships at sea. The Japanese, infuriated by the deed, themselves responded by stirring up a major firefight on the summit. Meanwhile, on a Higgins boat headed for the beach, Forrestal is said to have turned to Smith with an utterance which would not be lost on any of its auditors then or later. "Holland," he observed, "the raising of that flag on Suribachi means a Marine Corps for the next five hundred years" (Marling and Wetenhall 51).

As part of the excitement, both symbolic and official, a representative of the flag-raising party was duly ordered offshore to receive congratulations. Schrier declined and sent Thomas, who proved unsuitably heroic in his insistence on a bland forthrightness about the event.[50]

Meanwhile, a battalion officer on the beach, Lieutenant Colonel Chandler Johnson, had arrived at a personal command opinion that the first flag was too hard to see. A much larger flag was duly gathered from an LST locker and sent up the hill with a battalion runner, Rene Gagnon, who was already preparing to set out with radio batteries. Also in attendance by this time, and deciding to accompany Gagnon, was the photographer Joe Rosenthal.

At the top, Schrier, now superintending the new affair as well, did his work thoroughly and according to regulation.[51] The second flag began to go up, with the raising timed so as to coincide with the first one going down. Meanwhile, combat photography was making history in every sense of the term. Rosenthal took a new picture in what he called a grab shot. Then he took a few more, just to make sure, over the protestations of his subjects that they were not "Hollywood Marines" (Marling and Wetenhall 71). The whole batch was sent off to Guam for development. And within a day the results were well on the way to making themselves part and fabric of American remembering.

Rosenthal's shot was easily the most celebrated and widely disseminated photo of the war. The official worldwide military newspaper, *Stars and Stripes*, gave it the entire front page. At home, newspapers and magazines could not reproduce it fast enough, even hurrying into print new special issues, which sold out on the spot.[52]

Three available Rosenthal participants, John Bradley, Rene Gagnon, and Ira Hayes, were brought home, enlisted in bond and monument drives, and otherwise generally paraded around as instant celebrities — in some cases suffering considerable guilt over what they felt to be a false representation of any personal heroism, and in others rather opportunistically trying to parlay it all into new kinds of fame and fortune. As a result, albeit with widely differing personal outcomes, the three figures themselves, like the image they came to represent, seemed for a while to become nearly ubiquitous. As late as 1954, they would all make a final platform appearance at Arlington National Cemetery for the dedication of the great Marine Corps monument for which they had literally served as models. And, as is well known, in 1961 one of them, the Pima Indian Ira Hayes, would become the subject of his own movie, *The Outsider*, itself a recapitulation of the Iwo Jima story and a fable of Hayes's subsequent encounter with tragic and ultimately fatal celebrity.

Meanwhile, of course, a whole new saga of production and commodification, equally complex in its own metanarrative involutions, was about to be set in motion by the movie project. And what remains most striking here too, curiously, is the degree to which what might be called tactical desperation seems to have preceded any notion of high mythic symbology on the film project as well. To put it simply, it was Hollywood that now stood as an embattled institution in need of both a quick operational victory and a morale boost.

The new enemy here was the House Un-American Activities Committee and various other Red baiters and would-be blacklisters; and the desperate, wide-ranging battle now joined was over Hollywood's seeming postwar lassitude in continuing to make films in which Americans appeared as sufficiently heroic. On Hollywood's part, this, of course, had been in large measure a common-sense marketing decision. By the late '40s especially, filmmakers had simply assumed — and rightly — that in the lengthening wake of victory and the natural decline of fervor for the war effort, with film as with other popular media, the American public was tired of celebrations of the American fighting spirit through graphic depictions of combat. To put it directly, the Good War had for the moment worn itself out as entertainment.

What no one could have anticipated were the consequences of such decisions in new contexts of international political upheaval and the resultant anti-Communist hysteria abroad and at home, into which Hollywood's newly found pacifism would find itself playing. The year 1947 had seen the birth of the House Un-American Activities Committee; and 1948 had confirmed many Americans' worst paranoiac fears of global conspiracy with the Russians' Berlin Blockade and the specter of the imminent defeat of Chiang Kai-shek's Nationalist forces by Mao Tse-tung's Chinese Communists. Americans had been linked to Communist spy networks; and broader allegations of Communist sympathizing had become rife among government agencies and the liberal intelligentsia, with writers and other practitioners of the creative arts among the most visible targets. In sum, an atmosphere had developed overnight in which the film industry came under extraordinary pressure to prove anew its loyalty to American institutions and values (Marling and Wetenhall 127). And one of the most readily available responses seemed to be a return to highly traditional, patriotic war movies of the sort at which 1941–45 filmmakers had become so thoroughly practiced and adept.

Response quickly followed on a grand scale across the industry. MGM scored with *Battleground*, Fox with *Twelve O'Clock High*, and Warner with *Task Force*. A new cycle of production began.[53] Further, as suggested by

Garry Wills, there was also the canny inclination by filmmakers in most cases to let the heroism depicted do double duty. While depicting World War II situations, that is, these war films would also concentrate on psychological portraits of "men under stress," and on the necessity of "discipline" and "organization" in standing up to the challenges of "protracted conflict." As Wills points out, then, including in his analysis emphasis on Wayne's imminent portrayal of Stryker in such a role, the studios could imagine themselves at once rewinning the big war and "waging the cold war" (154).

In the meantime, smaller producers, less flush and less flexible, struggled to get into the act. One of these was Republic Pictures. This was essentially a "B" producer, now in need of an "A" hit to mend its lagging postwar fortunes but short of resources to finance a big-budget spectacle, and especially a cast-of-thousands saga complete with heavy troops and authentic equipment.

On the other hand, given the already demonstrated public-relations possibilities of such films as those from the major studios, which had all been service-specific, Republic did not have to look far for a corresponding poor relation and potential partner in the military finding itself in comparably dire postwar circumstances. That partner, of course, was the Marine Corps, by anyone's reckoning the war-movie glamor arm among World War II ground forces, but now itself threatened also with severe budget cutbacks and perhaps even elimination in the proposed defense reorganization act.[54] Indeed, what the marines needed in the military and political eye was exactly what Republic could provide: image refurbishing in the form of a guts-and-glory, up-from-the-beaches film that had been the hallmark of their representation in wartime. And what Republic needed, of course — base facilities, uniforms, troops and equipment, authentic training and realistic combat simulation — the marines could not only provide but justify from a utilization and readiness standpoint as part of their operations budget.

One may perhaps wonder, therefore, about the rather more aestheticized account of the film's genesis in a widely reported epiphany of the producer Edmund Grainger, who claimed his reading in a newspaper of the phrase "sands of Iwo Jima" had simultaneously brought to mind the idea of the Rosenthal photo grandly reenacted as a movie climax.[55] On the other hand, no one could deny the public-relations triumph that ensued for both parties once they realized they had basically the same idea. As a production saga attempting to reproduce a great symbol of historical remembering in a new popular-culture icon possessing a comparable visibility and importance, the making of *Sands of Iwo Jima* proved to be a combined-operations story — both cinematic and military — conceived in some Hollywood screenplay heaven.[56]

Success was enormous and enduring. *Sands of Iwo Jima*; guts and glory; John Wayne: the phrases still string themselves together in mythic conjunction, a litany of remembering.

Never mind, as to issues of cinematic or military logic, that in the final result the great Iwo Jima scene would wind up being more or less summarily tacked on to a movie that has been almost in its entirety about Tarawa. Or that the same grand moment — popularly regarded as the ultimate John Wayne guts-and-glory scene in the ultimate John Wayne guts-and-glory movie, the crown of an entire genre,[57] would itself also be used more or less summarily to kill off the John Wayne character with a single inglorious shot from a sniper's spider-hole. Or even that John Wayne barely got into the film in the first place, shamelessly lobbying himself into a role intended for Kirk Douglas.[58] From the moment it was decided there would be a movie classic entitled *Sands of Iwo Jima*, all particulars of process and product seemed to become invested with some strangely self-originating aura of grand mythic synthesis and symbiosis.

Central to the quality of self-originating myth would of course be the complete identification of the featured actor with the central character. As he had pursued the part, Wayne in turn pursued the character with almost mystical devotion. It was a "beautiful personal story," he reflected nearly a quarter century later, a story making for "a different type of war picture" in which the big scenario could be devised almost exclusively from the intimate depiction of a small unit (Marling and Wetenhall 128). In between, he also negotiated rough spots in the civilian-military production relationship, becoming in his description "the 'Richelieu' of Republic" (Suid 98).

To guarantee almost reverential authenticity, the rest of the Hollywood cast, caught up in the same spirit of identification, were provided with a special boot camp. For stateside drill and barracks scenes, the company was also given the full use of Camp Pendleton, the main West Coast training facility for marines. On-post battle re-creations were staged on a mockup Mount Suribachi rising from an artillery observation point and in a moonscape quarry sprinkled with cosmetic volcanic ash. According to various needs, personnel from the Seventh Marine Regiment participating came to as much as a full battalion, complete with necessary equipment — uniforms, weapons, jeeps, planes, tanks, and landing craft. In any single shot at least a company was kept in background attendance for the various principals (Suid 97).

The marine command and advisory cast supplied was also imposing. The chief technical advisor, assigned full time by the marines, was Captain Leonard Fribourg. Wayne also spent great amounts of time shadowing a veteran warrant officer whom he deemed a suitable image of Stryker. Colonel David Shoup, winner of the Congressional Medal of Honor on Tarawa, and Lieutenant Colonel Henry "Jim" Crowe, one of his decorated battalion commanders at the seawall, were brought with much fanfare to handle authenticity matters on the significant part of the film devoted to that operation. As to Iwo Jima, however, no one would do but Holland M. Smith himself (Marling and Wetenhall 128–29). And when the time came, also brought aboard were the actual commander of both Suribachi flag-raising parties, Lieutenant Jim Schrier, and the three Rosenthal photo participants, rounded up from their labors in what would amount to almost a decade of ceremonies. Finally making a star appearance as well, with great public-relations impact, was the Rosenthal Iwo Jima flag, brought out of safekeeping at the marine museum at Quantico and handed over with much pomp and fanfare.

As might be expected, the movie quickly assumed its own metahistorical logic. In the big view the story of Tarawa was absorbed into the story of Iwo Jima, with the first, a wholly avoidable bloodbath, now augmenting the status of the second, at the time itself considered largely a companion piece to Okinawa. Meanwhile, in the close focus, the culminating dramatic event, the Suribachi flag raising, found itself being reconstituted in the image of its own iconic representations.[59] In this respect *Sands of Iwo Jima* has continued to be rightly grouped with wartime epics such as *Pride of the Marines* and *To the Shores of Tripoli* and others of the postwar period including *Halls of Montezuma* and *Battle Cry* as films in which, of all military forces involved in the war, the marines continue to hold their mystique and heroic luster. Indeed, historically, it is not too much to say that for most Americans of the postwar era, such films still constitute the marine war.

On the other hand, and less noticed, although the story of Stryker and his men may celebrate marine victory in the war in the big view, it also remains the great World War II marine movie classic with a difference. And that difference lies in its emphasis, at the more closely personal focus, on equally hard marine facts about the making of soldiers capable of achieving victory in such terms. For, out of the aura of the combat scenes, and after the customary melting-pot squad hijinks, the preponderance of the movie is really devoted to the decidedly non-guts-and-glory shaping up of the unit; and it is thereby heavily oriented as well toward Stryker's own drunkenness, anger, abuse of trainees,[60] abandonment of a spouse, estrangement from a son, and mastiff professionalism. John Wayne, that is, becomes and remains a decidedly problematic character throughout — perhaps *the* most problematic played by him in a long movie career.[61] Accordingly, for the sake of the marines and everyone else, it becomes essential in just these terms that he is rather gratuitously and pointlessly — if cleanly — killed off. For this is the real stroke of genius in the Stryker-and-his-marines story, with the flag raising providing the ceremonial bridge, the moment of mythic passage: that it is finally, just at that moment, subsumed into the story of another marine, in this case the John Wayne hero subsumed into the John Agar hero. The latter has been the platoon intellectual, the questioner, the officer's kid as reluctant warrior. Now he assumes leadership in a single imperative — "Saddle up."[62] These, of course, are themselves Stryker's words. Agar has just earned them in his moment of decision. But it is important that we also know, already, that he will never be a lifer. Rather, he will just have had that grand moment as a team-working American who saw it was time to pick up the mantle of leadership. Actually at the expense, then, of Stryker and, by implication, other professional marines such as the officer-father, is achieved here once again the really best and happiest and most familiar story to come out of each of the Good War's greatest hits: the story of the World War II citizen-soldier.

The message would thus seem to be that Stryker is useful, even necessary, in wartime, but he is a problem back in the world. The John Agar character, in contrast — the civilian who makes the transition to soldier — must become the real hero of the war *and* the peace. To be sure, sometimes he will have the melodramatic good fortune to be killed — a Doug Roberts, a Joe Cable, a Robert Hearn — before having to experience civilian readjustment; but he is equally likely to make it back, albeit a more complicated but more likely character: the civilian who has made the transition to soldier at least possibly now the soldier who can also make the transition back to civilian — an Al Stephenson or a Michael Whiteacre. As for the necessary killing off, this will always be the inevitable fate of a Stryker, a Prewitt (and most likely a Warden), a Croft, a Two Gun Shapiro. These people, made for the military, may be needed in time of war, but they must remain disposable in time of peace. Or, with luck, their heroism allows them to dispose of themselves in a concluding blaze of glory.

One must infer that the version of such a moral contained in *Sands of Iwo Jima* largely got lost on viewers hell-bent on continuing to mythologize John Wayne *and* American men in marine utilities, not to mention conflating the two mythologies in some eternal identicality. It was not, however, lost on the marines, who if anything seem to have seen a benefit in allowing it to subtly reify into a quasi-official self-characterization, with films as late as the 1955 *Battle Cry*, as will be seen, still hewing to the hard-core model, albeit in somewhat sanitized, Technicolor updating. Of all the World War II military services, indeed, they retained for decades the most consistently heroic image by making it a point of blazoning the rigor and — for Western armies at least — even the brutality of their training methods; and of the firmness of the indoctrinations whereby they could still program American boys to do what is required of U.S. Marines, which is to sacrifice themselves, of course, for a mad belief in their sheer military utility. And so it seemed to work in some strange reciprocity of art and life. Who else but a crazy marine like Chesty Puller could have gotten away in 1952 in the middle of a military disaster by describing the frozen retreat from Korea's Chosin Reservoir as an advance in the opposite direction? And who else but dug-in, outnumbered marines, even as late as 1967 and 1968, could still look heroic in places like Con Tien and Khe Sanh? Even Vietnam could not kill off the marines. The popular aesthetic — what another service would have called an image problem — of hard-core self-mythologization would remain their capital, then, now, and beyond.[63] In the midst of all the latest awfulness, a mystical thing called the corps would continue to be as big as its own iconography.

Life's Picture History of World War II

If World War II, as evidenced by its classic texts of postwar representation, was a war made for the big novel, the big Broadway play, the big Hollywood movie, or the big TV documentary, it was also probably the last great war made for the big picture-history volume. For the war itself was the last great pictorial war. Americans may have gotten regular and memorable reporting from newspaper copy and radio; and they may have seen more than their share of film footage in newsreels and movies. But they got their most vivid and enduring images of the war from pictures. In the great illustrated magazines, especially — *Time, Life, Newsweek, Look, Collier's,* the *Saturday Evening Post* — they saw the war *pictorially* to an almost overwhelming degree: in cartoons, drawings, sketches, and paintings; in poster and propaganda art; in illustrated stories, articles, and public information messages; and in dramatic artwork associated with wartime advertising. But above all they saw the war through golden-age photojournalism: that of the newspapers and wire services, to be sure; but also that made widely available — sometimes by reprint but as often by staff or commissioned original — through the weekly and monthly magazines. And when it came to the photojournalism usually remembered best as somehow catching the whole grand sweep of the war, it was likely to be that of the greatest of all the great photojournalistic magazines, Henry Luce's *Life*.

Accordingly, given the vast archival accumulations of the Luce enterprise, not to mention its thoroughgoing political and psychological identification in the public mind with the Allied war effort, it must have seemed inevitable that the publishers of *Life* should have chosen to celebrate the victory with a great, ambitious, commemorative photojournalistic volume.[64] And so they did, in 1950, with one of the most visible, popular, and enduring of all the classic texts of postwar representation in any major medium or genre — a text indeed that continues to be almost invariably cited to this day by Americans of the immediate postwar era as one of the two or three most prominent sources of their remembering.

It was entitled, simply, *Life's Picture History of World War II* — although, to be sure, like everything else bearing the Time-Life imprimatur, it might as easily have been called *The War According to Henry Luce*. Further, in this case, as will be seen, the Lucean hand would now also make itself equally visible through significant attempts at Cold War revisionism. Still, the latter notwithstanding, the *Life* compendium quickly became an omnipresent cultural icon, a text in which history, so recently spilling forth as actual event from the weekly pages of the great magazine itself, now seemed preserved as permanently at one with actual memory. Indeed, *ubiquitous* might have served as the operative term. It was a standard in libraries. And within months of publication, it lay in prominent view on bookshelves and coffee tables in countless homes.[65] Further, unlike novels or even popular print histories, which were often read once, if at all, or plays and movies, which were most frequently experienced and remembered from a single viewing, it made its peculiar presence felt as the convenient subject of repeated perusal. Thereby it served its own dual function as at once commemoration and commodification; and again, the result was one that Henry Luce himself could not have devised more expertly. As a textual commodity proving endlessly revisitable, it became in itself a primary and continuous medium of remembering of the war; and, as events would show, it proved almost as endlessly replicable in new formats and presentations. Thus the project became an ongoing historical confirmation of the degree to which the war according to Henry Luce, before, during, *and* after, would for countless Americans always somehow be the war.

From the beginning, indeed, *Life* and the war seemed themselves, almost in some fated way, made for each other. Or, as the editors proclaimed as late as the preface to a 1977 volume entitled *Life Goes to War*, World War II "was the longest story" the magazine "ever told." And eager as they may have been to promote the new book, they were also speaking accurately about the ground-floor identification of the great conflict and the correspondingly enormous journalistic enterprise carried out by the publication.[66] Of the war they wrote, "It began in 1936 on the blood-stained barricades of Madrid and Barcelona, and the wind-swept plains above Peking." But they might have been as easily writing about the magazine, as from the same year onward it began to survey across what it called "the newsfronts of the world," the gathering cataclysm.

To be sure, as to initial production values, even momentous world affairs seemed subsumed within a kind of brawny, American, journalistic muscle-flexing. Everything in the magazine, it seemed, came invested with a stamp of sheer national bigness. The first cover — Margaret Bourke-White's classic photograph of massive concrete pilings at a dam project in Fort Peck, Montana — quickly achieved monumental status of its own as a modernist icon. And inside, an accompanying photographic story, while celebrating the huge construction effort as an epochal WPA enterprise, pursued with a rumbustious, Whitmanesque appetite the lives of the workers and their families, the camp followers and the taxi dancers.

On the other hand, with more cosmopolitan matters back East, the same application of the big pictorial view could create an aura of detached sophistication, of an almost Olympian social and political urbanity. *Life* followed people in the news in the major centers of culture and power. It also accompanied them to parties and other major celebrity gatherings, in this social aspect often remaining distinctly Anglophile, with the recording of romances and marriages, biographical profiles and family lives of nobility. And in the United States, it likewise devoted itself mainly to the WASP upper crust, debutantes and college beauty queens, the Ivy League, the eastern women's colleges, the service academies. In politics, keeping a cool ambivalence toward Roosevelt, as might be expected of its already legendarily pro-Republican and anti-Communist publisher, it nonetheless acknowledged his powerful presence, devoting an entire weekly section to presidential news along with close coverage of Washington events — domestic politics, legislative and foreign affairs, defense issues.[67]

Meanwhile, it capitalized on the visual possibilities of the new pictorial format to address large cultural developments in the arts and the sciences. It lavishly reproduced works as diverse, for instance, as those of Edward Hopper, Vincent Van Gogh, and Thomas Hart Benton, as well as apprentice water colors from the World War I western front by Adolf Hitler. It also endlessly photographed birds, spiders, and monkeys. And in a celebrated 1938 photo essay, it followed step by step, right down to the process of clinical delivery, the birth of a baby.

Indeed, as suggested in the later aspect, *Life* often seemed a magazine at once brash and canny enough to get away with much that would have elsewhere in the popular domain been considered downright risqué. This was especially true of its attitude toward the female form. The preferred mode was what might be called seminudity, seizing the opportunity for tastefully revealed bare breasts — of bathers or undraped studio artists' models, for instance — or of leg shots of dancers, skaters, bathing beauties. It almost always portrayed such glamorous Hollywood stars as Paulette Goddard, Merle Oberon, and Betty Grable in a decided pin-up aspect. And again, perhaps most prominently *and* memorably, it also made magazine history with a notorious early photo essay on how and how not to undress seductively for one's spouse.

All in all then, early *Life* truly could be said to subscribe to the photojournalistic philosophy aptly encapsulated by Bernard DeVoto in *Saturday Review*: along with its snappy texts, sidebars, and captions, it developed a trademark visual style, "a formula that called for equal parts of the decapitated Chinaman, the flogged Negro, the surgically explored peritoneum, and the rapidly slipping chemise" (Wainwright 95).

At the same time, from that same first issue, of November 26, 1936, onward, *Life* found itself sharing its fascinated gaze on the American scene with a lurid, nearly obsessive interest in the rise of the great dictatorships and events on the gathering international scene of global military upheaval.[68] Already, great attention was given to nations in the midst of conflict — most notably Spain and China — and to a host of others on the eve of crisis — Austria, Czechoslovakia, Hungary, Poland, Singapore, the Philippines. The magazine reported comprehensively on early major events that would later read as a catalog of opening acts to global war: Barcelona, the Anschluss, the Sudeten crisis, Munich, the Russo-Japanese clash on the Mongolia-Manchukuo boundary. It also gave profiles of major Axis and Allied leaders, including, in the third issue, of December 7, 1936, a long biographical feature story on Hitler, and then going on in later ones to Mussolini, Goering, Chamberlain, Churchill, Stalin, Chiang Kai-shek, Madame Chiang, Mao Tse-tung, and Manuel Quezon.

Once major hostilities were in progress, *Life* may be said basically to have named the war and claimed it, at once representing and essentially constructing it for Americans according to the Lucean world view. By September 25, 1939, with Germany and Russia dividing the spoils from conquered Poland after the Germans' September 1 invasion and the quick honoring, on paper at least, by Britain and France of treaty commitments bringing most of Europe officially into the conflict, the editors were calling it "the Second World War." In short order there followed dismally extensive coverage of the French defeat. On the other hand, much was also made of the embracing of a new ally after the German invasion of Russia.[69] And, as had been the prewar custom, particular attention continued to be paid as well to developments in a long-favored theater, the ongoing Sino-Japanese war, including accounts of the internal political struggles of various Chinese factions and power groups.[70]

Meanwhile, *Life* prepared American readers for the likelihood of their own war with profiles of U.S. military services, weapons development, strategic defenses in Hawaii, the Canal Zone, and the Philippines, and other features on issues of military and industrial readiness.[71] Personally, Luce made his own position clear on such matters as the increasing danger of world conflict and the threat of international totalitarianism in a famous February 17, 1941, essay entitled "The American Century." And in the ensuing dark night of the soul just after Pearl Harbor, with the equally famous "WAR" and "Day of Wrath" issues of December 15 and 22, it steeled Americans for their own long struggle and quickly assumed the position of preeminent popular information and morale resource for the duration. Accordingly, from the first steps back on the march toward victory, *Life* kept its own commitments to the war effort. It was in completely and in for good. Guadalcanal, Midway, and other early successes in the Pacific; the African invasion, the opening of new fronts in the European theater such as Sicily and Italy, and the bombing war from England — in its devotion to these American stories, *Life* did a job of global proportion. Story material seemed to arrive from all theaters, large and small, much of it involving combat action on various fronts — land, sea, air. There was also extensive and continuing coverage of civilian suffering, bombing casualties, victims of Nazi and Japanese terror. Joining earlier *Life* photos that had already become legendary — a Maginot Line poilu (slang for French soldier) patiently waiting out the phony war everyone called the Sitzkrieg; a solitary, crying Chinese baby, sitting burned and upright in the blazing ruins of a Shanghai train station — were a collocation of new documentary images permanently imprinting themselves upon the national memory: George Strock's anonymous GI bodies washed up on the beach at Buna; Robert Capa's D-Day recordings of the first wave ashore on Omaha; W. Eugene Smith's U.S. infantryman, his buddy vigilant in the background, tenderly handling a baby plucked out of a deadly cave on Saipan.[72] Apace, in addition to Strock, Capa, Smith, and Bourke-White, all the other great names would emerge: the photographers Carl and Shelley Mydans, Eliot Eliosofon, George Silk, Ralph Morse, Alfred Eisenstadt; the war artists and illustrators Tom Lea, Peter Hurd, Fletcher Martin, Paul Sample, Floyd Davis, Edward Lanning, Barse Miller, Aaron Bohrod, Reginald Marsh (Wainwright 137–38).

Thus the war according to *Life* became a massive, world-ranging, indefatigable extension of the war effort itself, a total production. And so, for countless Americans, the industrial-strength experience of reading and rereading *Life* week after week in wartime became indistinguishable from the day-by-day and week-by-week experience of the war.[73] Further, as to active political influence on the conduct of affairs, all the prewar jokes about Luce Inc. as already something of a branch of government — albeit venting itself frequently throughout those years in blasts of Olympian opposition — were now reified into quasi-official fact.[74] In its massive production shift into a wartime mode, as one historian has phrased it, the magazine also moved politically into a preeminent role as "more often than not a great weekly cheering section in pictures and words, a voluble, reassuring, earnest, admonishing, indignant, aghast, tender, hugely admiring witness to a conflict whose victorious outcome for America it never doubted" (Wainwright 122); and in so doing, it would also come full circle in self-awareness, even as the war continued, of its nearly absolute production success and political preeminence as a wartime institution. It was an institution, that is, finally making history in a way as important as the sweep of events it recorded (Wainwright 168).

Such institutional self-awareness was openly described in a preface to the classic 1950 *Picture History* as a central motivation for creating the volume. For the permanent record, it was suggested, *Life* basically owed the world a commemorative classic, a standard, judicious, perhaps even definitive overview in picture and print of the epic struggle just concluded. Further, the text concluded, it could also thereby seize the occasion justly to celebrate both heroic efforts: the Allied march to victory itself, and *Life's* own epic effort — the work of its photographers, writers, and editors — to chronicle it and document it.[75]

At the same time, however, the date was now 1950, with the threat of the old wartime Fascist totalitarianisms already replaced with the specter of the new Communist monolith. Accordingly, Henry Luce being Henry Luce, the same preface also carried up front important new attempts to construct postwar geopolitical agendas, chief among them the revising of old enmities into new alliances and old alliances, when necessary, into new enmities.

Thus, somewhat shockingly, it opened on the first count by proceeding from a prefatory tribute to Americans fallen in combat and to their allies, to an explicit honoring "too, of those millions of enemy combatants who, however wickedly misled, fought courageously and who found wounds and death and all the miseries of war no less bitter on their side than on ours." It went on: "To all those who fought honorably and died, we say: God rest them and God forgive us all" (v).

On the turn of recent geopolitical events, it was even more direct. Although billing itself as "strictly a book of military history" and eschewing analysis of "political and social forces," it nonetheless delivered the unhappy judgment that "the U.S. and her Allies" had obviously "displayed more skill and valor in the military war than in the political conduct of the war" (v). Especially, it concluded, if the war had been "essential to keep open the possibility of decent civilization on this earth," surely "the principles of political freedom have yet to be established as the law of mankind." To put it simply, World War II may indeed have been the Good War; but new, unblinking acceptance of Cold War realities was already being required to tell us what it had really meant — and, by implication, how far it was from being over.

The result of this hybrid focus, part commemoration and part retrospective construction, would be a politically hybridized text. To be sure, the prevailing spirit would be that of celebratory remembrance. We truly had just been part of a world at war; it truly all had been a case of do or die. All the great themes were there, along with all the major divisions of the great dramatic scenario. At the same time, the text was also distinctly a late 1940s and early 1950s political projection, a form of historical argument thoroughly invested with Cold War revisionisms. If the *Picture History* was an attempt to recapture the way it was, it was equally the construction of a different world making the war itself already a different war.

Mainly, this was a structural achievement. Pictures and text were divided into twelve chapterlike units. Each section was given an introductory essay by John Dos Passos;[76] running text was under the authorship of a Time-Life senior editor, Robert Sherrod, with the help of assistants. The units themselves merged chronology with topical organization. With succinct descriptive titles, they seemed to combine the best features of "straight" and "thematic" history: I, The Conquest of Europe; II, The Siege of Britain; III, The Axis Strained; IV, The Arsenal of Democracy; V, Japanese Conquests; VI, The Axis Contained; VII, The Axis Reversed; VIII, The Axis Broken; IX, Invasion; X, The Home Front; XI, Victory in Europe; XII, Victory in the Pacific.

The format led to a remarkably efficient and coherent managing of the enormous story line. The opening blitzkrieg against Poland was followed by the Battle of the Continent, the fall of France, and the evacuation of Dunkirk; a separate division was given to the Battle of Britain; new German aggressions were traced in Greece, Crete, Malta; these were followed by a long feature on the Nazi invasion of Russia; and in the last of the opening chapters, increasing American involvement in global crisis was shown culminating in the Pearl Harbor disaster.

At this point, the text moved appropriately to corresponding earlier scenes of Japanese conquest — China, Hong Kong, Singapore. Then came a spectacle of nonstop American disaster — Guam, Wake Island, the Philippines — culminating in Bataan and relieved only by the bright example of the Doolittle raid on Tokyo. In depictions of the gradual turn of global events in favor of the Allies, coverage included the Coral Sea, North Africa, the Atlantic, Stalingrad, and Midway; miscellaneous other topics involved the Torch landings, Casablanca, the ongoing Russian war, the Aleutians, submarines, the China-Burma-India theater, and flying the Hump. Finally, it was back to the main action: Sicily and Italy; Guadalcanal; Tarawa and the Marshalls; the European bombing war; D-Day; the home front; the Normandy breakout, the Bulge, the Rhine, the Ruhr; the German retreat from Russia; the death of Hitler, fall of Berlin, and German surrender; new Pacific victories at Saipan, the Philippines, Leyte Gulf, Iwo Jima, and Okinawa; kamikaze warfare; the atomic bombing of Hiroshima and Nagasaki; and the final Japanese surrender.

A brief epilogue attempted to address directly changes and aftereffects at home and abroad, postwar geopolitical reorientations, and the responsibilities assumed by the United States. There was brief mention of increasing international frictions in general, of the Berlin Airlift in particular, but *nothing* about specific Cold War antagonisms. Freedom was still imperiled, the editors could note in conclusion, but their volume pointedly does not specify *by whom.*[77]

Appendixes followed, including national casualty statistics and an assessment of the financial cost of the U.S. effort compared with other U.S. wars. Finally, there also appeared "A Selective Glossary of World War II Personalities." This was a listing, ostensibly, of major dramatis personae, with names, nationalities, and capsule descriptions of roles; but here, especially, selection seemed to have a distinct Cold War flavor. The entries numbered 155. The Axis, predictably, was dominated by Germans and Japanese, with the Italians sharing brief space with such celebrated toadies as Vidkun Quisling and Pierre Laval. The Allies, on the other hand, were overwhelmingly American, British, and French — down to Colonel Oveta Culp Hobby, director of the Women's Army Corps; Admiral Sir Bruce Fraser, commander of the British Home Fleet; and the Vichy French vice-premier, Jean Darlan. Only four Russians made the list: Joseph Stalin and Marshalls Konev, Timoshenko, and Zhukov. Two Chinese remained: the deposed Generalissimo Chiang Kai-shek and his foreign minister, T. V. Soong.

Yet this too, one realizes retrospectively, has also in some degree been part of the story line, itself structurally proportioned down to page and picture count. The Russian contributions, for instance, although they were recognized as being of sufficient historical importance to require substantive recording, have also been given carefully constructed editorial contexts. A fairly large proportion of *combat* coverage has been actually from German command archives; in materials from Russian sources, emphasis has been on the personal bravery and sacrifice of Soviet soldiery and on the larger suffering of Russians as a people.[78] On the other hand, the treatment of Chinese war participation, although comparably massive on a global scale, has simply been minimized out of existence[79] — and this, of course, after an unbroken record of service by *Life* and other Luce publications as essentially house organs for the Chiang Kai-shek regime in its struggle against Japanese invasion from without and Communist menace from within.

Further, as opposed to the visibility accorded Roosevelt, Churchill, De Gaulle — not to mention every member of the U.S. Joint Chiefs of Staff, with a section devoted to them in full portraiture, we suddenly realize also that we have not seen *a single photograph of Stalin or Chiang*. And this is the key, of course. For both had by now become bitter reminders of what had been lost to the aggressions of a new Communist world-historical totalitarianism in the short five years since victory had been so gloriously declared. Of all the wartime giants, Stalin now remained as emblematic of the new Russian menace, the disarray of the old Allies in the face of postwar Soviet triumphs and consolidations of Eastern European hegemony. And Chiang, of course, had become the burning image of the other great Communist triumph of the immediate postwar era, with the mainland lost to Mao Tse-tung's Communists in the disaster of 1949 and the champion of Holy China now reduced to tinpot despotism on a fortified island. It was indeed a new world, after all. Accordingly, the story of the war itself had already begun to take on its own new Lucean reflection.

Whatever the chemistry of these twinned rhetorical functions of text — the attempt to combine overt appeal as straight historical celebration, coupled with a less obvious role as a new Cold War lens on Good War events, it surely made for good book business. The volume enjoyed wide commercial success and gained overnight cultural status as a popular classic. Moreover, success bred success, with the first work's extraordinary visibility as a Time-Life production — not to mention further, vast, untapped riches of Time Inc. holdings — parlayed as inexhaustible capital into an endless series of ensuing productions.

A lavish two-volume 1959 reprise, for instance, combined impressive photo essays with Winston Churchill's history, itself initially produced in three massive volumes and now specially abridged and edited for American readers.[80] To be sure, as if to remind readers of the appeal of the 1950 book, much of the photography was familiar. In addition, however, the Churchill property ran heavy with elaborate color reproductions, dramatic war art, and in some cases important new photography.[81] The physical design also emphasized prestige, with coffee-table size, colorful dustcover, and custom binding.

The new text brought to bear Churchillean perspectives and emphases, on leaders, conferences, the crucial evolutions of relationships among the Allies. But the story format of the documentary divisions remained familiarly Lucean. Out of twenty-two sections, embattled Britain again got a chapter. Two more were devoted to the eastern front. On the other hand, here was nothing of China save now for a page on Singapore, Hong Kong, other bastions of British Far East that fell early in war. For the intransigent Christian Sinophile and Cold Warrior Henry Luce, it was as if the consequences of the war for the Asian continent had now become almost too hard to talk about.

In the 1960s and '70s, *Life* went to a host of productions in the picture-and-text genre of which the World War II books had been the prototype in editorial and market format.[82] And in many of these — especially the great historical retrospectives — *Life* and the war according to *Life* continued to be inevitably conflated as major subjects. *The Best of Life* (1973) was followed by *Life Goes to the Movies* (1975) and *Life Goes to War* (1977). These were followed by *Life: The First Decade* (1979), *Life: The Second Decade* (1984), and *Life: The First Fifty Years, 1936–86*.

But the great, commercial Time Inc. reprise on the war was yet to come; and when it appeared, it also turned out to be the most expansive, ambitious, and comprehensive Time-Life classic ever: a full, hardbound, thirty-nine-volume set, produced between 1976 and 1980, advertised extensively through magazine and television offers and distributed by mail-order installment. It was entitled, simply, *World War II*. Each volume now followed its own microcosmic version of the standard picture-history format, with elaborate scenario-like divisions. Further, each was centered on a commissioned text by an established historian or a respected writer of general nonfiction. On the other hand, it was mainly just the commercial conceptualization and packaging that seemed to have changed. The photos were the familiar ones, and the volume titles still told the old Lucean story: *Prelude to War, Blitzkrieg, Island Fighting, The Italian Campaign, China-Burma-India, The Battle of the Atlantic, Across the Rhine, The Road to Tokyo*.[83]

Naturally, there would also come fiftieth-anniversary volumes. The first would be *Life's WWII*, an updated combination of photographic and historical text (1989), serious enough to run with new competitors but familiar enough to strike the old appeal. The second, on the other hand, edited by Philip B. Kuhnhardt, was impossible not to recognize. There, cycled up to the front cover now, was the valedictory photograph of the grim, hard, confident GI, beard and mud and cigarette and helmet still in place, from the old photo history of forty years earlier. And inside, in mirror image of its predecessor, came the old familiar contents, a final recycling and harvesting of the treasure of remembering. The war according to *Life* had assumed an existence of its own, far outliving the event, the magazine itself, even the age of the magazine, the age of the print book, and the age of the vast majority of persons for whom the experience is still an actual memory. Henry Luce had dreamed a political turn of journalistic genius undreamed by Clausewitz: the postwar classic had become the continuation of the war by other means. This is to say, then, that the history of the war and the history of the magazine finally did become conflated into an identification whereby the war became an event remembered through style of popular representation. Our memory of the way it was became of a piece with the memory of the way in which it was imaged; accordingly, the history of a whole style of remembering finally came to look like history itself. For many persons from the era, the war would continue to be what it had always been: the war according to *Life*.

Victory at Sea

"Of course. It's my father's absolute favorite. He was there, you know." Thus a friend replied when I told her I was writing about *Victory at Sea*, the classic NBC television documentary of U.S. and Allied naval operations in World War II. The father in question, moreover, was no ordinary judge of the material, but an old navy chief who *had* actually been there for much of it, before, during, and after. Nor was the friend — a career journalist of long acquaintance with sea stories — an uncritical interpreter of the information. Still, as regards the forms and processes of cultural mythmaking, the exchange could be said to contain a familiar parable of World War II and American remembering, about some of the particular and identifiable ways in which Americans from the generation of 1941–45 and their successors have come to conflate the experience of the war with certain popular-culture texts achieving classic status among its postwar representations. To put it more directly, one could not help thinking that for both father and daughter, as for me and other Americans who "remember" World War II, "there" — or at least a significant portion of it — has actually become *Victory at Sea*.

To this degree, of course, the case at hand is but one instance of the basic production story of the postwar classic and American remembering. As with corresponding texts of the era from print literature, drama, and film — not to mention, as here, from such emergent media as television and high-fidelity musical recording — it is at once a parable of representation and, in the fullest degree, of cultural commodification. At the same time, as will be seen, it is one especially notable both for its own complex politics of origin and for the complex politics of its relation to national developments ranging from the rise of the electronic media to major postwar defense reorganizations. As the "creative" work, that is, of writers, researchers, editors, advisors, consultants, technicians, engineers, producers, directors, designers, composers, arrangers, and performers, *Victory at Sea* also comes into being as corporate work in the fullest sense, in this case as the collaboration of a pioneering communications network testing out new possibilities of media entrepreneurship and a venerable, once dominant military service fighting for its life amid radical postwar realignments.[84] It is as a production in this composite sense, then, at once as artistic and techno-political and economic artifact, that *Victory at Sea* becomes nothing less than the reified body of American remembering.

Victory at Sea: an epochal thirteen-hour, twenty-six-part television documentary, produced by the National Broadcasting Company in official partnership with the Department of the Navy, and assembled, with full diplomatic cooperation, out of sixty million feet of film gathered from the vast archives of Allied and Axis nations, including the United States, England, France, India, Japan, Germany, and Italy; an accompanying text, by a young researcher and writer, Henry Salomon, in collaboration with the journalist Richard Hanser, with narration by Leonard Graves; and an original musical score by the composer Richard Rodgers, with symphonic arrangements and orchestration by Robert Russell Bennett, who also conducted the NBC Symphony Orchestra in performance. After decades of media huckstering, even to sketch out the dimensions of the original property is still to suggest the set of extraordinary coincidings of cultural vectors that brought it to pass; and it is also, not surprisingly, to invoke a post-1945 American production saga so complex in both its artistic and its institutional politics as to be worthy of a Renaissance Italian city-state. But best of all, as a quintessential American story, it may also be said to come down to the bright idea of a single unlikely innovator, a staff historian employed in the most drudging kind of anonymity, in whom suddenly flowered a marriage of the practical opportunist and the prophetic technologue that Benjamin Franklin could not have improved on.

That figure, mentioned briefly above, was Henry Salomon, a former student of the eminent historian Samuel Eliot Morison at Harvard, who, while serving as a naval officer during the war, had been recruited as part of the in-uniform historical research team assembled by Morison; and who, in that capacity, had then and afterward worked with Morison, along with a cadre of fellow researchers and writers, on the latter's magisterial fourteen-volume *History of U.S. Naval Operations in World War II*. And what got Salomon started, appropriately, on his passage from teamworking factualist to techno-visionary was an essentially utilitarian horror of waste — a horror specifically awakened, as he toiled under Morison, by his awareness of incredible *film* resources being bled of their documentary content for absorption into the official print history. Further, such an awareness seems to have been spurred not by any particular appreciation of film as a medium so much as by the sheer mass of an inventory that came to his attention, a listing, compiled as part of Morison's overall research plan, of all documentary footage in the possession of the navy. Indeed, according to Pat Weaver, it was this catalog of core material that Salomon appropriated as his capital, so to speak, in seeking independent support to broaden his researches into other Allied *and* Axis archives.

To be sure, questions of scale aside, the idea of such a major "artistic" film documentary was hardly new. During the war itself, for instance, had already appeared the legendary *Why We Fight* series and such memorable feature documentaries by major Hollywood directors as Leland Heyward's *Marines on Tarawa*, Louis de Rochemont's *The Fighting Lady*, John Ford's *The Battle of Midway*, John Huston's *Report from the Aleutians* and *The Battle of San Pietro*, Darryl Zanuck's *At the Front in North Africa*, and William Wyler's *Memphis Belle*. Further, already in circulation for postwar audiences were two major newsreel compilations from *The March of Time*, *Crusade in Europe*, and *Crusade in the Pacific*.

The distinguishing feature of *Victory at Sea* lay in the fact that *this* massive documentary artifact, from its first stages of planning onward in late 1947 and early 1948, would be devised exclusively for television — itself, at the time, a potential mass-information and entertainment technology so little understood as a production medium or an audience venue as to require for today's reader a whole other definition of the concept. Certainly, it was anything but current television, that cornucopia of overload, with cable, premium channels, network and special-interest programming — with new networks entirely devoted to movies, sports, news, weather, even shopping. Nor did it even much resemble TV of the broad middle era, with its standard big-three network slates: star vehicles, variety shows, dramatic series, news, sports, specials, and seasonal programming — along with game shows, giveaways, soap operas, sitcoms, cartoons, Westerns, detective series. Perhaps, at most, one might correctly think of *Victory at Sea* — or at least by the time of its first appearance in late 1952 and early 1953 — in something of the context of an early golden age, with TV already familiar as a commercial medium having achieved popular success but at the same time still trying to carve out a distinct intellectual niche: TV, that is, with such varied favorites as *I Love Lucy*, Milton Berle, Bishop Fulton J. Sheen, and *Dragnet* joined by public affairs programming in the vein of the army-McCarthy hearings or Nixon's Checkers speech; with early attempts, in competition with both Hollywood and Broadway, to make live drama a TV staple, emphasizing professional writing, acting performance, production, direction, and design; with the first attempts at network news; and, in perhaps a closer intellectual paradigm for the artistic-documentary model at hand, with topical treatments of politics, history, and what we used to call "current events" — *You Are There*, for instance, a "news" dramatization of great historical incidents; the classic *See It Now* (1951), in which current news was mixed with reporting on cultural affairs;[85] or, in an extension of that concept, *Omnibus*, in which information and entertainment might extend themselves further into education and even art.

But even this analysis of contemporary contexts of production and reception in early television broadcasting would be only partially correct as pertaining to the largely unvisited technological landscape still awaiting the documentary conceived of by Salomon nearly five years earlier. For, as to the forms of production described above, something as simple as these basic categories of programming in their relation to audience interests would not yet have been available to be conceptualized. And to all this, as hard as it may be to believe now, we would also have to adduce the public perception — in the late '40s and early '50s largely accurate — of the TV set as a function of class status associated with television equipment itself, the actual homeviewing apparatus, still relatively expensive and hard to get. Moreover, again emphasizing the differences between television and movie viewers, it would still have been considered predominantly a "live" medium in which prerecorded forms of production would not seem much of a novelty.[86] And in both these connections there would also have been the related exclusivity of a broadcast area strictly urban and anchored to major cultural centers, with national hookups a thing of the future.

For his part, Salomon seems not particularly to have cared, having already somehow moved beyond any extant notions of both genre and medium into a new, potentially all-encompassing concept of viewing experience: the saga of Allied victory, to be recaptured in bold artistic documentary, thus re-creating on a grand scale for the generation of the war *and* creating anew for the generations to come after them the sense of the whole, vast, communal experience of it, as in the era itself that experience had been rendered through newspapers, magazines, radio, film; but now also with the saga to be endowed the unprecedented immediacy of an extraordinary new broadcast technology, a technology, by its nature, capable of reproducing that sense of vast, collective, truly popular and national identification through the essential quality of the TV experience itself. Here would be the great epic of victory again, but now with the sense of documentary excitement enhanced by communality *and* simultaneity in a family setting. In homes across America, that is, at the same hour, on the same series of dates, with those dates publicly heralded and anticipated, would the newest and most dramatic of communications technologies render through its exclusive electronically "living" potentialities the old national identification, even communion of spirit, to an immediate, immense audience, once again intensely "present" in several senses of that word: at the debut of a documentary project of unprecedented historical scope and artistic ambition; at the viewing experience as itself an epochal national event perpetuated through continued immersion in weekly segments; at the subsequent celebration of its nearly immediate rebroadcast under commercial sponsorship; and then, eventually, in ways at the time no one could have imagined, through the ongoing communality of reference made possible by endless syndication.[87]

At the same time, as Salomon moved in late 1947 and early 1948 through the concept stage and into the preliminary production process already with television explicitly in mind, he met with the bit of serendipitous good fortune without which no saga of young American enterprise would be complete. That came in the form of a friendship with Robert Sarnoff, a college classmate, himself a junior television executive casting about for the chance to do something independently under the NBC regime of his magisterial father, General David Sarnoff.[88] As a result, NBC funding of five hundred thousand dollars shortly became available. This in turn allowed Salomon to take the crucial step of organizing an independent production unit in direct coordination with the navy.

Three long years followed of assembling materials. Meanwhile, the main film scenario was devised by Salomon with assistance from M. Clay Adams, a Hollywood writer, producer, and director, and Isaac Kleinerman, a Hollywood technician. To achieve this by the end of the "rough" stage, sixty million feet of film had been winnowed to sixty thousand.

Apace, Salomon and the newspaperman Richard Hanser wrote scripts — albeit, one should add, not without serious professional harassment and legal hectoring from Morison. Indeed, especially with production growing near, as Morison had hoarded credit for his massive history project, so he now claimed financial compensation for use of the film resources which had been gathered to exclusive purposes of research on the official history. Further, he challenged NBC over the absence of his name, as "author" of the great history, from Salomon's film credits. (On the first point, the matter seems to have been settled by a five-thousand-dollar honorarium; on the second, Morison and his lawyers were apparently left to stew.)[89]

Still, as Salomon and the production group persevered in massive film editing and in academic and legal squabbles over the script credits, so in the conceptualizing of an accompanying musical score they continued to engage in more inspired, even visionary multimedia thinking that would pay immediately by bringing an added luster of both artistic seriousness and popular visibility to the project — not to mention pay enormous new material dividends, as with evolving video technologies, in entertainment markets created by other new sound-reproduction technologies just down the road. For, instead of mere musical background, perhaps "period" material or a running accompaniment drawing on military and patriotic standards, an exclusive, original work of serious musical composition, they decided, should also be devised as dramatically and thematically integral to the film work and the narration. The question was, of course, where one might find a major composer right for the demands of such an extraordinary project — a composer willing to sublimate creative ego to the demands of documentary accompaniment, and, given the length of the programming, also do an astonishing amount of work without running out of creative ideas. Again, the answer was at hand, albeit not without more New York power networking, as it might be called now, coupled with some fast sales talk by a new participant in the project, NBC Vice President Pat Weaver, who managed to interest the celebrated Broadway composer Richard Rodgers, renowned for such popular scores as *Oklahoma!*, *Carousel*, and, most recently, his own musical celebration of wartime events in *South Pacific*. As it turned out, Rodgers was much receptive to the idea of enlisting his talent and his celebrity in a matter of distinguished public service.[90] Accordingly, he too signed aboard, accepting along the way surely one of the strangest technical challenges ever presented to a composer — of writing music to fill the roughly thirteen hours of massive, in-progress documentary presentation. And duly he arrived at an impressively architectonic set of basic themes and various other internal musical motifs designed to fit with the proposed segments in the story and the drama line augmented by narration. Further, by now he had been joined on the production team by the well-known arranger and orchestrator Robert Russell

Bennett, himself the veteran of more than three hundred Broadway musical shows, who at that point essentially took over and put together the final score. With that score in front of him on the podium, Bennett also conducted the NBC Symphony Orchestra (for whom the senior Sarnoff had earlier imported Toscanini) for the sound track. Then the music was finally married to the twenty-six segments and thirteen hours of voice text, narrated by Leonard Graves.

The result might be best described as the greatest and longest musical commercial ever written for a television-network production team and a military service,[91] not to mention for a country, a war effort, a set of victorious military powers, and an increasingly wistful prospect of a geopolitical future that had seemed so recently the fruit of victory, only to be undercut by an astonishing collocation of postwar crises at home and abroad.[92] Most important, in terms of the new technologies of representation portended, it was also applauded rightly at the time as an importantly evolutionary version of the future of television, of television in a set of conflated roles as a public information, entertainment, education, even art medium.[93] In short, *Victory at Sea* proved one of the first great media events before we had such a nomenclature. It attracted an enormous, admiring audience. And it was treated with impressive critical reverence. Both *Time* and *Newsweek* pronounced it magnificent. The *New Yorker*, still the reigning voice of eastern urbanity, billed the series as "certainly one of the most ambitious and successful ventures in the history of television" (77–78). And Bernard DeVoto in *Harper's*, speaking from Howells's old easy chair, could hardly find words for his admiration, calling it "a drama, a work of the imagination, art of a high order. . . . and new under the sun" (8).[94]

But here, as will be seen, in its moment of being lauded both popularly and critically as proof of the artistic possibilities of the new commercial medium, what one might call the material history *proper* of *Victory at Sea* had barely begun. Within months, after a second, equally well received commercially sponsored run, the whole twenty-six-segment package went into widespread syndication, appearing continuously as a freestanding series throughout the decade and well into the next.[95] Also, a condensed, ninety-seven-minute version of 1954 proved successful as a feature presentation in movie theaters. And by 1959, following the enormously successful example of numerous postwar photodocumentary volumes,[96] a picture-history text also appeared in print, with the publisher, Doubleday, astutely promoting the feel of the TV tie-in: scenes and events featured in the series were encapsulated in representative photograph selections; the text, a sequence of essays offering a synopsis of the narration, and accompanied by a dedication to Salomon, with mention of his recent death, was attributed to Hanser; captions and running commentary were identified as the work of Salomon and Hanser; even the breathless sequencing and highlighting of main titles — "Barometer Falling," "Upwind Beat," "Tides Turning," "Landfall and Harbor" — seemed an attempt to capture on the page the feel, pace, drama, and general atmospherics of the Graves narration.

The most visible, however, not to mention the most commercially lucrative and long-legged among the inventory of by-products emerging from the project turned out to be yet another extremely popular commodity in the marketplace of yet another exploding entertainment technology. This, of course, was the musical sound track, in new performances by Bennett and the RCA Symphony Orchestra, on the 33⅓ RPM long-playing phonograph record — itself a medium opened up, not surprisingly, in the late '40s and early '50s by Rodgers and his collaborator Hammerstein, as well as arrangers such as Bennett, in original-cast albums of such Broadway classics as *Oklahoma!* and *South Pacific*, and installed in an important middlebrow niche, elevated but not overbearing, popular but not plebeian, situated between opera and classical in multivolume 78 RPM sets and the "pop" or "hit" single. Further, in the present case, given the particular marriage of materials and evolving technologies, the musical resources proved not only uniquely abundant but also almost limitlessly marketable. When a first RCA Victor disc, appearing in 1959 coincident with the print volume, proved successful, it was quickly followed by a volume 2, both initially recorded in high-fidelity and later in stereo. And these, in turn, proved so popular that through a set of new program reconfigurings a third was issued in 1961.

Further, in all cases the design of the product was again carefully engineered to summon up — if not actually re-create — the cachet of the larger project. In the visual dimension, for instance, each record jacket recalled the film and book forms by carrying a spectacular war-art cover, with the third also containing its own actual portfolio of combat photography.[97] And in the arrangement of musical tracks, each, by its use of dramatic sequencings and entitlings, was at once made to recall the original while creating its own vivid scenario — with the "drama" abetted, in the last two cases, it should be observed, as audio technologies became more ambitious, by various sound-effect features. Further, in elaborate liner copy, each likewise reprised the project's textual history, often reproducing text and commentary by original participants and early reviewers, but also increasingly promoting, through content and design, its own creative role as textual apparatus.[98]

To be sure, as is known to anyone who reads record catalogs, eventually such audio material would also make its way from vinyl to tape and now, most recently, from tape to compact disc, with remastered versions of the earlier discs often most visibly featured in marketing guides published by the Corporation for Public Broadcasting, both radio and television divisions. And accordingly, in the latter connection, with the advent of videocassette, the complete film series has now also made its way back into popular home screen circulation, available now in virtually any rental outlet or for purchase from numerous distributors.[99]

Naturally, in all venues the material proved to be an especially hot fiftieth-anniversary property.[100] And as a result, the production enterprise once again does seem to have come full cycle to connect with the experience it was supposed to create. We attend once more to the flickering black-and-white luminosity of the screen, the sonorous Leonard Graves narration, and the sweeping Richard Rodgers–Robert Russell Bennett score. We scan the titles, themselves evocative of grand structures and rhythms of presentation: "Design for War," "The Pacific Boils Over," "Sealing the Breach," "Midway Is East," "Mediterranean Mosaic," "Guadalcanal," "Rings Around Rabaul," "Mare Nostrum," "Sea and Sand," "Beneath the Southern Cross," "Magnetic North," "The Conquest of Micronesia," "Melanesian Nightmare," "Roman Renaissance," "D-Day," "The Killers and the Killed," "The Turkey Shoot," "Two If by Sea," "The Battle for Leyte Gulf," "The Return of the Allies," "Full Fathom Five," "The Fate of Europe," "Target Suribachi," "The Road to Mandalay," "Suicide for Glory," "Design for Peace."[101] We ready ourselves for the opening, the night sea, the moon upon the waves, the light and shadow of their great heave and swell. We see the big white V. We hear the opening bars of the great theme music, rising to a great melodic crest, the Song of the High Seas. We catch the *in medias res* takeup on the narration, and watch the attendant visual drama unfold, quickly plunging into crisis eventuating in dramatic climax issuing into pregnant closure, the familiar period that marks the falling off into silence, the end that prepares us for the next beginning. In turn, the cycling of the episodes themselves issues into the old, ongoing communality. It is all there. We are all there. With *Victory at Sea* we are at the Good War; simultaneously we are at the alternately good and desperate years when *Victory at Sea* came to us after the Good War — TV, Eisenhower, shiny cars, the suburbs, but also Korea, Khruschev, blacklists, the bomb; and somehow, we are also strangely present now at the post–Cold War future that the Good War may actually have made possible. Whatever the locus of history, it is all there, we are all there, and "there" has once again become *Victory at Sea* — at least as it is remembered.

CHAPTER 3
BIG WAR, BIG BOOK,
BIG MOVIE

The breathtaking final race of the Allies to win World War II shortly had its postwar literary correlative in the race among American writers to produce *the* great novel of the war. The new figures emerging within less than a decade to provide the most visible entries in the contest were Norman Mailer, Irwin Shaw, James Jones, Herman Wouk, and Leon Uris — each of whom would go on to careers involving literary prominence in varying degree but with noteworthy popular success.[1] What they all had in common, though, was that each would write a "big" novel of the war forever identified with a "big" movie of the same title. Norman Mailer's *The Naked and the Dead* would also become *The Naked and the Dead*, directed by Raoul Walsh and starring Cliff Robertson, Raymond Massey, Aldo Ray, Dorothy Malone, and Lili St. Cyr. Irwin Shaw's *The Young Lions* would become *The Young Lions*, directed by Edward Dmytryk and starring Marlon Brando, Montgomery Clift, Hope Lange, Dean Martin, Maximilian Schell, and Mai Britt. James Jones's *From Here to Eternity* would become *From Here to Eternity*, directed by Fred Zinnemann, with

Montgomery Clift, Burt Lancaster, Deborah Kerr, Frank Sinatra, and Donna Reed. Herman Wouk's *The Caine Mutiny* would become *The Caine Mutiny*, also directed by Edward Dmytryk, and starring Humphrey Bogart, Van Johnson, Fred MacMurray, and José Ferrer. Leon Uris's *Battle Cry* would become *Battle Cry*, also directed by Raoul Walsh, and starring Van Heflin, Tab Hunter, Aldo Ray, Raymond Massey, and Dorothy Malone.[2] And what these authorial figures in the big-war big-book big-movie genre would likewise all share afterward was the reliance on such a production model or new variants thereof as the basis of enormously successful careers featuring authorship itself as a kind of ever-enlarging literary-commercial commodity. In each case the appearance of a new literary property would become a major publishing event, and the occasion for extended production activities often extending as far as the eye could see. Book club adoptions would be followed by paperback issues. And all this, often with careful coordination of design and time of release involving the sundry artifacts, would invariably eventuate in a movie, most often dwarfing the print original in attendant publicity and commercial success. Afterward, of course, would also come a new life on television, perhaps as a network movie or in endlessly syndicated reruns. Further, as the medium developed, there might be movement from print to TV special or mini-series, both devised expressly for the form.

Mailer would get there by a nose with the first "big" novel.[3] And with his prodigal endowment of intellectual and stylistic gifts *in conjunction with* his star-quality instinct for literary self-promotion, he would become and remain the biggest book personality, with each text, to use his own phrasing, an increment in a set of advertisements for himself: controversial political novels including *Barbary Shore* (1951), *The Deer Park* (1955), *An American Dream* (1965), *Why Are We in Vietnam?* (1967), and, more recently, *Harlot's Ghost* (1991); monuments of the new journalism including *The Armies of the Night* (1968) and *The Executioner's Song* (1979); unclassifiable experiments ranging from *Of a Fire on the Moon* (1970) and *Marilyn* (1973) to *The Prisoner of Sex* (1971), *Ancient Evenings* (1983), *Oswald's Tale* (1995), and *The Gospel According to the Son* (1997). On the other hand, from the outset he remained dubious about Hollywood as an artistic venue. His big novel of the war eventually got to the big screen, to be sure; and in some measure it cashed in on the remembered notoriety of the book. Of all the film projects, however, from start to finish it would remain singular for the absence of interest or involvement on the part of the original novelist. Mailer was seeking his business elsewhere.

Shaw, the closest competition in the 1948 race, also had to wait nearly as long as Mailer to see his big novel reach film. But when it did, no one had to doubt that this novelist from the outset had also known how to write a movie property. The screen treatment of *The Young Lions,* in contrast to the somewhat slapdash and cursory treatment of Mailer's book in its screen version, had really only to take its lead from the slick, multiply plotted, big-screen scenario laid out by the book to effect an effortless transition to comparable Hollywood success. Nor, as Shaw's subsequent career would show, was early evidence of this knack for multipurpose construction accidental. Already an admired New York playwright and short-story writer before the war, and a correspondent in the European combat theater among the great celebrity journalists and literati, Shaw knew the formulas and how to make them work. Accordingly, as a literary writer, he continued an impressive short-story career in major "smart" magazines and in well-received collections. As to novels, he more readily exploited the popular, often with immense commercial success, and, as the medium of TV developed, often bypassing Hollywood with garish sagas including *Rich Man, Poor Man* (1970), *Evening in Byzantium* (1973), and *Beggarman Thief* (1977), proving readily adaptable to the new form of the miniseries.

In contrast to both previous figures, with *From Here to Eternity* Jones found himself almost simultaneously an overnight celebrity in both the novel and the movie business. The novel was a literary and commercial success, winning the National Book Award and selling endlessly in hard cover and paperback; and the film, if anything, topped the book's success as both an artistic and commercial triumph. The act was hard to follow, however. Jones, like Shaw, forged a career as a popular novelist, with best-selling but often critically disparaged volumes including *Some Came Running* (1957) and *Go to the Widow-Maker* (1967). He would write about the war more successfully in *WWII,* a collection of wartime combat art, and in such novels as *The Thin Red Line* (1962), eventually the basis of a moderately successful film, and *Whistle* (1978), a nearly completed work published shortly after his death.

Wouk, after some notice as a promising New York novelist of the postwar generation as the author of *Aurora Dawn* (1947), in turn trumped all the previous competition. *The Caine Mutiny,* once it achieved publicity momentum, became a runaway literary best-seller. In turn, the movie became an instant classic, rivaled even today only perhaps by *From Here to Eternity* as the best-known film of the war to have come out of a popular novel. Meanwhile, Wouk had also contrived to have a Broadway hit out of the novel as well, with a much-acclaimed dramatic distillation entitled *The Caine Mutiny Court-Martial*. Wouk's success across multiple config-urings of genre and mode continued with best-selling novels such as *Marjorie Morningstar* (1955) and *Youngblood Hawke* (1962) translated into equally popular films and eventually with a globe-girdling two-volume saga of World War II conflict, *The Winds of War* (1971) and *War and Remembrance* (1978), both developed as installments in one of the most ambitious, star-studded, and heavily publicized offerings of the TV miniseries on record.

Uris followed *Battle Cry*, a popular work that made few pretensions about a technicolor Hollywood-marine style that ensured its quick transi-tion, virtually intact, to the screen, with a series of popular epics — *Exodus* (1958), *Mila 18* (1961), *Armageddon* (1964), *Topaz* (1968), *QB VII* (1970), *Trinity* (1976), and *The Haj* (1984). Further, over the ensuing years several of the latter would as easily make their way to the movies and, eventually, television.

To be sure, other figures besides these five jostled for attention in at-tempting to join the ranks of "the new war novelists," as John Aldridge called them (133) — sometimes even before hostilities had formally con-cluded. Out of the Italian campaigns, Harry Brown produced the 1944 com-bat classic *A Walk in the Sun* and John Hersey the tragicomic *A Bell for Adano*, which won the Pulitzer Prize for fiction in the same year. The year 1946 in turn, as detailed earlier, brought the extremely popular *Mister Roberts*, as well as Alfred Hayes's *All Thy Conquests*, noted by Aldridge as one of the first postwar books taken seriously as a corrective to the "hygenic productions of Marion Hargrove and Ernie Pyle" (133), and shorter works in a similar vein such as Gore Vidal's *Williwaw* and Robert Lowry's *Casualty*. The year 1947 produced John Horne Burns's *The Gallery*, a set of art-ful, astringent vignettes that quickly achieved cult status among postwar literati; Vance Bourjaily's more traditional *The End of My Life*; and, also discussed earlier, that year's Pulitzer Prize winner, Michener's *Tales of the South Pacific*.[4]

Likewise, similar processes of book-to-film transmission had occurred with earlier, wartime classics such as *Thirty Seconds over Tokyo* and *They Were Expendable*, as did Hollywood versions of nonfiction favorites such as Bill Mauldin's *Up Front* and Ernie Pyle's *Brave Men* and *Here Is Your War*, with the latter two conflated under the title *The Story of G.I. Joe*. Also, in a rehearsal for some of the politics of production involved with the "big" books, Hollywood at least made an attempt to begin dealing with the war in the kind of understated critical realism of such print originals as Hersey's *A Bell for Adano* and Brown's *A Walk in the Sun* — the first a satire and the second dispiritingly matter-of-fact in its depiction of combat.

Still, *A Bell for Adano* and *A Walk in the Sun*, though both have been much admired then and now by literary and film critics, had nothing of the social impact of the five big war novels of Mailer, Shaw, Jones, Wouk, and Uris, which found themselves within the next decade enshrined in both the literary and the popular-culture canons as the great novels of the war. And "social impact" was the key phrase. Given the expectations of both critics and the novel-reading and novel-buying public — not to mention the ambitions of the rising new novelists of the war — the literary stakes could hardly have been higher. The Big War had been, after all, the great American experience of the century, perhaps the greatest American experience ever, at least the fulfillment of what Henry Luce had called the vision of "the American Century." The great American novel of World War II was thus equally a candidate for the great all-time American novel. Further, there was also the more immediate example — and the source of a deeply felt competition as well — of the great generation of twentieth-century American writers already on the scene. To a person, their greatness seemed to have come directly, in one way or another, out of the scene of the earlier war or in the assessment of its cultural aftermath. Hemingway, Faulkner, Fitzgerald, Dos Passos, Stein, Eliot, Pound, Cummings. And beyond them, of course, lay the American tradition of Crane, Melville, Cooper, and the whole epic record of a country quite literally born of war.[5] Combat had always been seen as the ultimate crucible of the American soul. Indeed, as Tom Englehart has brilliantly pointed out, it was the ground and origin of the concept that had already come to be seen as Victory Culture: a national vision of heroic individuality persistently triumphing against impossible countervailing odds. And now, of course, that same belief in the innately heroic capabilities of the American democratic spirit seemed in some near-absolute sense vindicated once and for all by total victory over Axis powers who five years earlier seemed exactly on the brink of plunging the world into a new age of darkness.

At the same time, aspiring postwar novelists labored under conflicting literary-cultural imperatives. Victory Culture was in the air. But because of their close relation to the great American high modernists of the post–World War I era, they also confronted the legacy of deeply ironic forms and attitudes arising directly out of the larger twentieth-century vision of war. Regimentation; mechanization, brutalization, dehumanization, industrial-strength slaughter; political mendacity, economic profiteering, moral and patriotic sham: through the translation of these experiential legacies of 1914–18 and the decades just following into the great tenets of high modernism came a theology that carried its own catechism of literary commonplaces: the wasteland, the death of love, the religion of *nada*; the utter dissociation of fact from meaning and value; the failure of civilization as a sustaining force in people's lives.

Or, at the very least, there was antiwar writing as itself a kind of literary categorical imperative. The nineteenth century alone — Tolstoi, Crane, Zola — had basically used up war as naturalistic metaphor. And then had come the more immediate masters, the Americans and Anglo-Europeans writing in the wake of the war to end all wars: in America, novelists such as Ernest Hemingway, John Dos Passos, Thomas Boyd, William March; in Britain, a whole array of novelists, poets, dramatists, memoirists — Siegfried Sassoon, Robert Graves, Edmund Blunden, Frederick Manning, E. C. Sheriff, Wilfred Owen; in France, Henri Barbusse; in Germany, Erich Maria Remarque.

The World War II writers by any definition as literary intellectuals would thus have to assimilate the liberal critique of war already mounted by their direct generational forebears. Further, as to techno-war, industrial war, global war, machine war, extinctionary war, they would have to confront the apparatus of geopolitical mass slaughter on a scale even those forebears had never dreamed. The Nazi death camps; German and Japanese atrocities against conquered peoples; English and American strategic bombing of cities; the American introduction of atomic weaponry: all these seemed to reduce the mythologies of an earlier lost generation down to the level of literary conceits. Here was something beyond a bungle, a fraud, a hideous sham; arms merchants, dugout generals, lying politicians; life as endless prospect of waste, art as fragments shored against the ruins.

Yet facing them as well now was a certain legitimate vindication, in the abstract at least, of many of the old dreams of geopolitical hope that the conflict of 1914–18 had but a generation before seemed to have declared dead on arrival. The new Axis dictatorships had threatened the world; and Allied peoples had banded together to achieve a victory that had saved the world. For the moment, at least, it was factually that simple.

The available avenue seized by most of the big novelists of the war proved equally simple. Largely eschewing the radical modernist experimentalisms of their immediate predecessors, although with a frequent assimilation of modernist ironies, they reassumed the more traditional function of the novelist as popular realist, with wartime military culture in itself and in its complex relationships with the civilian world serving as sociopolitical and economic microcosm of world-historical struggle. Accordingly, in this way, it could become possible to write an antiwar novel about an ultimately just war; an anti-Fascist and pro-democracy novel about a war in which the chief ally was Communist totalitarianism; a humanly compelling novel about a war in which the Allies finally won over Fascist automatons by building themselves into a better fighting machine. It became possible, that is, to expose the horror, folly, and waste of war while at the same time not denying that the victorious Allied war effort against the Axis powers had been a worthy human cause, a basis for satisfaction, perhaps even optimism, as opposed to high modernist reflexes of disillusionment or despair.[6]

This turned out to be precisely the formal and thematic middle way chosen by most of the "big" novelists. Their approach was consciously microcosmic, with the emphasis on individual units, the small heroisms and cowardices of average men, their yearning lives, their frequently brutal and ironic deaths. The chief characters often proved possessed of a human quotient of intelligence, discrimination, decency, even good will, albeit equally as often fated and undone. They became modernist eirons, to be sure, but in most cases not reduced to the existential cipher, even as they faced the requisite ironies, injustices, outrages perpetrated by the war-breeding system and its eager minions. To put this another way, emphasis was kept on the closely political, the working of ideology in the fullest sense of the everyday and quotidian. Often this came with a twist of '20s and '30s radical-liberal intellectualism. *The Naked and the Dead*, for instance, would have an explicitly Marxian edge; and *The Young Lions, From Here to Eternity*, and *The Caine Mutiny* would be explicit in their depiction of sundry fascisms, racisms, and class antagonisms in the American military services. A homegrown populism-proletarianism in footsoldier novels generally would exalt enlisted men, dependable NCOs, and junior officers — perhaps the odd lieutenant or maverick captain — as opposed to company and battalion commanders, staff officers, and, of course, generals. These latter were often portrayed as the enemy within, martinets at least, brutish, arrogant, decadent; gender and class oppressors, anti-Semites, racists. Similarly, in navy books, junior and middle-grade officers often became partisans of the enlisted crew against the tyrannical captain. Only in Uris did one find the sanitized exception. But that of course was a marine book, essentially a wartime guts-and-glory movie resurrected as a postwar novel so it could be turned back into a movie.

In all cases, of course, the cultural packaging of the film versions became more or less automatically a matter of popular-market considerations. Movie audiences were simply less ideological by nature, and far less interested than reading audiences generally in forms of social and intellectual critique. They were also more given to popular mythologizings of the war effort, precisely because they had been schooled in wartime documentary and Hollywood productions, and their long familiarity with film itself as part of the war effort continued to carry mainly positive associations. There was some question, to be sure, about their possible weariness with depictions of the war. And a further problem, peculiar to Hollywood, was the diminishing technical and logistical support, because of massive postwar defense cutbacks, of the individual military services.

Certainly, the material aspects of the big-book-to-big-movie transition would chart their own courses and often find their own peculiar complications. Mailer's text rather quickly passed out of his hands, for instance, and into a long sojourn as an independent production property. Jones and Wouk, on the other hand, found their works delivered back into the hands of the military, with heavy critical censorship rights exacted in exchange for technical and logistic support. Shaw maintained certain creative control over the script but had little influence on casting.

Transitions were affected by the simple factor of cultural timing. Both *The Naked and the Dead* and *The Young Lions* took a decade to reach the screen. Why? Nineteen forty-eight may have been a big year for big war novels, but it was a bad year for nearly any kind of war movie. It was also a bad year, as would be the next several to follow, for liberal intellectuals, particularly if their subject matter was the totalitarianism of the officer class and the brutalization of the proletarians. With Jones and Wouk, on the other hand, the book-to-movie transition seemed to partake of its own inevitability only to run head on into major service jitters about image problems in the midst of ongoing postwar defense reorganizations. Uris, on the other hand, translated almost immediately, but in a film that had the good fortune seemingly to partake as much of enthusiasms about new marine heroics in Korea as any actual remembering of the generic World War II action depicted. Ironically, it would be of course the films, with their advantages of condensation and entertainment value in a passive audience medium, that would prevail. Coupled with these would be new advantages of familiarity and increasing availability, especially in television rerun and, later, videocassette recording. The movies, in sum, with the decline of reading, and the ascendancy of the visual and electronic media, would increasingly become the reified body of memory. The books, on the other hand, would find themselves lost somewhere between memory and, like the printed word itself, history.

The Naked and the Dead

Although Norman Mailer may have been credited with producing, in *The Naked and the Dead*, the first of the splashy "big" war novels to come out of World War II, a bare two decades later the fact seemed to have been lost on many Americans — including, most notably, the family of his wife-to-be, Beverly Brown. This was made clear by their response to intimations of the impending match. "Beverly called," a brother, Charlie, remembered, "telling us she's coming down to Georgia with her ace new boyfriend, a famous writer named Norman Mailer." He went on: "We said, 'Who?' 'Norman Mailer. He wrote *The Naked and the Dead*.' I said, 'Yeah, I saw that — damned good war picture. But who the hell is *Norman Mailer?*'" (Manso 381).

Once more, in the odd anecdotal exchange, one finds a kind of fractured parable of the World War II classic and American remembering, in this case a real-life lesson in what might be called at once the cultural heroics and the cultural vicissitudes of the big-war, big-book, big-movie model of production. For in Mailer's case, as will be seen, the process proved unusually discontinuous; as a result, so did the particular trajectory of American remembering comprising the successive evolutions of his text. At each stage, the identity of the cultural artifact in question was deeply conditioned by the circumstances of its own production and commodification. The story of *The Naked and the Dead*, that is, may have begun for many Americans as that of a literarily ambitious and intellectually complex 1948 novel of World War II combat by an author named Norman Mailer, emerging to the applause of an important critical audience and a large book-buying public as one of the first major young writers of fictional narrative to come out of the war. But it continued equally for others as the story of a sensational 1958 movie, also entitled *The Naked and the Dead* — and by then almost entirely dissociated from the author or novel serving as its point of origin — setting itself forth in the American entertainment market of the late '50s and early '60s as an immediately recognizable genre film of the era in an immensely popular genre. In any event, given the model, it becomes a clear case of the exception actually proving the rule. Here, the big-war, big-book, big-movie production model of history and memory had been essentially allowed to create its own serial versions of American remembering, with each almost exclusively a function of its contemporary critical and popular-culture contexts.

Indeed, as far as Mailer was concerned, things had probably turned out for the best. That is, to Mailer himself it probably seemed fairly inconsequential if not downright irrelevant that it was the film evolution of the property that had dictated his standing with his latest in-laws-to-be. For by 1958 or 1968 for that matter, the only fact really of consequence to Mailer in art or life was that in *The Naked and the Dead* he had turned the big war into an indubitably big novel by any objective standard then or now; he had, at least by common opinion, gotten there first; and he had also found large literary and popular success. The making of *The Naked and the Dead*, to put it simply, had always been first and foremost, in Mailer's mind at least, the making of a writer.

In 1948, the year of the novel's appearance, it had rapidly risen to number two on the best-seller lists, selling 137,185 hardbound copies in stores and another 60,000 through book club offerings. And nearly thirty years later, it would still be counted among the all-time best-sellers, with total sales of 2,816,662 copies, including 2,443,662 in paperback.

As promptly, the book had been sold to Hollywood. The movie, on the other hand, took a decade to appear, showing up in the same year, and in distinctly inferior relation, with the film version of Irwin Shaw's *The Young Lions* — by coincidence Mailer's only real 1948 competitor for big-novel honors. Unlike Shaw, however, or Jones, Wouk, and Uris, who in the early '50s had all seen their big novels of the war turned rapidly into screen blockbusters, Mailer, after some initial efforts in the same direction, wound up more or less happily severing any direct ties to the film version of his book. For by now the big war and the big book had set Norman Mailer on a trajectory he saw as leading to something bigger than any movie: the making of a figure whose own life and career, beyond any or all of his texts, would repeatedly show him to have been his own foremost literary and popular-culture production. That figure, of course, would be Norman Mailer, who had already chosen to write his own version of the production model: big war, big book, big author.[7]

Indeed, in retrospect, the particular film artifact in question was already so peripheral to that larger project that its notoriety must have surprised even as canny a judge of cultural property as Mailer had turned out to be.

On the other hand, the same could be hardly said of the novel. There, Mailer seemed even before the beginning to have been in charge of the basic process whereby the engineering of a great war novel would also become the engineering of a great, even exemplary author of the generation of war. To use the titular phrase of John Aldridge's groundbreaking critical study of Mailer and his literary cohort — to which Mailer would later give his own literary-critical imprimatur — this novelist was going to point the direction of literature "after the lost generation."[8] Honoring his great modernist forbears, that is, he was going to write the big war novel of the new war generation; he was going to do it first; and he was going to do it best to the degree that he would be immediately set forth as their stalwart and shining heir.

Whether the novel succeeded in all these respects remains debatable. On the other hand, whether the underlying cultural strategy of author making delivered the basic goods can hardly be doubted. Witness, for instance, the pronouncement of Alfred Kazin, dean of post-1945 scholar-critics:

> Norman Mailer's *The Naked and the Dead*, published in 1948 with enormous success of every kind, was the first "important" — and is probably still the best — novel about Americans at war, 1941–45. Mailer at twenty-five was so thoroughly launched by his first book — it was exactly what people brought up on novels and films about the First World War expected of the "new war" novelists — that he was to make many later efforts to disconcert his admirers. But even jealous older novelists — Hemingway called the book "poor cheese, pretentiously wrapped" — understood the book in terms of their own expectations. The moment was still ripe for a novel that would honor war as a test of the literary imagination. (71)

To put this all more simply, no author of a *novel*, at least, destined to become one of the Good War's greatest hits ever started out with so firm an idea as Norman Mailer's of how the war itself was going to be his material. And none ever saw the experiential and literary dimensions of the task through more resolutely. This was, after all, the Norman Mailer, the aspiring "author" who, when finally drafted after a long wait, was happy for the Pacific, it is said, because he feared the European theater would be written over.[9] (Further, according to Kazin, the Pacific may have interested him as a first choice because "he also had a certain vanity about his ability to handle the many technical problems created by war — he had been interested in aeronautics and engineering at Harvard" [72].) On top of that, of course, there was also the cultish veneration of experience inherited from such immediate examples as Hemingway, Dos Passos, Malraux, and others. This would be enough to account further for the Norman Mailer who intentionally got himself transferred from a clerk's job to just enough infantry action — during mopping-up operations on Leyte in an intelligence and reconnaissance (I&R) platoon like that depicted in *The Naked and the Dead* — to feel (rightly, it turned out) that he could write convincingly of jungle infantry combat.

But the chief motive that brought Mailer the novelist together with the war as his subject was the one that more than fifty years later would sustain his vision of the author as culture hero and media celebrity: his unassailable belief from the beginning in his own genius and in his work as that of a true literary prodigy. As early as fall 1940 at Harvard in Robert Gorham Davis's story-writing class, for instance, he had committed himself to the idea of being a writer (Rollyson 16). He had also served a rigorous apprenticeship on the *Advocate* (16–17). With a story written in his sophomore year, "The Greatest Thing in the World," he had won first prize in the 1941 contest conducted by *Story* magazine (20). Attempts followed to cultivate writerly "experience." Mailer bummed around the South on a boxcar and worked in a mental ward, while making several starts at novels. He also attempted a play, about the mental hospital, which was rejected by the Harvard Dramatic Society. Its title was "The Naked and the Dead" (25). And well it should have preceded the text. For the issue, Mailer had quickly come to see, was truly "experience"; and as early as 1942, he knew the one he had to have, the "experience" that would be the crucial, defining one for his generation.

To be sure, as a former liberal noninterventionist, Mailer himself felt compelled to explain his new commitment to war experience by espousing a moral and political change of heart. For a Jew, he said, Hitler made the difference. "I'm going to enlist and get into the goddam army and get it over with," he claimed (28). On the other hand, the literary motive was strong. He seems to have known it, and so did everyone else. According to Hillary Mills, "although Mailer had begun to accept the inevitability of war, the young man who was to write the first great World War II novel then viewed the conflict primarily as dramatic input for his work-to-be." Sy Breslow put it even more directly: "Rather than thinking about the horror of war or the fact that he might get killed, he looked at it as an experience which would feed the novel he wanted to write afterward. He was desperately searching for experience at that time, because he came to the realization that you can't write if you don't experience" (Mills 60). Or, as Karl Rollyson summarizes, by the end of the years at Harvard, "Norman Mailer found in the subject of the war the crucible of his conviction as a novelist. In order to know what he really believed, he had to know what was worth dying for" (28).

Nevertheless, by Harvard commencement in June 1943, Mailer had stayed on about as long as anyone in his class had managed to do. He was now a cum laude graduate with a major in aeronautical engineering; yet the chief claim his experience at Harvard had made on him — and, with no small irony, perhaps the chief reason for the delay — was clearly his identification of himself as a great writer-to-be.

Thus Mailer described himself as he waited to get drafted in summer 1943: "a little frightened of going to war, and a good deal ashamed of not going to war" (Rollyson 30). He worked on *Transit to Narcissus*, a novel written in elaboration of the mental hospital play. And there, the war already seemed to be writing itself in advance through Mailer's self-described encounter with the theme that would "stalk" him all during his "writing life" — "What is the relation between courage and brutality?" (30).

By January 1944 Mailer was still working on his novel and waiting to be drafted. Then, in February, the notice came. One of Mailer's first responses was to elect immediately not to become an officer. According to Beatrice Silverman, whom he had by then married, Mailer "was determined to write the great war novel and didn't want the responsibility of rank" (Mills 75). He also felt, according to Bea, that an enlisted man would stand a smaller chance of being saddled with a desk job and missing combat.

In this he was incorrect. After basic training he was shipped in January 1945 to Leyte and, at the end of the Philippine campaigns, on to Luzon during mopping-up operations; along the way he had learned to hate officers and had also run afoul of the anti-Semitism of 112th Cavalry Texans with whom he was assigned. As to job assignments, however, he had thus far been balked of straight duty. He had been a telephone lineman, a typist, and a clerk in photo interpretation. For background he read *Infantry Journal*. But in his behind-the-lines leisure, he also seemed to have enough time for a four-volume set of Spengler's *Decline of the West* and thrillers by Chandler and Hammett.

Providentially, a call went out for volunteers to join the regimental I&R platoon, officially a headquarters-level unit but frequently assigned to dangerous and important patrols, themselves most often secret and unsupported by regular units. Mailer joined (Mills 77). "I was brought up on those war hero novels," he alleged later. "Of course, all the war ideals you had were quickly lost about a week after you got into the Army. But all the time I was overseas I had these conflicting ideas — wanting, the way everyone else did, to get the softest, easiest job, to get by with the least pain — and also wanting to get into combat and see it. The only time I could make up my mind was the time I asked to go to Recon" (Rollyson 37).

More important, Mailer got the experience he wanted but not in excess. "He saw just enough action to feel he could write convincing war scenes," writes Rollyson (37); and three years later, in the *New York Star*, Mailer seemed to concur, saying he had been in "a couple of firefights and skirmishes" (Mills 78).

While in the I&R platoon, Mailer kept the equivalent of a diary in letters he wrote to Bea.[10] Meanwhile, the experience of the jungle seemed to sap all energies, including the desire for fighting and even the desire for writing (Mills 79). Even with minimal combat, life as an infantryman proved to be just plain hard, miserable, and exhausting. As Mailer confessed somewhat melodramatically, if correctly, to James Atlas, "Your horizons come down and down and down, until you don't much care whether you remain alive or not. So I really did give up the idea that I'd ever come back and be a writer" (Mills 79). On the other hand, he also heard in great detail from fellow unit members who still seemed able to speak with the authority of experience about a legendary three-day patrol behind enemy lines that the platoon had taken before he joined.

That patrol, of course, was to become the "experiential" basis of *The Naked and the Dead*. On the other hand, it seemed to have taken late-1945 occupation duty in Japan, according to Mills, for Mailer to undergo the pivotal experience that laid the philosophical basis for the novel (80). By now Mailer had become a cook, a T-4, or sergeant fourth grade. As a first cook he had some small authority. He also got into a serious quarrel with the mess sergeant. For this he was ordered to apologize by the captain commanding the unit. And Mailer knuckled under. "It was a week before I was going home," he said. "I crawfished — the way Hearn did in the book" (Mills 80).[11]

To restore his self-respect, Mailer the next morning tried to "give" his stripes back. Unfortunately, the captain, unusually clever for his rank it seemed, one-upped him at least semantically by agreeing to "take" them back instead.

It was one of Mailer's last encounters with an officer, and it cemented his loathing for all of them. It was also, as will be seen, to have enormous immediate consequences for the thematic and formal evolution of his big book, which by June 1946, in Provincetown, Massachusetts, he was at last beginning to write.

For he had begun, on the basis of his I&R memories, with the idea of writing a scaled-down novel about a patrol, perhaps on the model of spare realism already made prominent by such war books as John Hersey's *Into the Valley* and Harry Brown's *A Walk in the Sun*. Still, the chapters grew and the patrol episode seemed increasingly delayed. Some new engineering was clearly going to be required; and Mailer quickly addressed it anew, he claimed, in just that fashion (Rollyson 38). He drew charts, wrote biographies, and assembled dossiers on characters. But most important, on the advice of a friend and editor, Ted Amussen, he found the specific means of engineering to accommodate the political, ideological, even metaphysical superstructure that the long patrol simply could not carry. He added the whole second narrative line with General Cummings and Lieutenant Hearn (43). Apace, he seems to have come into a grasp of all the other particulars that would weld the book together as ingeniously composite order of production. Mailer's somewhat obscure experiences in the Philippines were translated in the book to a scene resembling much more heavily publicized — and thus much better known to prospective readers — island warfare of the marine variety. Anopopei was made to look like Guadalcanal, Tarawa, Pelilieu. Like Iwo Jima, it had a dominating volcanic peak. Like Okinawa, it boasted the "Toyaku line" that had to be assaulted head-on.[12]

Publishing and editing would involve more practical engineerings of a composite order. Charles Devlin, Norman Rosten, who was a family friend and an editor at Little, Brown, and Adeline Lubell all read early portions with a growing conviction that Mailer had written *the* great novel of the war. Little, Brown senior editors countered by finding the book's obscene language totally unacceptable — "fuck, shit, motherfucking, . . . son of a bitch" (Mills 90). The editorial judgment was confirmed by Bernard De-Voto, who was asked to give outside opinion. A new contact was then made at Rinehart, through Rosten's editor, Ted Amussen, who, unknown to Rosten, had already turned down Mailer's *No Percentage* and *Transit to Narcissus* (Mills 91). Stanley Rinehart himself signed the novel for a $1,250 advance (Rollyson 42). Meanwhile, a cousin, Cy Rembar, also an attorney, supposedly came up with the important "fug" compromise (Mills 93).

The famous bar scene from *The Best Years of Our Lives* using an unprecedented three planes of focus: foreground, Hoagy Carmichael and Harold Russell; middle, Fredric March; background, in phone booth, Dana Andrews. Used by permission of the Metropolitan Museum of Art Film Stills Collection.

Academy Awards photo of Samuel Goldwyn, producer, Harold Russell, disabled soldier-actor, and William Wyler, director, receiving Oscars for *The Best Years of Our Lives.* Used by permission of the Academy of Motion Picture Arts and Sciences.

Title page of original hard cover edition of *Mister Roberts*, with cartoon art by Samuel Hanks Bryant. Used by permission of Houghton Mifflin.

Henry Fonda enlisting in the U.S. Navy. Used by permission of Springer/Corbis-Bettmann.

Henry Fonda as the character Mister Roberts.
Used by permission of Springer/Corbis-Bettmann.

Columbia LP album cover for the original Broadway cast recording of *South Pacific*, featuring Mary Martin as Nellie Forbush and Ezio Pinza as Emile DeBecque.

RCA Victor album cover for the stereo recording of the *South Pacific* movie sound track, featuring Mitzi Gaynor as Nellie Forbush and Rossano Brazzi as Emile DeBecque.

Front portrait of Mary Martin and Ezio Pinza from the
Technicolor Columbia LP album cover, updated to compete
with the movie sound track, for Broadway cast recording of
South Pacific.

Back cover of updated Columbia LP featuring Mary Martin
as Nellie Forbush and Ray Walston as Luther Billis in the
"Honeybun" number.

Marine Corps memorial sculptor Felix de Weldon instructing Iwo Jima flag-raising survivors Ira Hayes, John Bradley, and Rene Gagnon on how to re-create their actions in a movie scene so as to resemble his statue. Used by permission of *Leatherneck* magazine.

Title page of *Life's Picture History of World War II*. Used by permission of Time, Inc.

LIFE'S PICTURE HISTORY OF WORLD WAR II

TIME INCORPORATED · NEW YORK · 1950

Tom Lea's "Going In," Peliliu, 1944, depicting a young Marine in camouflage paint on his way ashore, and representative of war illustration featured in *Life's Picture History*. Used by permission of the Defense Department Center of Military History.

RCA Victor album cover for volume 3 in the *Victory at Sea* LP series. Billed as a "pictorial edition," with bound-in pictures and text selected from the 1959 book, it also featured stereo reproduction of live combat sound effects.

Dust jacket design for the first edition of *The Naked and the Dead*. Given advance release in advertising copy, it was designed to project an "existential" look.

Biography and photo of Norman Mailer on the back of *The Naked and the Dead* dust jacket, promoting Mailer as the prototype of a new breed of literary novelist emerging from the war experience.

Photo by G. Maillard Kesslere

norman mailer · Brooklyn, Harvard, Leyte, Japan; soda-jerk, usher, flat-painter, rifleman; *Story Magazine*, *Cross Section*, a first novel—Mr. Mailer's itinerary, literary and otherwise, reads like the traditional background for the novelist. But this twenty-five-year-old author bids fair, with the publication of **The Naked and the Dead**, to establish a literary tradition of his own.

Double-page *Variety* ad from Wednesday, February 5, 1958, for the movie *The Young Lions.*

Publicity photo of James Jones, looking uncharacteristically authorial in a suit, and Montgomery Clift, wearing a Prewitt-style Hawaiian shirt, around the time of the movie release of *From Here to Eternity.* Used by permission of Gloria Jones.

A *Variety* ad from June 30, 1954, on the box-office success of *The Caine Mutiny*, featuring a telegram from a grateful theater owner. For emphasis, the studio possessive is spelled with a dollar sign.

Biography and photo of Herman Wouk on the dust jacket for the 1953 edition of *The Caine Mutiny*. The publisher seems at pains to project a slick, corporate, eastern-establishment image of the author.

Herman Wouk graduated in 1934 from Columbia College, where he edited the *Jester* and wrote *Varsity Shows*. Thereafter he served five years on Fred Allen's writing staff. Before the war he was a dollar-a-year man in the Treasury Department's defense-bond radio section. He served four years in the Navy and was executive officer of the destroyer-minesweeper *Southard*. He entered the literary field with the novel *Aurora Dawn* (1947), a Book-of-the-Month Club selection. This was followed by *City Boy* (1948), a humorous novel about eleven-year-olds, and the Broadway drama *The Traitor* (1949), produced by Jed Harris. The movie about Navy weather fliers, *Slattery's Hurricane*, which he wrote in 1948, stemmed from research for THE CAINE MUTINY.

THE CAINE MUTINY

An ad for Leon Uris's *Battle Cry* in the
New York Times Book Review, May 3, 1953.

Robert Capa photo of the American assault on Omaha Beach. Included among the illustrations in Cornelius Ryan's *The Longest Day,* and one of the few action shots taken during the first wave, it is probably the most famous photo of D-Day. Used by permission of Wide World Photo.

The cover of the June 15, 1970, issue of *Time* magazine, featuring *Catch-22* movie director Mike Nichols and Alan Arkin as Yossarian.

More important was the novel's growing "radical" reputation, set out against the general mood of victory, as an American testament of resistance in the grand intellectual-literary tradition. While it was in press, Mailer himself described it to Fig Gwaltney as "an antiwar job." The general, he said, was a "beaut of a villain — a homo, a reactionary, a sadist" (Rollyson 47). What he also knew was that Cummings's powerful mystery and threat carried a long cultural provenance. From Melville came the legend, under a West Point class picture — perhaps "a little ambiguously, 'Handsome is as Handsome Does.'" (*Naked* 412); from Nietzsche came the apostolic invocations of world-historical destiny (321), "organization" (321), "power" (323–26).[13] From Emerson came the clothing of it all in an American uniform. "You know," Cummings calmly remarks to Hearn at a crucial point in their Faustian struggle for spiritual mastery, "if there is a God, Robert, he's just like me." Hearn elaborates helpfully: "Uses the common denominator technique." "Exactly," Cummings replies (183). And later, he approaches pure Emersonian apothegm. "Actually man is in transit between brute and God" (323), Cummings says. His deepest need, as Hearn again helpfully elaborates, is "omnipotence" (323). It is our greatest disappointment, he says, that we unlearn our lesson of birth: "In the final analysis there was only necessity and one's own reactions to it" (402).

Further, even the enlisted men seem to know this. "Listen, Polack," asks Wyman after Hearn is killed and Croft takes over the patrol, "you think there's a God?" "If there is," Polack replies, "he sure is a sonofabitch" (607).[14]

In the heavily ideological portrait of Cummings as the Nietzschean-Emersonian fascist, the monolithic world-historical totalitarian essence of the Right, Mailer seems to have personally surprised himself as the archetypal "Jew Radical" (Rollyson 47). On the other hand, for all their trailing of the apparatus of Dos Passos–like realism-naturalism, the melting-pot cast of enlisted characters are hardly depicted as proletarian ciphers. Rather, as in more conventional novels and films of the era, the emphasis seems to be on their general representativeness within the army itself as social microcosm: Polack, Gallagher, Red Valsen, Martinez (Japbait), Brown, Stanley, Ridges, Minetta, Goldstein, Roth, Wyman, Hennesey, Toglio. Even Croft, as Mailer surely knew, was less a cut-rate Ahab than a clearly recognizable military type, the tough, mean soldier who just gets into the habit of liking to kill people (Mills 87).

As to "radical" characters, Mailer could likewise hardly have done a better job of defusing ideological caricature. Hearn, the voice of the left in the book, is a richly inefficacious WASP, an upwardly mobile, prep-school,

Harvard, eastern liberal establishmentarian, vaguely literary, full of flirty critiques (*Naked* 328–53) of "bourgeois morality" (343).[15] Even he knows it. "Hearn and Quixote," he finds himself reflecting at one point. "Bourgeois liberals" (586). And it is exactly for that reason that he, in contrast to a Marxist college friend who has written to him about the inevitability of postwar Red-baiting by frightened reactionaries, reads establishmentarian power like a book. "There would be a witch-hunt after the war, all right," he muses, but in the hands of people like Cummings "it would hardly be a frightened witch-hunt." He goes on: "History was in the grasp of the Right, and after the war their political campaigns would be intense. One big push, one big offensive, and history was theirs for the century, perhaps the next one. The League of omnipotent men" (391).

If nothing else, the novel seemed to buttress Mailer's belief in his credentials as literary antifascist: "Every time I turned on the radio and looked in the newspapers, there was this growing hysteria, this talk of going to war again [with the Russians], and it made me start looking for the trend of what was happening. It seemed to me that you *could* get men to fight again" (Mills 84–85). On the other hand, when one looked at the picture closely, the emphasis still seemed to be on the term *literary*. For Mailer was, above all, a war naturalist, with obvious debts to Dos Passos, Hemingway, and Crane, interspersed by frequent nods to the metaphysical school of Melville.[16]

This was certainly the tendency of extremely positive reviews appearing immediately upon the novel's spring 1948 publication, which itself had been surrounded by literary hoopla involving previews of artsy cover design and news of "an unprecedented piece of flap copy" (Mills 100) written by no less than Stanley Rinehart himself.[17] If anything, they outdid Rinehart in hyperbolic mirror image.

Orville Prescott, for instance, in the daily *New York Times* called *The Naked and the Dead* "the most impressive novel about the second World War that I have ever read. . . . Mr. Mailer is certain to become famous as any fledgling novelist can be." Despite "unnecessarily offensive language," he could only remark on Mailer's "brilliant self-assurance" (Mills 100). Maxwell Geismar likewise in the *Saturday Review* averred, "Mr. Mailer is a new novelist of consequence" (Mills 101). And next in the *New York Times Book Review* proper came David Dempsey, "who called the book 'undoubtedly the most ambitious novel to be written about the recent conflict. . . . It bears witness to a new significant talent among American novelists.'" *Time* invoked Tolstoy's *War and Peace*; and *Newsweek* simultaneously anointed "Mailer 'a writer of unmistakable importance'" (Mills 101).

Mailer still professed himself "dumbfounded," while receiving such reviews, to see himself simultaneously at the top of best-seller lists (Rollyson 52) and then to find himself staying there for nearly three months. By the end of the first year, 197,185 hardcover copies had been sold. Mailer had earned one hundred thousand 1949 dollars. "My life," he said, "seemed to have been mined and melted into the long reaches of the book" (Rollyson 53). A past self was gone, with no choice but "to step into the war of the enormous present" (Mailer, *Advertisements* 71–72).

In New York, Mailer likewise professed embarrassment at being treated like "a movie queen" and refused to be photographed by *Life*, suggesting it "much better when people who read your book don't know anything about you, even what you look like" (Rollyson 55). One may be struck, says Mills, by such behavior from "the man who would become such a notorious self-promoter" (106). But Mailer was terrifically uneasy with it all. "I kept walking around saying, 'Nobody treats me as if I'm real'" (106).

To escape, Mailer sought involvement in Henry Wallace's political campaign and in his relief remained unaware of fellow-traveler manipulations. He made speeches for the Progressive party. Further, at a "Cultural and Scientific Conference for World Peace" at Waldorf in late March 1949, he denounced both the United States and the Soviet Union as both aiming toward "totalitarian state capitalism" — promoting thereby basically a Trotskyite position. He also formed a friendship with Lillian Hellmann, who had unsuccessfully tried to adapt *The Naked and the Dead* into a play. Mailer's political visibility, then, had increased exponentially in ways that had little to do with his big war novel. His socialism, his Marxism, his Trotskyism, all became wrapped up in a garish ideological-ness. He was getting ready to flop into the bathetic disaster of a new novel entitled *Barbary Shore*.

As it turned out, by 1949 he was in Hollywood, working on that new novel but also doing some experimenting with screenplays. Still, according to Mills, Mailer had no particular illusions about why he was going there. Ambition was surely important, as were the possibilities of the big-screen venue; but he also knew what he might be in for, as with the lesson of F. Scott Fitzgerald. Accordingly, "Mailer indulged his ambition and went to Hollywood, but from the moment he got there he steeled himself so completely against its temptations that he was able to accomplish nothing" (117).

If nothing else, he met Shaw, similarly there on the basis of *The Young Lions*, to whom he openly said that he would like to write for the movies or make his own film and that his interest went back to precelebrity days. He would sell *The Naked and the Dead*, he said; but only if he could write the screenplay.

No one for the moment seemed to want *The Naked and the Dead* on such terms; but meanwhile, he had gotten a contract offer from Samuel Goldwyn to write an original screenplay, which "he readily accepted" (Mills 117; Berg 477). On one side was Goldwyn's wife, Frances, who had increasingly become, according to Scott Berg, his self-appointed "chief scout for talent and material." On the other were Mailer and Jean Malaquais, his mentor in outlaw existentialism. The deal, dubious from the beginning, was to make a screenplay based on Nathanael West's *Miss Lonelyhearts*, but to do so, by Goldwyn's insistence, with a happy ending. Suffice it to say that things did not work out. (Allegedly, the novel's central concept of a columnist offering advice to the lovelorn and miserable was to be gimmicked up further with TV sponsorship by a burial-products manufacturer [Mills 117].) In any event, here and in other dealings Mailer made a name for himself as someone "so anxious to protect himself against the lure of Hollywood ambition that he wore integrity as a kind of chastity belt" (Mills 120).[18]

Still, he was "the first important novelist of World War II, and Hollywood ached for a great war picture" (119). Further, he and Malaquais were considered war specialists: the latter remembered perhaps fifty meetings where producers beseeched them to help make a "happy" war picture (120). On the other hand, Mailer was also thought of as a kind of political prize, one of the very few postwar writers of some popular visibility "who had no compunction about being identified with the left" (120).

Meanwhile, through intermediary work by a Hollywood friend, Mickey Knox, *The Naked and the Dead* finally sold as a screen property to Burt Lancaster, who had formed a new movie company and who wanted to play Hearn (Rollyson 63). Also, by another account, John Garfield was interested in playing Croft (Mills 121; Manso 145). But script approval, which Mailer had secured through his cousin, Charles Rembar, an attorney, proved a sticking point. According to Rollyson, "neither Lancaster nor his producer, Harold Hecht, provided a version of the novel that pleased the author, even though they enjoyed dealing with this 'brilliant' writer who insisted on 'creative control' of the picture" (63). On the other hand, according to Hecht, the author himself seemed to have fairly minimal interest in getting the project off the dime. *"The Naked and the Dead* was such a strange, difficult book for film that probably Burt and I were the only ones in Hollywood interested in doing it, so that's why Mailer wanted to go with us," he recalled. "I don't think Norman was going to write the screenplay," wrote Hecht; "but he had certain creative control and insisted that we couldn't do anything that departed significantly from the philosophy and attitudes" (Manso 146).

In any case, by June 1950 Mailer was on to Provincetown and to further encounter with his refusal as a novelist as well "to write the sequel he called 'The Naked and the Dead Go to Japan'" (Rollyson 65).[19] The result, of course, was *Barbary Shore*, a bleak ideological parody of Arthurian romance and allegory of left-existential politics, something like bad Sartre filtered through even worse Kafka into what a *New Yorker* review described aptly as "monolithic flawless badness" (Rollyson 71).

As to the ongoing saga of the Lancaster-Hecht *Naked and the Dead*, this, in turn, surely must have fed increasing anxieties in Cold War Hollywood about addressing American institutions in general through ideological critique; and by now, for the production team in question, there were also the concrete money problems faced increasingly by anyone likely to give even a relatively negative view of the military in the years 1948–53. In sum, as reported by Knox, Hecht simply ran head-on into "a lot of trouble with the government." One just "couldn't make a war picture without getting tanks and uniforms and guns." And "they refused to give all this to him unless he changed the title and made various changes in the story" (Mills 122).

Mailer's version, in a letter to Fig Gwaltney, told the same basic story. "*Naked* isn't going to be made into a movie," he wrote. "The story is too long and too complicated to go into, but the short of it is that the War Department let go a Colonel's Request to the effect that they would be happiest if said film property, blah, blah, were not to be made. And since without their approval nobody can raise money, and the guy who was going to make it was a small producer, the thing ended up with no money for me and the producer spending lots of dough on scripts, none of them good, for the No man's land between the War Dept. and myself was pretty rough." On the other hand, it was again a resolution that brought a certain perverse creative peace. "I'm kind of relieved in a way," he concluded, "because I have a sort of affection for *Naked*, and I'd of felt pretty cheap to have seen it fucked up on the screen" (Manso 154).

Indeed, according to Hillary Mills, the relief was such that when Hecht was forced to call Mailer and tell him about the impasse, Mailer did something almost surely without parallel in Hollywood history. As the author, he offered to buy back the book. Hecht readily accepted.[20] "It's better that I get the book back," Mailer rationalized (Manso 155). And years later, the explanation remained the same. "Well, if Hecht had kept it," Mailer told Knox, "the movie never would have been anywhere near the book" (Mills 122).

In this context, it almost seemed an afterthought when Mailer sold the property again after four years to Charles Laughton and the Hollywood producer Paul Gregory. And so it largely was. After a new set of discussions with Mailer, they too found the novel unworkable.[21] Shortly, they in turn sold it to Warner Brothers. And when that studio got around to doing something with it, another half decade had passed. The property had been out of Mailer's hands for a long time, and as Knox puts it, "Norman had no say whatever" (Manso 155). Moreover, by now he was the author not only of *The Naked and the Dead* and *Barbary Shore* but also "The White Negro" and other essays that had earned him status as the patron saint of the eastern hipsters; and, most recently, he had added a third novel, *The Deer Park*, a Hollywood exposé of unrelieved seaminess which had made him permanently persona non grata in the film capital. To put it simply, by now he could not have cared less about the movie odyssey of his first novel.

On the other hand, as is well known, the 1958 film that eventually did result turned out to be one of the best movies an author ever had the good fortune to be dissociated with. Any fears about the novel — the sexual preoccupations of the characters, the profane language, the military totalitarianism of high-level commanders such as Cummings, the liberal-intellectual cynicism of junior officers such as Hearn, the depiction of the GI Joe as a killing machine like Croft, or in the alternative as Jew, Polak, Wop, Irishman, Mex, as miserable, scared, isolated, stupid, mainly driven by terror and lust, love of pleasure, fear of pain — got lost in the totality of the movie's disaster as genre cliché.

The basic casting told most of the story. Cliff Robertson was cast as Hearn, Aldo Ray as Croft, and Raymond Massey as Cummings. Dorothy Malone and Lili St. Cyr figured tempestuously in sexual interludes salvaged from the novel's "time machine" sections as flashback love interests. (Meanwhile, one kept thinking, Barbara Nichols has to be in here somewhere.)

As to general effects, the spectacle was filmed in the grainy Technicolor used more or less indiscriminately in such period war films[22] — with the lurid process a kind of correlative to the frequent appearance, in many analogs, to the appearance of "Hell" somewhere in the title — that is, *Hell*

Is for Heroes, Hell Squad, Hell to Eternity, To Hell and Back, From Hell to Victory, Between Heaven and Hell, etc., etc., etc. This is to say that *The Naked and the Dead* became in some nearly absolute sense a generic war movie, essentially undistinguished and indistinguishable in process and design, completely interchangeable with others of the era in plot, casting, and production values of the late '50s to early to mid-'60s. Basically in "look" and "feel" a kind of scaled-down *Battle Cry,* it could as easily have been entitled *The Proud and the Profane, The Thin Red Line, Darby's Rangers, Merrill's Marauders, Kings Go Forth, Never So Few, No Man Is an Island, None but the Brave, In Love and War, Up from the Beach,* or *First to Fight.* Most of them were, after all, the same movie.

As to vestigial similarities to the novel, there is the Hearn-Cummings conflict followed by the Croft-Hearn long patrol. Further, Massey, at least, is a passable Cummings, although he goes light on the Nietzsche-Emerson and basically plays late-villain Raymond Massey. Ray steps out of the sturdy GI/noncom niche he perfected in a career extending from *Battle Cry* through *The Green Berets* to play the brutal Croft and in the movie gets killed for his sins. In contrast, Robertson, as Hearn, wounded and stretcher-borne, survives the movie version of the long patrol with two other platoon members to deliver a moral and a homily: "There's a spirit in man," he intones, "that will survive all the reigns of terror."

As late as the writing of *The Armies of the Night* — published on the twentieth anniversary of the publication of *The Naked and the Dead,* Mailer was still making roughly ten thousand dollars a year on royalties from his first novel. Its academic cachet, also, beginning with John Aldridge's early ranking of the novel with Crane's *The Red Badge of Courage* (134), had continued to grow, and by the late '70s it still ranked high on lists of top ten novels included in contemporary American fiction courses. Meanwhile, Mailer had still kept trying to write the big novel of America as megapolitical conspiracy: a vast authoritarian nexus of paranoiac congruencies — where the shadowy, Cummings-like godlike fascists are in control; and where Hearn-like existential protagonists wreck on the seemingly infinite capacity of such tin gods, as in *Catch-22,* to do anything we can't stop them from doing. This had underwritten the achievement of *An American Dream,* for instance; and it would also be secret history of the Republic in *Why Are We in Vietnam?* and, nearly two decades later, *Harlot's Ghost.* Forty years after *The Naked and the Dead,* Mailer would still be on the long patrol: the voyage to the center of the existential darkness of our times, to which is inevitably attached the grand geopolitical plot. Nor would any of the later versions result in the making of a major motion picture.[23] But they would continue the making of Norman Mailer, and that had been the point from the beginning.

The Young Lions

Although a first novel — and intentionally touted by its publishers as such — Irwin Shaw's *The Young Lions* appeared in 1948 with some degree of critical and popular recognition as the work of a writer who had already established a considerable reputation on various other grounds. Shaw was considered, for instance, a revolutionary prewar playwright, often linked with Clifford Odets and others (Giles 4) and a major '30s figure in the Theatre Group (31); and he had also become known as an accomplished practitioner of the literary short story, publishing prominently, again especially in the second half of the '30s, in the *New Republic, Collier's, Esquire, Harper's*, and, most important, the *New Yorker*. Collections had included *Sailor off the Bremen* (1939); *Welcome to the City* (1942); and *Acts of Faith and Other Stories* (1946) (31).

Shaw was also known as a liberal intellectual who had gone to war out of a deeply sensed awareness of the dangers posed by European Fascism. He had contributed to the Spanish Loyalists; and he was on record for his approval of Roosevelt's prewar admonitions about Fascist threats posed by Mussolini and Hitler. Still, with prewar Hollywood connections likely to gain him classification as a worker essential to war effort (5), he probably would not have been required to do military service. According to his biographer James R. Giles, "This was never an option for Shaw, however. In fact, only family responsibilities kept him from enlisting as early as he would have preferred" (5).

That enlistment came in June 1942. Shaw served until October 1945. Most of that time, writes Giles, he worked as part of "a camera crew; and while he never did any actual fighting, he was quite often under fire. He arrived at Normandy two weeks after the Allied invasion and helped photograph battles for the liberation of towns throughout France." At one point, he remembered, "'a bullet went between me, right behind my neck, and under the chin of the guy sitting in the jeep behind me.' In addition, he was present at the liberation of Paris and recounted, in *Paris! Paris!*, photographing a battle over the Chamber of Deputies from the top of the Comédie Francaise" (5–6).[24]

In the three years after his discharge, Shaw worked on his panoramic novel of the European war, *The Young Lions*. Accordingly, given his previous reputation in the theater and for the short story, the book was "much anticipated" (6), according to Giles. More to the point here, considerable gossip and ink were also spilled on its likely competition with Mailer's simultaneously heralded *The Naked and the Dead.*

Unlike Mailer's book, which made it into print first, Shaw's was attacked by the critic John Aldridge, who had set himself up as something of a gatekeeper of new war fiction. But generally it was "well received" (6). Better yet, it sold and continued to sell. It made the 1948 best-seller list at number ten, with 78,050 hardbound copies in circulation; and more than a quarter century later, with the help of Shaw's ongoing paperback popularity, it could be found on overall sales lists with a total of 2,185,201.

These figures suggest an uncommon measure of popular success for a novel in which the operative figure was, according to Giles, "allegory" — in this case, specifically, "the allegorical defeat of fascism by the decent common men of the United States and the world" (21). The better war-related phrasing, on the other hand, might have been "the big picture." For Shaw's great trick was to anchor his world-historical fable not in any single unit microcosm, as in *The Naked and the Dead* or later in *From Here to Eternity, The Caine Mutiny,* or *Battle Cry,* but rather in the trajectories of three separate protagonists, each essentially given his own novel-like experience of the war within a complicated plot design in which the three ultimately come together during the war's last days on the same battlefield. These included, in order of appearance: Noah Ackerman, a wandering, sensitive Jewish-American; Michael Whiteacre, a theatrical producer and Broadway playboy; Christian Diestl, an Austrian ski instructor enlisted in the Wehrmacht. All are introduced, launched in the courses of their individual lives, on New Year's Eve 1938. The ensuing panorama will include the war in North Africa; the invasion and conquest of France, culminating in the capture of Paris; and the final American assault into Germany, including the liberation of a death camp.[25]

Further, each main character is also given a major love interest. In Ackerman's case it is Hope Ploughman, the daughter of a Yankee widower living in a rock-ribbed New England village. In Whiteacre's it is Margaret Freemantle, a young New York cosmopolitan. In Diestl's it is Gretchen Hardenburg, the pleasure-loving wife of his commanding officer. In addition, Margaret Freemantle, as a world traveler, also serves to connect the fates of Whiteacre and Diestl. She meets the European first, on a 1938 New Year's skiing vacation in Austria, while waiting for the arrival of her lover, a Viennese Catholic doctor named Joseph, who, because he is Jewish on his mother's side, is soon to disappear in the Nazi holocaust. More immediately, she herself has also been nearly raped by an innkeeper's son in an establishment that turns out to be a hotbed of fervent Hitler worshippers. In political discussion with Diestl, a handsome young ski instructor, she in turn exposes the cynical corruption lying beneath his apparent civility (Giles 81).[26] Later, in New York, she meets Whiteacre, with whom she falls in love and whom she similarly serves as a kind of political conscience; and meanwhile, her previous relationship with Joseph has aptly foreshadowed, as Giles puts it, "the introduction of Noah Ackerman, an American Jew who is killed in Europe" (81).

The main difficulties attending the initial reception of the novel were the same ones recapitulated later by academic critics.[27] These centered on Diestl, presented as a basically good albeit politically undiscriminating man, eventually brutalized by war, who dies in an evil cause. To contemporary reviewers, especially this soon after the war, he still recalled too closely other controversially "humanized" Germans of wartime novel and film, such as the downed pilot in Jan Struther's *Mrs. Miniver* or the occupation troops in Steinbeck's *The Moon Is Down*.

Years later, Shaw was still defending himself against the charge, expressing indignation in a 1978 interview, for instance, about Marlon Brando's film portayal of "an innocent" when the "character" was in fact "a monster" (Giles 82). Further, as to the ways the character in question is actually allowed to develop in Shaw's very long and very detailed novel, the author had a point. Early in his duties, for instance, as Christian settles into occupied Paris, he reveals something of an ironic, even literary sensibility, remembering Hans Castorp at the end of *The Magic Mountain*, "running into French fire across the flower-spotted field, singing Beethoven." Now he thinks "the book had ended too soon. There should have been a chapter showing Castorp three months later, checking off size 12 boots in a supply depot in Liege. Not singing anything" (Shaw 142). And rounding up suspects, listening as "barbarian" police conduct interrogations, refusing his mistress's appeal to help her brother on the black market, he can still maintain, "I am not all the others" (151).

Three hundred–odd pages later, on the other hand, Christian largely has turned into an animal. At Normandy he coldly shoots a wisecracking American paratrooper entangled in a tree (456); shortly, he kills a boy for the sake of a bicycle to escape on (554); in Paris, after fleeing in a car provided by his old comrade Brandt, the photographer, he coolly turns the latter in as a deserter; and trapped near the end in a concentration camp he has stumbled into, he steals an inmate's clothing and personally cuts the commandant's throat (669) to clinch the impersonation. Shortly, in the nearby woods, he finds himself humming pleasantly, he recognizes, like his old commander Hardenburg the day they massacred the British in Libya.[28] He then opens fire on Ackerman and Whiteacre, killing Ackerman and causing Whiteacre to kill him, after first wounding him with a grenade, by shooting him point blank. Diestl's cynical last words are "Welcome to Germany."

Also doing more literary justice to his book than most critics, Shaw objected as well to Dean Martin's playing Whiteacre "strictly as a playboy," when "he's supposed to be an intellectual, to a degree at least" (Giles 100). This too is borne out by the novel. While in Hollywood, for instance, Whiteacre feels genuine revulsion at the whole California scene (180–96); during boot camp he assumes an active role in trying to do something about the anti-Semitic hazing of Ackerman and later enlists the help of influential New York friends to get the latter off on a desertion charge; and as he moves from duty in London through a series of experiences in the war zone, we do witness a progressive growth of consciousness culminating in his maturation as a combat soldier. Surely he is, as Giles suggests, the dramatized image of "a liberal intellectual who is perennially tormented by an inability to follow through on his decent impulses" (100). On the other hand, the image is a complicated one. Or, as the character himself sees the predicament near the end, thinking as usual, always thinking, "Michael Whiteacre, the inadequate man" (599).[29]

A major cause of such lack of serious interpretive attention on the part of early readers may have been the marketing image created for the book from the outset as essentially a popular production of a composite literary or perhaps quasi-literary order. Suggestions had been made, for instance, about Shaw's going to school as an American popularizer of Balzac and Tolstoi (Shnayerson 41) with all the vast human drama, a vision of the huge, pulsing social organism rendered within the framework of world-historical martial spectacle. Certainly, moreover, there was literal truth to the latter, with some obvious *War and Peace* appropriations — the most direct being Whiteacre in the Pierre role and Gretchen Hardenburg as an updating of the rapacious Helene Kuragin. On the other hand, more to the point as reading analogs probably were Margaret Mitchell and *Gone with the Wind* or Ernest Hemingway and *For Whom the Bell Tolls*, in both cases with admiring glances by Shaw at both the immensely popular novels and the classic Hollywood versions as well.

Where Shaw could claim credit for bold liberal sociopolitical critique, however, was in his assault on the fascist authoritarianism practiced by World War II military Americans against other Americans. As with Mailer, for instance, and shortly Jones as well, the officer class was depicted as relentlessly obtuse, decadent, bigoted, inept, and self-interested. And so Whiteacre, as with Mailer's Lieutenant Hearn, presented the failure among the intelligentsia of liberal good intentions. But most important was the crucial role played by Noah Ackerman — far beyond Mailer's Roth and Goldstein, for instance, in establishing and maintaining a central thematic concentration on anti-Semitism in the U.S. Army. Indeed, in both the book and the movie, the basic training of Noah Ackerman, not to mention the relentless physical violence and mob hatred visited upon him, seemed to go on literally forever. Further, in the book at least, the company commander, Colcough, gets away with simply looking the other way;[30] meanwhile, Rickett, the vicious NCO, goes on engineering it all for the "Jewboy, Ikie" (301) comprehending him within a virulent, all-purpose bigotry. "Niggers, Jews, Mexicans, or Chinamen" (302), they are all the same.[31]

No one could dispute, however, the breadth and catholicity of the novel's appeal. A quick paperback sale was made to New American Library, which had also picked up *The Naked and the Dead*. Both proved so popular as fifty-cent Signet double volumes that the company openly bragged about sales in promotional copy sent by the founding editor-in-chief, Victor Weybright, to hardbound publishers from whom he hoped to solicit similar new properties (Bonn, *Heavy Traffic* 28).[32] Further, Bennett Cerf at Random House shortly deemed Shaw's book so important a property that by 1950 Random House had bought it from NAL for yet another printing in the Modern Library series.

After more than five years of good sales — not to mention, as Shnayerson puts it, Shaw's enjoyment "of international stature as the author of *The Young Lions*" (228),[33] work finally began on a movie version in January 1954. The agent was Swifty Lazar. The price was reported to be more than a hundred thousand dollars. The buyers were a New York tax attorney, Jacques Braunstein, and a producer, Robert Lord, who planned an independent production for that summer. By the arrangement Shaw was also to get a percentage of the film's profits and, for an additional sum, write the screenplay (Shnayerson 227).

But by spring 1955 there was more bad Hollywood writing news. "Shaw learned that his work of the previous year on *The Young Lions* was for nought: the Braunstein-Lord package had collapsed for lack of financing" (239).[34]

After a new sale to Twentieth Century-Fox, *The Young Lions* finally moved to the shooting stage, but only after a decision by the director, Edward Dmytryk, to abandon Shaw's script, which seemed — like the novel, he thought — to center too heavily on Whiteacre. Rather, with a new scriptwriter, Edwin Anhalt, he tried to set up a firmly tripartite balance among the main male characters as a way of making the film's "real" subject the larger issues of war and what it does to people. Accordingly, with a further nod to Brando's box-office vanity, it was decided to make Diestl more attractive. As quickly, Shaw must have realized that the film was no longer his text in any sense of the term. During an interview with David Schoenbrun at Maxim's while filming was in progress, Shaw quarreled openly with Brando over proprietary rights to Diestl. "It's my character," Shaw said. "I gave birth to him. I created him." Brando informed him otherwise. "Nobody creates a character but an actor," he snapped back. "I play the role, now he exists. He is my creation" (Shnayerson 252–53). The two nearly came to blows. Then, later the same day, Shaw tried to press the point with his sometime friend Hemingway. The latter, pontificating on his own Hollywood experience, only made matters worse. He had long ago learned what to do, he said, after selling a book to the movies. "You don't think about the movie, you don't look at the movie, you know it's going to be a piece of shit. The idea of selling a book to the movies is to make money" (253).

If nothing else, for once Hemingway was dead right. Moreover, Shaw's problems with any personal artistic investment only got worse after the film's April 1958 release. Although largely attended by audiences, it was scorned by critics.[35] Still, it did help validate the worth of at least one risky technique increasingly uncommon in big-budget features of the era. That was the continuing use, in "serious" World War II films, of black-and-white filming, which quickly manifested itself again in a number of big-screen imitators — including one dreadful neorealist analog, *The Victors*, but also the highly successful *Longest Day*.

But surely the Hollywood *Young Lions* would always be remembered, then and now, for mainly the wrong things. Brando, promoted from sergeant to lieutenant, would flaunt a head of flaxen hair and a very, very bad German accent. Maximilian Schell would prove a filmgoer's dream of the crazed, decadent, high-strung, overbred, officer-class Prussian aristocrat, as would the golden Scandinavian love goddess, Mai Britt, as his rutting sensualist wife. Dean Martin, after the disaster of an earlier try at serious acting in *Some Came Running*, took the risk of another straight role with Whiteacre. One might have hoped it to turn out as had Sinatra's long shot with Maggio, but Martin wound up mainly walking through the part of the New York theater-intellectual-playboy. Clift played jumpy, harrowed, brooding Noah Whiteacre pretty much in the manner of late, jumpy, harrowed, brooding Montgomery Clift. Still, his performance in the role surely provided the most effective acting in the film, with Clift a rootless, ethnic Prewitt to Hope Lange as his New England small-town princess, Hope Ploughman.

About the only good thing for Shaw that seemed to come directly out of the film version of the novel was Cerf's announcement of big sales from a new paperback tie-in (Shnayerson 261). Still, it is hard to hold to an unqualified judgment that the 1958 *Young Lions* was a "bad" movie — except to the degree perhaps that it fell somewhere between the way *The Victors* was a thoroughly "bad" movie and *The Longest Day* somehow avoided completely being a "bad" movie. Beyond all else, the film's one worst consequence was surely the injustice that it helped to perpetuate regarding the long-term reputation of the book. For, as Mailer's was a tour de force, a huge, but astonishingly well engineered book assimilating his realism-naturalism and its sundry experimentalisms into something very centered and tight, so *The Young Lions* took the alternative path of traditional social panorama as a meticulously craftsmanlike, fully developed novel-reader's delight, with heavy realistic concentration on the personalities of the major characters and the changes wrought upon them by the experience of war. It also offered literally hosts of fully developed minor figures, with attendant painstaking attention to dialogue, scene, large-scale continuity. From beginning to end, it remained full of energy, a complete and sustained creation. Noah Ackerman's growth of courage; Christian Diestl's deepening cynicism; Michael Whiteacre's emergence as a soldier: these major developments were mirrored with equal care of execution in the dissolute animality of Gretchen Hardenburg or the weariness of the prostitute Simone. At the end, the homey domesticity of the photographer Brandt, ever the soft civilian in Wehrmacht dress, is as convincingly rendered as his surprisingly instant evolution as a soldier in his first ambush.

To be sure, with the eventual commingling of vast scenarios of love and war, the novel's plot implausibilities, considered from a distance at least, become staggering. Margaret Freemantle meets Christian Diestl; Margaret Freemantle meets Michael Whiteacre; Michael Whiteacre meets Noah Ackerman; everybody separates for a long time. At the end, Michael Whiteacre, still in love with Margaret Freemantle, joins Noah Ackerman in the combat infantry. Together they encounter Christian Diestl, who kills Ackerman and is in turn killed by Whiteacre, who carries Ackerman's body back to the concentration camp.

Still, the novel's achievement would always be enough for a permanent, if at times bizarre, legacy of reputation that Shaw would alternately enjoy and struggle against. In spring 1961, for instance, when he was sent to Jerusalem as a feature reporter to cover the Adolf Eichmann trial, he was touted by the *New York Journal-American*, his employer, as the author of *The Young Lions*, who had there "plumbed the labyrinthine thinking of Nazis like no other fiction writer" (Shnayerson 272). On the other hand, when *Rich Man, Poor Man*, Shaw's sixth big novel, launched him in 1970 on a popular and literary comeback, it was excoriated by Christopher Lehmann-Haupt as a prostitution of Shaw's talent. The reviewer's measuring stick? *The Young Lions*, of course (Shnayerson 330).

Perhaps finally a fitting last word did come, in a 1980 Player's Club tribute from Shaw's fellow World War II veteran and fellow novelist Kurt Vonnegut. He called *The Young Lions* the best novel to emerge from World War II (Shnayerson 386) and suggested that perhaps the time had come to republish it, this time under the original title planned by Shaw, *The Bloodletters*. One had to agree with Vonnegut. Thereby it could again be read as a novel; and at the very least, no one would automatically confuse it with the movie.

From Here to Eternity

Among the five properties achieving production status as a postwar classic in the big-war, big-book, big-movie tradition, James Jones's *From Here to Eternity* was also the first to go more or less directly into a major film, with the 1951 novel and the 1953 movie both achieving extraordinary success with popular audiences and critics alike. Moreover, it did so without being actually *about* the war in the sense that *The Naked and the Dead* or *Battle Cry*, for instance, as novels and films are about World War II combat, or *The Young Lions* and *The Caine Mutiny* are about wartime military experience interfused with more conventional attempts at social panorama. Rather, as is well known, the focus of depiction in *From Here to Eternity* is the prewar garrison army in Hawaii during the months leading up to the December 7, 1941, Japanese attack, which itself receives brief representation just at the end.

Still, at every step of the way, it made its own kind of history as an exemplar of the genre. Purchased initially by 240,000 readers, the hardbound book topped the national best-seller lists in 1951 and then returned to sell 68,500 more in 1953 in conjunction with the movie. A first paperback run of 2 million copies sold out in the same year. Combined figures after two decades would exceed 3 million, with revivals facilitated by other Jones best-sellers, often distinctly related in theme and topic.[36]

Among critics and reviewers it was also set apart from likely competitors in large talk about artistic permanence. As David Dempsey wrote in the *New York Times Book Review*, "Make no mistake about it, 'From Here to Eternity' is a major contribution to our literature, written with contempt for the forces that waste human life, and out of compassion for men who find love and honor and courage in the lower depths" (106).[37] And it is a view that has continued to find validation in both the popular and critical canons. As a mass-culture artifact, *From Here to Eternity* truly does seem to extend the great vernacular tradition of realism-naturalism, of Crane and Dreiser, Lewis and Wolfe, Farrell and Steinbeck. And in its reach of statement as existential argument — beyond, ironically, even so flashy a competitor as Mailer's *The Naked and the Dead*, with the latter's homages to Emerson, Nietzsche, Dos Passos, and Hemingway — *From Here to Eternity* has also continued to be understood as the most properly ideological novel to come out of the war in its depictions of sexuality and violence, of power, money, and class relationship. For as a novel of World War II, it is uniquely able to locate the American experience of the war in its actual ideological provenance: the world of the army as a teeming microcosm of depression-era castoffs and misfits, time-serving professionals and cynical fascists, wallowing in their routinized misery, with solace only in the clubs, the bars, the brothels, the gambling sheds, all waiting for the end somewhere out on the edge of the empire.[38]

To be sure, as a film *From Here to Eternity* found itself deflected considerably from much of the most controversial content in the book. Still, it quickly proved a box-office sensation, by 1954 earning $80 million on a production cost of $2.5 million (MacShane 132); and by critical standards it was also a large success, winning major New York film awards and eight Oscars, including those for best movie, best direction, best screenplay, and best supporting actor and actress.

More than any competitor to date in the big-war, big-book, big-movie genre, then, *From Here to Eternity* succeeded at every stage of its creative and commercial evolution in presenting itself as a text made to order for all its cultural constituencies. And well it should have, moreover. From the ground up, it had been a prototype of the manufactured classic, in the fullest sense a genuinely corporate enterprise.

To put this another way, *From Here to Eternity* may claim the distinction of having succeeded as one of the Good War's greatest hits by being from the outset envisioned and devised — perhaps *engineered* would not be too strong a word — as a speculative property. And along the way, it would find the speculation repaid by having its own creative genealogy mythically and materially enshrined in the larger cultural narrative it helped create.

Memories abound as to how thoroughly the production of a history here became identified with the history of production. Indeed, any recollection of the title is accompanied almost inevitably by imagery of its popular promotions. In the case of the book, for instance, there is the unforgettable jacket, the dun olive-drab background, the upturned, corded bugle, the two raffish, loitering GIs in silhouette, one with a cigarette hanging on his lip, both in class-A khaki uniform. They are obviously at their leisure, on pass somewhere, maybe standing on a curb, or leaning against a lamppost, gentleman rankers off on a spree. At the time, it seemed to be everywhere, imaging itself in endless refraction: in advertising copy, in book-club news, in shop-window displays.

Of the movie, similarly what one surely recalls first are the posters and promotional stills. On one of the most memorable of the former, for instance, the novel bears its title in bold print, with the five movie principals — Burt Lancaster, Deborah Kerr, Montgomery Clift, Donna Reed, and Frank Sinatra — all seeming to appear in some magic three-dimensionality out of its centered bulk. (Above, the legend breathlessly announces, "From the stark, bold — yet tender — bestseller 5,000,000 readers gasped at!") And in the stills, Lancaster and Kerr have their torrid horizontal embrace in the surf; in the KP scene, Clift stands hunched over the pots and pans, as Lancaster grins sadistically in the background.[39]

Accordingly, given such a history of mythic evolution, surely the most extraordinary feature of the property must remain — in comparison with nearly any analogous text one might consider — that it originated in less than nothing; or at least in nothing resembling *From Here to Eternity*. Or, that it might all have ended before it began as one of the most pathetically familiar of writing and publishing stories, with James Jones, a wounded veteran of Pacific combat, out of the army since 1944, and since then mainly a drifter and aspiring novelist. By 1946 he had arrived in New York with a saga of returning veterans entitled *They Shall Inherit the Laughter*, which he insisted on submitting personally to Maxwell Perkins, the legendary editor of Fitzgerald, Hemingway, Wolfe, and others at Charles Scribner's Sons.[40]

On his part, Perkins seems characteristically to have recognized a first novelist's overblown labor of love, attentively reading it, for a time editorially encouraging it, but finally turning it down in the most politic and gentle way for what it was: unpublishable.[41] At the same time, however, with his uncanny instincts for matching literary talent with popular interest, Perkins also picked up rapidly on hints from the author about an alternative project, this one closer to Jones's own prewar military experience. And, after fourteen chapters and a detailed synopsis of the new work, he could respond with some encouragement, albeit getting the bottom line first. "I do not know whether this book will sell," he advised Jones, "and I think there will be a very hard struggle in cutting it and shaping it, but I think it exceedingly interesting and valid. The Army is *something*, and I don't think that anyone even approached presenting it in its reality as you have done" (MacShane 83).

A five-hundred-dollar option was offered on this second book while Jones was still working on the first. Another five hundred followed. And Jones, hoping to salvage a few stories from the earlier text, pressed on with the new one, all the while corresponding with the editor. The latter, in turn, also allowed Jones to embrace him as all-purpose father figure, at once a kindred creative soul and an impressively official literary-cultural guide. Perkins was upper-class, eastern, establishmentarian, in every sense the patron, the preceptor, and the patriarchal authority. The text had been duly authorized.

While writing, Jones led an itinerant life, bouncing mainly between trailer parks in Florida and his small Illinois hometown, where his work had already found an unlikely combination of muse, mistress, *magna mater*, and — through the largesse of her wealthy husband — full-fledged patron. This, of course, was Lowney Handy, the quondam Madame de Stael and Dragon Lady of Robinson, Illinois, with her own big literary aspirations, mainly involving proprietorship of an artists' colony for former World War II sailors and GIs where each was encouraged to fancy himself — like, eventually, Jones, Mailer, Shaw, Wouk, and Uris — as perhaps the newest celebrity author to enjoy fame and fortune through his latest big novel of the war. And it was in these circumstances of bizarre generation, then, that Jones parlayed Perkins's mentorship and Handy's grubstake into the text that would come to be known as *From Here to Eternity*.[42]

The strength and purpose, in fact, with which Jones worked in this somewhat gothic apprenticeship can be measured by the fact that by mid-1947, when Perkins died, his successor, Burroughs Mitchell, found a work sufficiently advanced that he could see the project through with a confident sense of continuity. And in turn, at the end of composition, when he eventually went back with Jones to start in on all the things an editor would normally do — cuts, redesignings, revised or newly suggested transitions — he found his chief problems to be not so much issues of literary craft as matters of public taste arising out of the novel's controversial sexual content and what seemed its inordinately heavy profanity. For by now it was the '50s, a period of retrenchment from the grim realism of depression-era and wartime life and its depiction in literature and film, and of redirection of public sensibility toward a new, sanitized happiness. Yet here, at least as it stood, was a book still full of depression-era and wartime sordidness, sex, and violence; and, most problematically, it was also a book written unblinkingly in the profane argot of the old-line soldier.

Compromises had to be made on all counts. Certain scenes were toned down, including one long sexual encounter between Prewitt and Lorene. Certain brothel lore had to be winnowed. And above all, of course, there was the whorehouse and barracks language. To be sure, thanks to the trail-blazing work of Mailer and others, certain indispensable words could now be permitted. The problem was, according to the Scribner's lawyer Horace Manges, that they would have to be rationed. And so, as in some strange metafiction of self-censorship, the parties involved sat down to work, Mitchell and Jones on one side and Manges on the other, with the lawyer keeping score. "There were 259 fucks, 92 shits, and 5 pricks," Jones reported. The editorial team reduced these to "146 fucks and 45 shits." For some reason, pisses were exempt. At this point Manges made a counter-offer. Jones withdrew angrily, leaving Mitchell to work on a little longer. Finally, he too felt compelled to halt the absurdity with a personal appeal to Charles Scribner; and in such a compromise of a compromise, *From Here to Eternity* was deemed ready to make its debut.

Meanwhile, in the commercial sphere careful attention was devoted to carving out a particular publicity niche for so particular a property. And here, the examples of foregoing analogs such as Shaw and Mailer proved especially useful. Like some secret-operations unit, Scribner's launched a campaign of prepublication rumor about the book and curiosity-provoking speculation about Jones himself. In a *Publishers Weekly* ad of late 1950, for instance, appeared a dramatic photo of the jut-jawed author with the brush cut, the beetling brows, the scowl. It was altogether a portrait of the artist himself as projection of the book to come, the literary newcomer as light-heavyweight, looking "tough and muscular in a striped T-shirt" (Garrett 95), the ex-GI as primitive existentialist. Further, there were also obvious attempts here to suggest more current bohemian resemblances, with beats such as Kerouac, for instance, and tough guys such as Mickey Spillane.[43]

If it all seemed something of a pop-epic annunciation, well it might have. The GI Homer in question had, after all, produced an enormous tome — nearly nine hundred pages' worth, to be exact. The copies soon pyramided in promotional shots of the Scribner's window also suggested a similar, epochal, even granitic permanence. And so immediately did the opening sales figures, even then stunning for a first novel in hardbound, both in the United States and abroad (Garrett 97).

In turn, an immediate paperback sale, to New American Library, was itself quickly enshrined as a major piece of publishing history, with its hundred-thousand-dollar sum nearly tripling the previously unheard-of thirty-five thousand paid by the same publisher to Mailer a few years earlier for *The Naked and the Dead.* The imprimatur of official criticism, with just enough controversy generated by questions of sensational content and language to keep the pot boiling, was simultaneously conferred in the form of the National Book Award; and, probably more helpful for sales, this was also paired with adoption by the Book-of-the-Month Club — as we may forget now, at the time a popular recognition still carrying a certain literary cachet as the choice of a board of well-known literary-critical "experts."[44]

As to all possible outcomes of so unlikely a publishing story, one can only say that the sui generis quality of composite genius involved in the making of *From Here to Eternity* somehow found itself even topped by the utterly original achievement of the text. As the only great book in our history essentially commissioned by a magisterial literary editor from a great and yearning, albeit untutored, American soul, it wrote its own version in socioliterary abstract or epitome of the national spirit. It bespoke at once the visionary democratic tradition of the great American romantics and the steady concentration of the homegrown realist-naturalists, them-selves, like Jones, small-town, middle-class, drifting. As a quintessentially twentieth-century work, however, it also partook of virtually all the great modernist iconographies: the wasteland; the death of love; the prolifera-tion of random, totalitarian violence; the failure of culture as a sustaining force in people's lives.[45] And it further, as a quintessentially post-1945 work, brought them all down to the mass-culture landscape of the utterly exis-tential and quotidian: the squad bays, the supply rooms, the mess halls, the bars, the brothels, the gambling shacks; the grimly efficient stockade; the luxuriant, manicured officers' golf course; teeming downtown Honolulu, with the whores, the cruising homosexuals, the aimless, drunken, brawling soldiers and sailors, the omnipresent, motorized, club-wielding MPs.

Further, for all the windy excesses, the crudities, even the illiteracies, the book finally does make itself out as largely an achievement of a vibrant, profoundly national style: the result of a typically incomplete American education, of a reading apprenticeship in the library stacks; yet also the prize of taking it all and making it in its way, somehow, great. For out of the whole dismal panoply, we truly do know and attend to the voices, the dreams, the angers of those afoot on the great '30s American sociopolitical landscape, the army and its hangers-on, all the cogs and bearings and ci-phers, straining away at once to make the system go.

At the putative top are the professionals, the West Point aristocracy: Del-bert, the regimental colonel, and Captain Dynamite Dana Holmes, his pet company commander. (But already out there beyond them, of course, and their petty authoritarianisms, are the others, shadowed, menacing, al-together in control, Nietzschean power figures such as the boy-general, Slater.) Meanwhile, NCOs actually run the business — career soldiers and professionals such as Warden and Stark, jostling with operators and system-racketeers such as O'Hayer, master of the supply room and concessionaire of the payday gambling sheds, and staying on the backs of dim old time-servers, Pete Karelesen, Ike Galovich, Chief Choate.

The enlisted men fend for themselves, scourings of the old, depression-era, blue-collar industrial and agricultural classes. Chief among them, of course, stands Robert E. Lee Prewitt, the novel's fully realized, even ex-emplary, proletarian hero, the untutored soul of the artist from the Ken-tucky mining country.[46] But they also include the more likely assortment by way of the melting-pot platoons so prominent in the war movies, new ethnic types like Maggio and Bloom, the spawn of the cities, punchies and jockstraps, tough, survivor-like, measured and promoted by their ability to keep the company and regimental trophy cases filled with athletic cups for the prestige of their cruel, obtuse commanders.

Against the male hierarchy in the novel, certain women may enact their own dramas of fated individual struggle. Karen Holmes, the officer's woman, is the status symbol, the regimental trophy in all senses of the phrase, the legendarily promiscuous wife of Captain Dynamite Dana Holmes, soon to become the mistress-lover of First Sergeant Milton Warden. Lorene/Alma, the prostitute, possessed of her own dream of status, seeks to make sufficient money to buy respectability as a society wife but instead makes the mistake of falling in love with a doomed thirty-year man, Prewitt. But most simply play their appointed roles: whores, madams, shack jobs, party girls, half-caste wives.

Thus we find arrayed before us the whole vast gamut, the complete socioeconomic apparatus, the microcosm on the eve, the inheritors of what Henry Luce was concurrently calling "the American Century" waiting for the inevitable blow to fall somewhere out on the westernmost Pacific extension of empire. By any cultural standard of the time, it was surely the most politically overarching of the big novels to come out of the war; and by the same standard, it was also surely the most existentially squalid in every respect, obscene to the degree that the entire war-breeding system is obscene.

In language it was easily the most profane and shockingly explicit of its era to make it to the general market, with enough "shit," "piss," and "fuck" to make it a truly groundbreaking work. And in its depiction of sexual relationships, sordid lives were somehow made to seem strangely grand and fated, something nearly like romance in a morass of unrelieved seaminess and depravity. Even the two main sexual situations depicted — the adulterous liaison between the first sergeant, Warden, and the captain's wife, Karen Holmes, rendered barren by gonorrhea she has caught from her husband; and the tragic love affair of Prewitt and the prostitute-princess, Lorene — are but large figures against the teeming backdrop of a world, truly far beyond any Hemingway conceit now, of men without women.[47] For the army itself is nothing less than a vast sexual engine formed out of a collocation of human detritus: misfits, isolatos, deadbeats, bums; drunken, violent, sex-starved, profane. Sex here is a behaviorist's dream, brief, sordid, pathetic pleasure in a world of fear and pain. It is a payday bender and a piece of ass from a prostitute; or going to the gambling shacks first to get enough for an all-nighter; or, more likely, losing the wad to the corrupt sergeants who run the games, spending another month broke, or deeper in debt; or, perhaps in final desperation, just to be somewhere, for the price of a good meal and a big drunk making the party scene with a rich Waikiki queer.

Here was America gone pathological in the fullest sense: a whole army as microcosm of its people, literally dying of love. The disease, everywhere, is venereal: crabs, gonorrhea, syphilis.

But beyond even this, there is worse. For here alternatively, at the center of the novel, we also find the army and its America as penal colony. Here, in the stockade, the masters are Fatso Judson and the MPs, and the forbidden pleasures sadomasochistic violence.

It is the army version of the death camps, the deeper microcosm. And one by one, the inmates arrive. First to be sucked in is Maggio, fed up with the chickenshit, screaming his defiance from a curb on Waikiki, daring the omnipresent MPs to find him and pick him up blind drunk and then making them almost kill him just to make the arrest. But then, suddenly, there is Prewitt, too, his refusal to yield pride of place to the head bugler's new punk, followed by his transfer to the infantry, followed by his refusal to box, to join Dynamite Dana's roster of company punchies and jockstraps, followed by the Treatment, followed by the great Waikiki queer-lover roundup, followed by the horrific fistfight with Bloom, followed by the one drunken punch it takes to fell the old raving sergeant, Ike Galovich. Suddenly it is the end of the line, the court-martial and the stockade. And it has all been for a belief in a simple credo, a line of American words, as Prewitt says it. "Every man has certain rights," he says; "in life, I mean, not in ideals." It is "my right as a man," he concludes, "to not be kicked around" (195).

In the stockade Fatso Judson and his minions Hayseed Turniphead Turnipseed and Handsome Hanson make an issue out of belief, blazoning on the stockade trophy board the clipping from *Ripley's Believe It Or Not* that memorializes the installation as the first place John Dillinger served time, the toughest joint in the army, the jail that made Dillinger vow "TO HAVE VENGEANCE ON THE WHOLE UNITED STATES SOME-DAY, EVEN IF IT KILLED HIM" (496). We witness the passion of Angelo Maggio, his descent into the incessant beatings and the eventual madness. We witness the breaking and killing of Blues Berry. We see the attempted recruitment of Prewitt as revolutionary by the old Wobbly organizer, Jack Molloy.

Prewitt, of course, will take the more direct route toward the settling of a blood debt, one more in keeping with his Kentucky hill-country credo.

On a Honolulu street he kills Fatso Judson with a knife. But by now, we realize, we have already had our glimpse into the real black hole of the book. The stockade is a reified moment of sublime iconographic recognition, the center of the metaphysical darkness of our times.

At the same time, the genius of the text lies in the quality of reification, the degree to which the stockade scenes or Prewitt's killing of Fatso are also no more or no less real than the playing of "Taps" or a barracks dispute among enlisted men over the relative merits of their favorite movie cowboys. For, whether in his own experience or in the cultivation of his craft, Jones had found within himself the indispensable instinct of the American realist, the gift for the faithful representation of democratic individuality. Or, as George Garrett puts it, Jones knew how to construct "all of his fiction, beginning with *From Here to Eternity*, from *character* outward, from character to event." He goes on: "Plot came from character and was designed out of the discovery of layers of being, the 'truth' of the characters rather than from the impact of events which, one might imagine, as his characters often do, is supposed to shape character" (80).

Now, this is obviously so of the principals. But one also sees that the same idea pertains in almost perfect egalitarian distribution to all the others as well. Maggio is as real as Maylon Stark, Jack Molloy as Fatso Judson, Mrs. Kipfer as the doomed Jewish boxer, Bloom, the mournful supply clerk Niccolo Leva, or the duty roster NCOs Ike Galovich, Chief Choate, Pete Karelesen, and the rest. Even the officers — Colonel Delbert, Captain Holmes, Lieutenant Culpepper — if left to sardonic caricature, carry the bite of a good Bill Mauldin cartoon.

Further, such focus on the relationship between character and event surely also has to do with how correspondingly focused and even oddly compact *From Here to Eternity* turns out to be for a book of its seeming length and sprawl. Composed of five basic units, "The Transfer," "The Company," "The Women," "The Stockade," and "The Re-Enlistment Blues," the text evolves carefully toward the cataclysmic surprise attack with which the war begins. And even the grand historical jolt of this stroke of upheaval, as Garrett again observes, has been in the fullest sense politically earned. For only "we know what none of these characters can imagine — the long, bloody road to victory in World War II and the end of much that seemed inherently characteristic in American life" (96). Truly, then, through the lost souls of *From Here to Eternity*, Jones had reckoned "the texture of the times," to use Garrett's phrase, the inevitability of the coming conflict, and the measure of the depression-era men and women about to be plunged into it. This great American novel of World War II ends just as the war begins. That would seem in many ways to be just the point.

Any extended literary-historical appreciation of the novel entitled *From Here to Eternity*, however, was quickly to be subsumed into the notoriety of the film — to this day, surely the version of the artifact remembered by most Americans. It was the one with Burt Lancaster and Deborah Kerr in the surf; the one that made a star out of Montgomery Clift and then left him never really able to get over having played Prewitt; the one where the unlikely casting of Donna Reed created an Academy Award–winning prostitute; the one where the leftover '40s crooner Frank Sinatra made a new career by getting himself cast as Maggio. It is also the one that won eight Academy Awards, starting with best film and including best script for Daniel Taradash, best director for Fred Zinnemann, best supporting actress for Reed, and best supporting actor for Sinatra.[48]

In some degree, that kind of creative capital had also been manufactured into the book property from the outset. Somehow the big movie deal would have to be attempted. The question was how much trouble there would be. Surely there would be no end of difficulty with the Hays office alone over violence, profanity, and sexual content. The army would surely balk, should its cooperation be requested. And more generally, all the politicians and public moralists could be counted on to decry any representation of the recently victorious U.S. military in its prewar condition as a miasma of human depravity and waste.

The purchase of film rights was something that made even the big Hollywood buccaneers nervous. In succession, Warner and Twentieth Century-Fox contented themselves, for instance, with simple, strictly pro forma approaches to the Defense Department to ask about the remote possibility of cooperation on a project involving Jones's novel. They were refused out of hand. After a spate of postwar movies, the guidelines had become firm and clear. "No film based directly on the novel," it was determined, "could benefit the Army"; hence "it did not qualify under the Department's regulations" (Suid 117). Both studios immediately quit the fray.

Neither studio, on the other hand, was run by Harry Cohn, who did things at Columbia decidedly in his own way. And in this case, his own way involved buying the property outright without asking anyone anything about government assistance deals. Those not consulted included nearly everyone at Columbia, where the New York office took the lead in protest.

Only after the Motion Picture Board and the Defense Department got done with them, it was claimed, would all the other federal law-enforcement and policy arms get started, and after they finished one could add on state authorities and religious organizations. Moreover, the immediate timing could not have been worse. McCarthyism was still rampant, and the integrity of federal authority was considered sacrosanct. In the words of Fred Zinnemann, the eventual director, "to voice doubt about any" of the great national symbols of that authority, "the Army, Navy, or FBI — was to lay oneself open to deep suspicion"; and thus even to consider "filming a book openly critical of the peacetime army . . . was regarded by many as foolhardy, if not downright subversive" (20).

Cohn's Washington representative, Raymond Bell, confirmed the nervousness on all counts. Asked to read the novel for its general moral tone, he emerged saying, "I felt like I spent a weekend in a whorehouse." On political matters he was even more pointed. The book contained, he said, "a lot of apparent communist doctrine" and, in the midst of the Hollywood Red scare, could cause Cohn to be regarded as a dupe. He also found it "anti-Catholic and anti-Jewish" (Suid 118); antiofficer in its depiction of the utterly useless captain whose top sergeant is sleeping with his wife; anti-NCO in the explicit brutality directed against Prewitt and Maggio; and decidedly nonconstructive in any image the army might wish to present to '50s recruits.

Undeterred, Cohn and his original choice for producer, Louis Sylvan, took the project to Washington anyhow. Again, reaction was completely negative. Cohn sought alternatives. He engaged Jones, of all people, to try his hand at an acceptable screenplay, after presumably briefing the novelist thoroughly on censorship issues. On his part, Jones, knowing nothing about movie work, returned a ridiculously sanitized draft. (Karen Holmes, to use just one example, becomes the captain's sister.)

Next, the project was handed to the screenwriter Daniel Taradash who, with Buddy Adler, the new producer, actually began to find openings for basic structural change that would finally make the project workable — and workable, in fact, with army assistance. First, the stockade scenes were simply eliminated. The cruelty would be left to the viewer's imagination. Second, the sexual themes would be reduced to concentration on the interweaving of the two main love plots (Suid 119–20).

In other, more specific sanitizations, the whorehouse in the book called the New Congress Hotel becomes a social club, a kind of fleabag USO, with Lorene/Alma a "hostess." Karen Holmes's sterility-inducing gonor-rhea gets traded in for a sterility-inducing miscarriage. Four-letter words were simply written out. Possible nudity was dismissed (Suid 120).

Still, with the military there remained a big catch. Though less ob-jectionable than before, *From Here to Eternity* remained a film project that could not possibly "benefit" the army. On the other hand, Cohn's bizarre obstinacy had achieved an effect. To the Defense Department in particular, Hollywood's determination had itself become a potentially embarrassing issue, with odds seeming increasingly in favor of Colum-bia's likely finishing of the film in a highly publicized way with or with-out support.

The army continued to hold the line. Negotiations dragged on for six more months. Meanwhile, Cohn went ahead and chose a director, Fred Zinnemann. Zinnemann now worked with Taradash, and new "changes" surfaced. Karen Holmes does not mention her previous affairs. It is strongly implied that the "Treatment" undergone by Prewitt is an aberra-tion. Dynamite Dana Holmes, in the book gaining for his sins a coveted promotion to major, is told in the movie to face court-martial or resign (Suid 123–24).

Now even the army was finally persuaded. The great military post de-picted in the book, Schofield Barracks on Oahu, was made available for lo-cation shooting. Disguised training planes were provided to stage the De-cember 7, 1941, attack. And a professional senior sergeant was assigned officially to instruct the male principals in military details (127).

Final sanitizations followed. For the code office, all mention of homo-sexuality was omitted. Warden and Karen Holmes were required to show obvious shame. The notorious beach footage got extra scissoring.[49] In one last sop to the army, scenes were also cut where Warden was allowed to be seen staggering drunk.

On the other hand, Cohn, with victory in his grasp, now seemed bent on frittering it away with idiosyncratic personal changes. He proposed a sentimental ending, with Prewitt actually dying in Warden's arms. Then he considered not letting Prewitt die at all. Next he convinced himself that the only possible Prewitt was Aldo Ray.[50]

The only real damage he probably did was during the filming, when, trying to score points with the local command, he roared up in midshoot-ing at Waikiki and gutted Maggio's famous provocation of the MPs — a scene rehearsed spectacularly by Sinatra that afternoon — by forcing him to deliver his insane philippic *while sitting on a park bench* (24). On the other hand, Zinnemann had already gotten something back by convincing Cohn to shoot the film, despite its Hawaiian setting, in dramatic black and white.

The result, especially for its time and the incredible constraints placed on its making, was both a brilliant film and a great movie. Its Hollywood status was affirmed by its thirteen Oscar nominations in the same year that saw formidable across-the-board competition in *Roman Holiday, Stalag 17,* and *Shane.* And its critical integrity was measured by outcries such as that in the *Los Angeles Times,* which branded it as "aid and encouragement to the enemy," and by the navy's refusal to show the film on ships and shore installations because of its status as "derogatory to a sister service" (Suid 128).[51]

In retrospect, one wonders how any person actually reading the book or viewing the film as a text of remembering could possibly have gotten it all as wrong as the *Los Angeles Times* or the navy did about *From Here to Eternity.* How could anyone have failed to see, that is, that the whole business was basically a love story ending with a death in the sandtrap? Death in the sandtrap. The image is an abstract or epitome of all that has gone before. At the end Prewitt, the thirty-year man, keeping his fine distinction between AWOL and desertion, tries to get back to the company — back from Lorraine's rented house in Wailea, where he has crawled, badly cut up, after his revenge murder of Fatso Judson. Now the war has begun, and Prewitt has to get back. Instead, he is shot down by the MPs on the officers' golf course, mistaken for a Jap or a saboteur, caught in the open and holed up in a bunker, when all he has wanted to do is get back and soldier. Instead he has found death in the sandtrap.

This is not *Death in the Afternoon,* a modernist conceit. Nor is it *Sands of Iwo Jima,* a guts-and-glory spectacular. Or rather, perhaps, it *is* just something of both, formed in Jones's possession — as Joan Didion affirmed it many years later in going back to all the old *From Here to Eternity* places in the islands — of "a great simple truth: that the Army was nothing more or less than life itself" (151). This is to say, of course, that Jones had finally been one of those writers who, by staking out an important part of the world with absolute patience and integrity, had made it so much his own that all the identities finally just got conflated — Hawaii, the army, America, a book, a movie. But in the process, he had made it all part of our remembering as well.

The Caine Mutiny

Among the five major World War II novels of the immediate postwar period to exploit the big-war, big-book, big-movie production formula into classic status as a literary *and* commercial icon of American remembering, Herman Wouk's 1951 *The Caine Mutiny* could make the simultaneous claim, albeit shared with earlier, groundbreaking works such as Michener's *Tales of the South Pacific* and Heggen's *Mister Roberts*, of generating a major stage property, the 1954 *Caine Mutiny Court-Martial*. Further, as if to cement the pattern of multiple developments, the production timing of the highly visible and acclaimed dramatic version could hardly have been improved on, the play being introduced into the public view concurrently with the preparation for release of the equally popular and celebrated 1955 film. As things turned out, the former, in its concentration on the novel's courtroom scenes, became a remarkably effective publicity vehicle, billing itself as a dramatic abstract or epitome of the novel's essential conflict, while also heralding the imminence of a big-screen Hollywood treatment sure to recapture the narrative scope of the original print saga. Indeed, here, as at every other stage of development, *no* other work of the period seemed so thoroughly engineered in every sense as a total production, so sure-handed in matching the increasingly adaptable commodity called the World War II popular classic to all possible configurations of genre and mode, audience and market.

To be sure, the production of a play insistently titled *The Caine Mutiny Court-Martial* as a high-profile theatrical project, itself commanding major critical commentary and mass-media coverage while the much-anticipated film version of Wouk's novel still awaited release, might have been considered a risky move for the prospects of both. Chief was the natural fear that the play, with the postwar American stage still enjoying considerable artistic prestige and audience visibility, would diminish the impact of the movie.[52] Meanwhile, on the stage project itself, plenty of things were managing to go wrong, often in their own well-publicized ways. Much had been made, for instance, of the star-director turn's being attempted by the legendary actor Charles Laughton, who in his new role often proved legendarily irritating and inept. Even more had been made of the appearance, in the choice role of the defense lawyer, Captain Barney Greenwald, of Henry Fonda, in a last stage appearance before his return to Hollywood for the much-anticipated screen reprise of his Broadway role in an earlier classic drama of the wartime navy, *Mister Roberts*. He had openly scorned Laughton throughout production for his pretense and mannerism.[53] Of decidedly lesser celebrity than either of the first two was the other major player, Lloyd Nolan as Captain Queeg. Yet this too proved a problem, at least with Fonda, who resented the play's last-minute rewriting to accommodate an enlarged role for Nolan.[54]

As to connections likely to be made by audiences between the new stage and screen properties, Hollywood representatives worried that the play's distillation of the novel's crisis into the drama of the trial scenes would upstage any comparable dramatic tension to be sought at the conclusion of the film. In practical terms, there was doubt that readers who may have plowed through the novel, only to be importuned into admiring the dramatic focus and concentration of the play, would care to go back through all the adventure-romance complication that the film would restore as a lengthy foregrounding.

Meanwhile, the film project had hardly been without its own troubles, chief among them a well-publicized dispute with the Department of Defense, without whose support, technical and material, any movie of the Pacific war at sea on the scale envisioned for Wouk's property was deemed impossible. To put it simply, navy image-makers in the late '40s and early '50s, with the navy's traditionally privileged position as the senior service under assault on various political and economic fronts, were paralyzed with fear. On the defense-appropriations scene at large, the navy had already been dethroned in its traditional role as the prestige, high-budget military service by the air force and had begun seeing big money for warships — destroyers, cruisers, battleships, even carriers — rerouted toward aircraft development and manufacture. And more immediately, in the Hollywood support arena, it had also just seen the army stumble profitlessly through the minefield of *From Here to Eternity*.[55] Here, in the opinions of both civilian and military managers at the highest levels of control, the case seemed equally simple. What good could possibly come of the depiction of an episode of mutiny upon any World War II U.S. Navy ship, let alone aboard one that the navy seemed to have rather routinely delivered into the hands of a twitching, dictatorial martinet and/or psychopath? (Actually, when one thought about it, in the book the problem was even worse, with an experienced prewar career navy officer — in fact, a 1936 graduate of the naval academy — pitted against an unruly bunch of civilian officers and reservists with a resident Freudian as archinstigator and a second-in-command not bright enough to deal with the mess.)

In the beginning there had simply been outright refusal. When negotiations were eventually allowed with persistent Hollywood representatives, they had dragged on throughout production. Still, an apparent victory had finally been achieved by the moviemakers, with the rewards including, by signed agreement, an official navy advisor and use of the Port of San Francisco and Pearl Harbor naval bases, with their backdrop of aircraft carriers, destroyers, and other combat vessels. Specific authorization was also given for deployment of two destroyer-minesweepers, one for scenes involving shakedown maneuvers after dry dock on the West Coast, and the other for those of tropical sailing out of Hawaii.[56] Yet they had been garnered, as far as the navy was concerned, at a price of serious rewriting and a sanitizing of various issues of command responsibility and military law, changes that would always brand the movie — or so the story would continue to be told — as answering to military censors in ways where the book or play had had to make no such concessions.[57]

Nevertheless, on all accounts production problems were quickly forgotten as both play and movie made their own way toward major success with a stunning near-simultaneity. The play opened in Santa Barbara, California, on October 12, 1953, toured across the United States for nearly four months, and then made its New York debut on January 20, 1954. There, in something very equal to a display of the attention rendered the book, the new *Caine* property continued to make theater headlines with its much-publicized director and cast until the end of May — within days, as it turned out, of the movie's June premiere — when Fonda left for the Hollywood *Mister Roberts*. In the critical and popular press, it was favorably written about nearly everywhere, with discussions and production accounts in *Life, The Nation, Time, Commonweal,* the *New Republic,* the *New York Times,* the *New Yorker, Saturday Review,* and *Newsweek,* to name just the most prominent. Even the play text itself found independent life in a hardbound volume, part performance script, part theater archive, with photo illustrations of original cast members in major scenes and accompanying documentation of its textual development.[58] Meanwhile, the movie moved effortlessly into the spotlight with star publicity for major players such as Humphrey Bogart as Captain Queeg, Van Johnson as the executive officer, Steve Maryk, and Fred MacMurray as the treacherous wardroom novelist, Tom Keefer. And much was also made of the film's bracing large-screen fidelity to the novel's atmospherics of seafaring adventure. "Thanks to the Navy," Bosley Crowther of the *New York Times* enthused, "the shipboard business is on the beam, the blue-water shots of the maneuvers are spanking, and the atmosphere is keen" (12). On both counts it gained immense attention and an ongoing popularity. To this day it likely remains the text of *The Caine Mutiny* best known to any American save the literary or theater nostalgist.

Such diverse market potential, on Wouk's part, seemed to have been written into the program from the outset. Insofar as possible, for instance, he had tried to propel the novel as a literary property into a new evolutionary niche by taking care to calibrate its publishing contexts and contexts of reception as closely as possible to those already established by foregoing models and likely competitors. Most important, it was to be a big war book expressly designed for the book clubs, flourishing again as sales outlets after the lifting of wartime paper and publishing restrictions, and for the moment retaining their prewar cachet as integrating the literary and the popular. It avoided, for instance, the ponderous ideologicalness and the showy experimentalisms of *The Naked and the Dead.* And as revealed in more closely contemporary publishing developments, it shared none of the negative publicity leveled at Jones's *From Here to Eternity* for its attempts to yoke existential inquiry with frank depictions of violence, as well as profanity and controversial sexual content. On the other, in its large literary ambitions and its complex intellectual critique of the wartime politics of command, it also avoided the resort to popular formula one so often senses in the bland reductiveness of Uris's *Battle Cry.*

If *The Caine Mutiny* had a close analog, it was, of course, Shaw's large and adventurously plotted *Young Lions,* which in its dextrous interweavings of war story and love story combined the do-or-die atmospherics of military life with social panorama — what Henry James would have called solidity of specification, density of detail, the air of reality. Or, to put this into a more contemporary context, the craft and urbanity — the New York slickness, one might call it — of both *The Young Lions* and *The Caine Mutiny* sent a distinct audience message: here would be none of the metaphysical atmospherics of *The Naked and the Dead* or the yearning proletarianisms of *From Here to Eternity;*[59] rather, here would be that popular kind of literariness preferred by most audiences, craftsmanlike and sophisticated but devoid of literary-intellectual pretension. On the other hand, even on this count Wouk had further trumped Shaw and all the others. For in the cosmopolitan, "smart" New York style, he had also made a big novel with a play inside it, here in the form of a courtroom drama detachable to the stage, a condensation of the basic moral and political conflict in which testimony could give basic narrative information.

Against all the competitors, however, Wouk had also simultaneously managed by stealth a major literary coup as well. And that was to work the seamless popular-culture assimilation into this big new book of conflict at sea of the author's direct homage to that most American of seafaring and writing geniuses, Herman Melville — and to do so in the bargain, moreover, by invoking *both* of the latter's acknowledged masterpieces, *Moby-Dick* and *Billy Budd*.[60]

To be sure, there had already been deep literary Melville in literary Mailer. The Cummings-Hearn relationship partakes, for instance, of a certain Ahab-Ishmael and/or Ahab-Starbuck dialogics of character and philosophical opposition; and Croft's mad pursuit of the deadly patrol mission providing the novel's dramatic core images the monomaniac quest after the whale. But in Wouk's novel it all seemed far more effortless — and pervasive. *Moby-Dick* was everywhere. The *Caine*, for instance, by its very naming, was another *Pequod* — part *Reluctant*, to be sure, another bucket plying its aimless ways as part of the grander mission — but also here, distinctly, in its mad command, a ship bearing a curse. Likewise, if Queeg is the shipboard totalitarian, Hitler or Mussolini or Tojo in khakis, he is also Ahab the old regular, with his tyrannies, despotisms, and insane arbitrarinesses. To him enters Willie Keith, the novel's *ingénu* as the center of consciousness — on which the whole drama turns, as Wouk is at pains to tell us in the preface, as a vault door turns on a single jeweled bearing. He, of course, is the Ishmael character, intellectual, dreaming, artistlike, a lover not a fighter. And to them both comes Maryk-Starbuck, who this time makes the choice to seize command and thus makes the book have its much more legally problematic ending.[61] So, in place of the quarterdeck, the compass, the corpusants, the log and line, the Parsee, the prophecies, we have the bridge, the wardroom nuttiness, and all the long unraveling into pure pathology — the yellow stain, the strawberries, the sand experiments, the messboy interrogations, the key collections, the typhoon, and finally the scene in the witness chair with the ball bearings. In the climactic vision of the paranoid psychotic with delusions of grandeur, it has all worked exactly as it should, the higher Melville reduced to the odd, creepy Queeg with his clicking metal marbles.

Meanwhile, *Billy Budd* is also there from the first pages onward. Or rather, *Billy Budd* is there even before the first pages, in the title, of course, but also on prefatory leaves where we find transcribed articles 185, 186, and 187 of the naval regulations governing the legal definitions of mutiny, against which are quickly cast, as in *Billy Budd*, most of the same higher legal, moral, epistemological, finally metaphysical issues: of military law versus human law, of military law versus natural law, of perhaps the very operation of anything like law in a world of war. And so, likewise, in redistribution of Melvillian roles, are assembled again the basic dramatis personae. Billy Budd becomes the callow Willie Keith, at first considered by his fellow officers "the Captain's pet" (232), gradually, unknowingly, blindly suborned here to the point where he finds himself on trial for *actually* having been solicited to a *real* mutiny.[62] In turn, the Claggart role of diabolical intriguer turns to Keefer, the Freudian novelist as amoral cynic, master artificer of the plot by sly suggestion and creative innuendo, and master evader of the consequences. Something of Vere, of course, albeit in limited conceptual reach, then becomes transferred to Steve Maryk, who must sort it all out on the spot, the military, the moral, and the metaphysical. But the major intellectual thrust of that inquiry is brilliantly reserved for the novel's legal interlocutor, Barney Greenwald. For here indeed, out of the American experience of World War II, is Starry Vere from all the necessary angles. A Jewish lawyer who is also a wounded and decorated Marine fighter pilot, a military officer who is also a resolute civilian, he is at once the exemplary American of the Good War and the outsider-intellectual who speaks far beyond the seeming conventionality of this smart, immensely popular novel for the great, tragic actuality of History.

For all this careful literary packaging, *The Caine Mutiny* still struck many potential publishers as something of a risk. For one thing, Wouk himself could claim the profile of neither a new novelist nor a new war novelist, having already published one moderately praised satirical novel of manners, *Aurora Dawn*, and then another, *City Boy*, which in 1949 had proved barely successful.[63] But more important, by the time in question, publishers had also come to feel fairly certain that the public wanted to stop hearing about the war. As a consequence, Wouk in turn found himself brushed aside by both Simon and Schuster, his former house, and Knopf, and only through a new agent, acquired through the offices of Fred Allen, for whom he had worked as a radio writer in 1936–40, did he acquire a decent deal with Doubleday. Still, sales started out slowly, with initial turndowns by book clubs including both Doubleday's own subsidiary, the Literary Guild, and its larger rival, the Book-of-the-Month Club. On the other hand, it was adopted with what proved to be considerable success by another, newly developing venue for middle-of-the-road fiction and nonfiction, DeWitt and Lila Atcheson Wallace's Reader's Digest Condensed Books.

Sales began to take off. The two book clubs both rushed back in, albeit belatedly. By August 1951, after initial publication in March, the book finally hit the best-seller lists. Once there, it stayed for almost a year. It also won the Pulitzer Prize for 1951. Within less than two years, sales totals rose to two million. And even by that point, in midspring 1953, it continued to sell between two thousand and three thousand copies a week (Tebbel 357).

Such success, one now sees, in retrospect, could not have been more fully a matter of total production. Down to such physical minutiae as the resplendent nautical heraldry of the cover and the careful subtitling as "A Novel of World War II," a market was at once being charted and confirmed. Even the back-jacket sketch of the author, with a tasteful eastern-establishment-style photograph, defined the constituency. For, again, the main target of authorial competition was obviously Shaw. It was well known, for instance, that Shaw prided himself on his urban Jewish origins and his Brooklyn College education. Here, Wouk was distinguished as a graduate of Columbia. He was also identified as having served as head writer on the Fred Allen radio show, thereby invoking the cachet of Allen himself, with his wry, intellectual style as the thinking person's radio comedian. Further, besides mention of Wouk's service as a naval officer, his wartime work was also played up as a dollar-a-year man (the phrase is direct from the bio-sketch) for the Roosevelt administration.[64]

Then one proceeded to the jacket flap copy, which took pains to detail the image of the book as an urbane blend of social panorama and wartime adventure. The reader, it announced proudly in advance, was really getting here two novels in one — the first, the story of the initiation of the eastern upper-crust ensign, Willie Keith; and the second the account of his eventual involvement in the dark drama of mutiny on the *Caine*. For the literati, there was also advance visual notice of the epic Melville connection. Inside the boards, front and back, a nautical map of the far Pacific traced the Pequod-like cruise of the *Caine* under the Ahab-like Captain Queeg. And for perhaps less cosmopolitan constituencies, there was also a careful note of disclaimer about shipboard military language. Complete reproduction was unnecessary, it averred, thus offering comfort to those concerned about reading on, *From Here to Eternity*–like, into a morass of profanity. On the other hand, for those concerned that sanitized language would result in a sanitized novel, Wouk asked for at least a deferral of judgment about naval realism until the work had been read.

Next came the passages quoted verbatim from the navy regulations framing the larger drama. And then, as quickly, in much the same format, came a transitional epigraph to the adventures of Willie Keith. The novel was launched.

Accordingly, the first two sections of the book proceeded as promised, with their focus on the military shaping-up of the unlikely hero. In "Willie Keith" we are plunged into the officer training of the Princeton dilettante previously whiling away a low draft status playing saloon piano, being doted on by his rapacious mother, and pursuing a torrid romance with the working-class heroine, the nightclub singer May Winn, née Marie Minotti of Brooklyn. And in "The *Caine*," we undertake the making of Willie as a junior officer aboard the *Caine* under its first skipper, De Vriess, while other dramatis personae are assembled for the Queeg mutiny-drama to follow. Willie continues by letter his romance with May Winn and frets with indecision over using his social status and musical talents to latch onto an easy, noncombat billet on an admiral's staff at Pearl Harbor.

By section 3, Queeg stands on the quarter-deck, although first stirrings of trouble are mixed with the crew's and junior officers' misguided relief at departure of De Vriess and what looks to be the shaping up of the *Caine*. But then follows a series of dubious incidents: the *Caine* runs aground in harbor, and Queeg dodges making a report; the *Caine* cuts a tow cable, and Queeg puts the crew in hack. Events of section 4, a return to the West Coast for dry dock and refitting, begin with more bizarre command behavior. Before setting out from Pearl Harbor, Queeg marches his officers en masse to buy out their overseas liquor rations, which eventually wind up on the bottom in San Francisco harbor during a smuggling fiasco. On-shore, Willie has dual reunions with May Winn and his mother, while back on the ship, Maryk becomes the executive officer and, in his first act while Queeg enjoys leave at home, lifts restrictions imposed by the latter on the crew. Most egregiously, he also allows Stilwell, the seaman blamed by Queeg for the tow-cable episode, and troubled as far back as Hawaii by fears about an unfaithful wife, to go on "emergency" leave when in fact Maryk and the entire crew know a Red Cross telegram about family illness is a phony. When sailing orders for the *Caine* are updated, Queeg quickly returns, and so does Stilwell, but just late enough for Maryk to feel he must confess to undercutting Queeg's authority. Queeg's response is for the first time a direct revelation of his paranoia: "I know damn well that the whole ship is against me," he says (218).

Back at sea, in section 5, events culminate in "The Mutiny." There is the deepening of Queeg's irrationalities: during the ship's support of the Kwajelein invasion, Queeg persistently stands opposite the landward side of the bridge. Then, within artillery range of the beach, he aborts an escort mission altogether, leaving landing craft to figure their own location from the dye marker and thereby gaining the epithet "Old Yellowstain." Next come draconian water rationing and the trumped-up court-martial of Stilwell, with the junior-officer board assessing the equally absurd punishment of six lost liberties. Finally, Keefer brings it out in the open: the hypothesis that Queeg may be insane (264–65). Maryk responds by reading up on mental illness and starting to keep a secret log (270).

Shortly comes Saipan, where the ship turns tail under battery fire while Willie pleads with Queeg to open fire in return. He now becomes the personal object of Queeg's constant hounding. Meanwhile, at the level of great command issues, there has also arisen the mystery of the strawberries stolen from the officers' mess, with interrogations of the mess boys and crew, mass key collections, and strip searches. Maryk and Keefer make a trip to the battleship *New Jersey* to seek Queeg's relief from no less than Admiral William Halsey, but Keefer talks Maryk out of the interview at the last minute. Now it is too late. In an ensuing typhoon, Maryk, having saved the ship while Queeg is catatonic with fear, relieves Queeg (339). The *Caine* mutiny has become official. Maryk commands. Willie, as officer of the deck, accepts Maryk's orders. The legitimation is clear: article 184. Maryk has it on his lips (341).

Section 6 prefaces the trial scenes with the introduction of Lieutenant Barney Greenwald, the badly burned Jewish fighter pilot and lawyer convinced of the mutineers' guilt but nevertheless with a soft spot, he says, for "dead pigeons" like Maryk (349).[65] Greenwald's immediate opinion: he can get the intriguers off, but they deserve conviction, because Queeg really could not be proven crazy. In response, Maryk at last encapsulates his version of the basic issues: "I may be guilty by the book but I don't feel like pleading guilty. Christ, I wasn't trying to take over the ship, I was trying to save it. If I was wrong about Queeg being nuts, well, that's one thing, but I was trying to do what I thought was right" (355). And with the conflict thus defined, the trial itself begins, the court-martial, first day, the court-martial, second day, the morning of the third, and so forth: a riveting hundred pages in which the passion of Ahab-Queeg is played out with the new operative word, *paranoid* (412); and then with all action and even language itself yielding to a final silence and the clack of a handful of ball bearings.

After the acquittal the officers take a certain chastened relief during a dinner at the Fairmont on Keefer's advance for the publication of his big novel of the navy war in the Pacific, *Multitudes, Multitudes*. But even here, the messy business of the trial follows, in the person of Greenwald, with his sodden angry tribute to Old Yellowstain on the picket lines, keeping old Momma Greenwald out of Hitler's soapdish; and, as significantly, also to Tom Keefer, the novelist, and "the author of the *Caine* mutiny," Greenwald says, "among his other works" (447).

Part 7 proves anticlimactic but satisfying. Entitled "The Last Captain of the *Caine*," it interweaves final installments in the shaping up of Willie Keith — Keefer has now succeeded to command, and Willie to executive officer — with kamikaze action off Okinawa. In the latter, Keefer executes his own last act of the poltroon, leaping Lord Jim–like from the damaged vessel with his precious novel manuscript (as usual, ever the novelist within the novel, Keefer himself supplies the precise allusion) while Willie stays aboard with an emergency party and saves the ship.[66] As a result, he in turn now actually becomes the titular hero of the final section. As the last captain of the *Caine*, Willie Keith brings her back to New York for decommissioning, finds May Winn, and is last seen watching a victory parade with high hopes that they can still be married and live on happily.

To put the whole big read in a nutshell, seldom had a novel seemed to possess something of literarily marketable appeal for everyone. Besides winning the Pulitzer Prize, it continued to sell widely in hardbound with long-term boosts from recurring book club successes. It also proved a strong seller in a paperback that reproduced in its cover art and layout many of the design features of the attractive original, and which benefited further in later editions from the binding in of sections of photo illustration from the film.

In the latter, even the producer Stanley Kramer, legendarily finicky for requiring the subordination of casting concepts to some artistic vision of the larger project, knew how to roll along with an unstoppable hit when he saw one, and here for once he proved more than agreeable to a big-name lineup, albeit in a number of cases rather adventurously cast against type. Humphrey Bogart became Queeg, and José Ferrer was chosen in the other big role as Barney Greenwald. Van Johnson became Maryk; and Fred MacMurray played Keefer. In retrospect one finds it hard to say who among the group seems the most definitive. Bogart, as Queeg, is simply astonishing throughout, alternatively tyrannical and and abject, loathsome and pitiable, holding to the lonely edge of pathology until it all unravels on the stand. On the other hand, a measure of Ferrer's work as Greenwald is the degree to which, as long as he is before our eyes, the movie — with the exception of Queeg's breakdown scene — belongs clearly to him. Of the two other principals, Johnson was given a role nearly as hard as Queeg's. His Maryk, in a performance praised by discerning reviewers for its "bluntness," came off as decent and well-intentioned but not terribly bright, perhaps even obtuse; terribly puzzled and frightened by Keefer's Freudian gibberish; but more than morally discerning enough to know the gravity of the deed contemplated and eventually carried out. On the other hand, MacMurray remains to be given the credit he deserves for playing the cowardly, cynical Keefer.

As for the fifth main performance, by Robert Francis as Willie Keith, in contrast to a book depiction that allowed room for some fairly persuasive character development, the movie part turned out to be just not that good a role; and Francis, more or less typecast in the confining role of the *ingénu*, and appearing in one of the few films for which he is even remembered, also turned out to be not that good an actor. Or perhaps, as a result of *Mister Roberts*, the role as scripted simply locked itself into the shipboard-comedy subgenre, with Willie here relentlessly eager and callow, in love *and* war, a lovable Pulver with Queeg just Old Stupid gone over the edge.

Against the work of the other four principals, however, the Willie Keith problem finally paled into significance, as did the May Winn and Domineering Mother subplots, which provided a not unpleasant romantic interest against the dark doings aboard the *Caine*. The core drama prevailed here, even as it did against the various other dilutions and emendations, alleged and otherwise, supposedly offered up to satisfy the navy. To be sure, the portrait of Queeg from the novel and the play seemed to be rationalized. If he remained crazy, with emphasis on an obsessive, paranoid personality, complicated by deep-seated insecurities, he was also credited with a certain heroism for not giving in to such demons while being worn out serving as the old regular on the first line of defense in the '20s and '30s, when everyone else slept or fished or went to college. Further, combat exhaustion received increased emphasis as a mitigating factor, with Keefer of all people made to drive home, after his own sorry tour at the helm, the point about the pressures of combat command and its absolute, utter, isolation. And by way of explicit preparation in the movie, Bogart was also given lines of reminiscence about the earlier war experience of antisubmarine combat: "The way those subs ganged up on us," Queeg says, nicely conflating his pathologies, "I thought they had it in for me personally" (Spoto 170).

Still, Spoto overstates it when he refers to the film as vexed by a "sudden shift in tone" toward the last, implying "that the crew, unsympathetic to Queeg from the start, was at least partially responsible for the conditions which made recourse to Article 184 necessary" and thereby rendering the film "a safe endorsement of the system, rather than the critical questioning of it which was quite clear in the novel" (174). (On the other hand, one did have to admit that the newly highlighted theme of between-the-wars service could also be seen as plumping resolutely for the value of a peacetime navy.)

In contrast, Suid probably gets closer to the truth. In the book Wouk had "in fact" not given "an unflattering portrait of the Navy as a whole"; rather, "until the military suggested otherwise," the author himself actually "believed he had written a complimentary story" (129). And so, after all the hubbub had died down, the film navy spokesmen "were praising" actually "did not stray very far from Wouk's book" (136).[67] As is often the case in debates over artistic integrity, whether the final product here represented mainly victory or concession depended on whichever party one happened to be listening to.

Meanwhile, the film would succeed on its own considerable merits. And eventually such questions of authorization themselves would be rendered absurd. At the end, all that would remain was an extraordinary chemistry of film creation, with the signature of the controversy and the genius of the artifice framed, on Kramer's part, in his compliance, by official acknowledgment, with surely one of the strangest pairings of stipulations ever to mark government and film-industry cooperation in a movie. The first required at the beginning of the film a statement that no mutiny such as the one depicted *or any other* had ever taken place on a U.S. Navy ship. This was duly provided. The second specified that no explicit acknowledgment be made of navy assistance. This provision too was easily accommodated with *Catch-22*-like precision. Grateful acknowledgment of the navy's help was made by eschewing acknowledgment of the navy's help. All that lingered was a final credit: a dedication to the U.S. Navy. If, as in the title, insubordination had likewise gotten a literal last word, the World War II navy mythologized in *Mister Roberts, South Pacific,* and *Victory at Sea* had still been joined in spirit by yet another testament of remembering entitled *The Caine Mutiny.*

Battle Cry

In terms of the big-war, big-book, big-movie production model at hand, it would not be inaccurate to call *Battle Cry* the ultimate property of its kind.[68] A best-selling 1953 novel by Leon Uris, it transferred effortlessly to the screen in a 1955 popular film starring Van Heflin, James Whitmore, Tab Hunter, Dorothy Malone, and Aldo Ray. Even down to an ingenious paperback tie-in — one of the first ever engineered in advance to play into a simultaneous movie promotion — it proved the final extension of the production synthesis, a seamless linear fusion of medium and mode.[69] To be sure, each of the other texts enacting the formula and — eventually, in their own ways — the process, had been devised with the near-certain expectation of serving as such properties-in-development. Even down to their resoundingly big-picture titles, they sounded like the big books of the big war inevitably destined to become big movies: *The Naked and the Dead, The Young Lions, From Here to Eternity, The Caine Mutiny, Battle Cry*; as opposed to *A Walk in the Sun; Into the Valley, A Bell for Adano; The Story of G.I. Joe*. If ever the phrase was appropriate, they seemed to say, as with such prewar analogs as *Gone with the Wind, The Grapes of Wrath*, and *For Whom the Bell Tolls*, they truly deserved to carry, from the jacket of the first edition onward into their various book-club printings and paperback issues, the telling inscription "Soon to be a major motion picture."

Still, Uris's most immediate predecessors, such as Jones and Wouk, though they saw their 1951 best-sellers quickly transformed into popular 1953 films, had struggled with demands for revision in various depictions of military life. In both cases, producers deemed the works impossible to transfer to the big screen without the cooperation of the armed services; and, suffice it to say, in both cases as well, the services in question found plenty to balk at. With Jones the problem had been the need mainly to sanitize language and explicit sexual content, although institutional army corruption and brutality also proved a tricky issue. With Wouk, the idea of mutiny itself, let alone the depiction of a commanding officer as martinet *cum* psychopath, was nearly enough to sink the film project.

Further, on many of the same grounds, coupled with late '40s and early '50s political repressions, such pioneering predecessors as Mailer and Shaw had basically given up on any possibility of seeing their novels rendered even relatively intact in any movie suggesting their original political or artistic intention. Rather, after early attempts at development, they had just let the properties pass to other hands and had moved on to other projects.[70]

Uris, in contrast to all the rest, would have to deal with virtually none of these problems. For his genius had been to create something, albeit first in print, at once essentially novel and film, with even minimal distinctions of genre and mode intentionally blurred from the outset. To put this another way, what *Battle Cry* did, as novel and film, was simply to enact its own generic self-reflexiveness, ensuring an uninterrupted transmission from one form of popular classic to another. The result was a relentlessly workmanlike imitation of a popular classic World War II war novel that plays into a relentlessly workmanlike imitation of a classic World War II war movie and vice versa.[71]

The conflation of modes is evident from the title onward. *Battle Cry.* By itself, it just sounds like the ultimate World War II guts-and-glory book and movie title. More to the point, it especially sounds like the ultimate World War II *marine* guts-and-glory book and movie title. From the outside in, one hears the call of Richard Widmark, sounding over the din of combat at the end of *Halls of Montezuma* and meeting its echo in the voices of fellow infantrymen rising up in massed charge: "Come on marines, give 'em He-l-l-l-l." And from the inside out one reimages the novel's climactic combat scenes on Saipan, the death of the legendary captain Max "Two Gun" Shapiro going down with pistols blazing, screaming with his last breaths, "Blood! . . . Blood! . . . Blood!"

Here, too, the other marines, in turn, take up the cry. The narrator tells us

Huxley's Whores rose to the heights of their dead captain. They no longer resembled human beings. Savage beyond all savagery, murderous beyond murder, they shrieked, "Blood!"

"BLOOD!" . . . "BLOOD!"

The enemy, who were mere mortals, fell back. (498)

Meanwhile, in terms of the political ideals being represented in more or less uncut military version, the same title strains toward its larger grandeur of historical reference. "Tramp, tramp, tramp the boys are marching," it says, "sounding the Battle Cry of Freedom."

And this is, in fact, what the novel and movie are about. It is about boys who become marines, often by marching;[72] and it is also, of course, about boys who learn, more often by fighting and dying, to keep sounding the battle cry of freedom.

As to the boys themselves, Uris manages to supply a full roster tallying with every war-novel and war-movie cliché one might imagine: Danny Forrester, the high-school football hero with the girl back home; L. Q. Jones, the humorous, indolent, drawling southerner; Andy Hookans, the rough orphan from the Oregon lumber camps; "Seabags" Brown, the midwestern farm boy; Constantine Zvonski, the "Feathermerchant," the Polish-Greek city kid too light to make the paratroopers, heavy enough to be the squad Dear John and the first example of selfless heroism in combat; Marion Hodgkiss, the aspiring literary type, with his classical-record collection and his book talk; Spanish Joe, the wily goldbrick, liar, and cheat, adopted by Marion, after the latter has administered a surprise boxing lesson, as a personal reform project; Speedy Gray, the Texan, squad redneck and all-purpose bigot; Levin, the Brooklyn Jew, the squad's first replacement, a draftee marine who earns his place by uncomplaining hard work and his eventual heroic death; Shining Lightower, the parody redskin with his stock of pidgin witticism.

The NCOs and officers for the most part form an equally familiar cadre, utility players with the standard big contracts, wandering interchangeably in and out of hundreds of novels and movies. Foremost, there is the narrator, Mac, the leathery old communications sergeant, ministering to his squad with a combination of rigid authority and paternal affection.[73] And along with him come his grizzled old wargoing and carousing buddies, the equally gruff but good-hearted Burnside, Parris, McQuade, and Gunner Keats, all of them constantly into their stagy complaint over the underage human dross they somehow manage to turn into marines. Then there are the officers: the larger-than-life battalion commander, Major (and later Lieutenant Colonel) Sam "Highpockets" Huxley, at once idolized and cursed for his driving, hard-charging style, in training and battle alike, of making the ultimate demands on the officers and men who proudly call themselves "Huxley's Whores"; the shirking, contemptuous, self-important lieutenant, Bryce, a former assistant professor at the University of Southern California, with his small pomposity and incompetence culminated by a complete breakdown in his first combat; and finally, claiming the spotlight near the end, the inevitable up-from-the-ranks maverick officer-hero, Max "Two Gun" Shapiro, wiseacre, chronic troublemaker, insubordinate, rear-area scrounger and wheeler-dealer extraordinaire, legendary combat fire-eater.

To summarize, in the book property — as in the movie, which, in its way, it has already become — literally nothing is left to the imagination. What one is conditioned to expect from the genre is exactly what one gets. In basic training the fuzzy-cheeked boys begin to shape up. The platoon bully, a big Irishman named Shannon O'Hearn, is dealt with by the quick-fisted Polish kid, Zvonski, and duly chastened. The latter, soon to be killed in the first combat on Guadalcanal, gets his Dear John. Marion "Sister Mary" Hodgkiss, the aspiring writer, eventually killed near the end on Saipan, seeks an intellectual companion among his fellow trainees. He finds in Milton Norton a brave, wise mentor who is shortly reported killed among the first casualties on Guadalcanal. On graduation day the drill instructor buys all the new marines a beer at the slop chute.

Basic training is followed by the West Coast assignment of the main enlisted characters to Mac's communications section as part of the headquarters company of Huxley's battalion. Danny betrays the girl back home — Kathy, a.k.a. Kitten — in a torrid affair with Mrs. Yarbrough, a society woman whose husband is overseas. Wiser heads bring him to his senses. Shortly, during a leave, Danny and Kathy get married, the latter having yielded up her virginity. The lovelorn Zvonski gets increasingly despondent, thinks about deserting, nearly gets slipped a mickey and robbed of his back pay in a bar, but is rescued at the last minute by Mac and the squad. Sister Mary, the writer, having shaped up the squad's bad actor, Spanish Joe, and thereby having earned the latter's utter fealty, meets a prostitute named Rae on a ferry and begins an ongoing platonic tryst. This ends when he encounters her in a whorehouse where she has just serviced Spanish Joe, whom Marion, against his better judgment, has accompanied there. Still, resolving to love her regardless, he goes back to the ferryboat. Soon Rae is writing to him from his parents' home in the small town where he grew up and where she has been sent to wait for him until the war is over.

Meanwhile, training continues, followed by shipment overseas to a staging depot in New Zealand. While there, the lumberjack Hookans sheds his misogyny — the result of abandonment by his mother and his initiation into the whores of the lumber camps — by meeting and falling in love with Pat Rogers, a soldier's widow he has met in a canteen. He thinks about deserting, but is brought to his senses by Mac and the squad.

Finally, there is combat, Guadalcanal. Zvonski is the first to sacrifice his life. Back in New Zealand, Andy and Pat get married and everybody gets drunk up at the farm. Highpockets, pleased by the troops' performance on Guadalcanal but knowing worse is in store, tries to keep the battalion hard by staging a heroic forced march that makes everyone curse and idolize him all the more. Meanwhile Levin, the Brooklyn Jew and the first drafted marine anyone has seen, arrives and earns his place on the squad. On Tarawa *he* shortly gets killed sacrificing his life for the squad and the battalion. Then, after Tarawa, everyone else goes back to Hawaii, this time to begin staging for Saipan. In the training plans the battalion is scheduled for the first wave, but they lose their ships. Huxley, nearly getting himself court-martialed for insubordination, gets them back the honor of spearheading the assault. On Tarawa he gets killed. His runner, Ziltch, also gets killed protecting the old man from a grenade. Even Two Gun Shapiro, the unkillable, goes down with pistols blazing. In the commo squad, everyone left gets killed except Andy, who loses a leg; Danny Forrester, the all-American boy; and of course Mac. Andy, wallowing in self-pity, despairs that he will be no good to Pat on the farm, but is shamed out of it by Mac. Mac and Danny get to go home. Naturally, along the way they visit as many of the families as they can. As they finally part ways on a station platform, a newsboy is shouting something about marines on Iwo Jima. Mac remembers the lines of poetry he found on Marion's body. It is Robert Louis Stevenson: "Home is the hunter, home from the hill, and the sailor home from the sea."

As one surmises from such a recitation, the whole project here becomes a triumphant conflation not just of book and movie but of a whole host of popular-culture images of the war, a genre essentially re-engineered as basic production model. Uris does not miss a connection. Marion Hodgkiss the writer sounds like Marion Hargrove the writer. Shining Whitetower reminds us that Marine communications units *did* in fact have Navajo talkers. Even the melting-pot platoon business — notwithstanding a racial homogeneity that in this instance is neither literary nor cinematic but a matter of simple historical accuracy[74] — reminds us that even the biggest clichés nearly always become clichés by being true in the first place. They are Pole, Mexican, Wasp, Redneck, Jew; high-school football hero, egghead writer, streetwise kid, con artist; and their names and faces are the high poetry of American remembering. It is a book thing; a movie thing; a popular mythology thing. Above all, here it is a Marine thing, from the big war, from the big war before that, from the war after the big war, from the next war, from the last war. *What Price Glory?* begets *Sands of Iwo Jima*. *Sands of Iwo Jima* begets *Battle Cry*, then *Marines, Let's Go!*, then *Full Metal Jacket*. The latest *Heartbreak Ridge* turns out to have nothing to do with Korea, but rather with the high-tech airmobile storming of a Caribbean trouble spot that looks a good bit like Grenada: Clint Eastwood is the hard-bitten but good-hearted sergeant; he shapes up the callow but ultimately brave and competent lieutenant; together they take the objective while putting to shame the ticket-punching middle managers; and, they do it all, of course, by making men out of a grab-bag platoon full of marines.

It is the basic production model. Intense depictions of combat are interspersed with rear-area carryings on, including liberty in places providing romantic interludes and communal drunks. *Everybody's* life history is filled in along the way in letters, flashbacks, conversations with buddies, fellow NCOs or officers, visits with the kindly chaplain. All the characters act the way they are supposed to act in that kind of war novel or that kind of war movie, including at least one risky customer turning out for the good, one rear-area asshole proving totally useless in combat, one good guy with no reason to get killed being arbitrarily returned home in a box to denote the senselessness of it all, etc., etc., etc. *Everything*, that is, turns out to be completely generic: the combat, the barracks, the bars, the beaches. They all look alike in the book and the movie. Even the sex scenes look all alike: the fumbling, the cries, the fade. And *Battle Cry* made it seem nearly effortless.

No matter, in the proximate case, as in virtually all the others, that the movie *does* differ in highly significant ways from the book. It's just that one instantly forgets in which ways — or rather, perhaps, one loses the ability to recollect. Mac just has to be James Whitmore. Highpockets has to be Van Heflin. Danny Forrester is Tab Hunter. Dorothy Malone is the predatory Elaine Yarbrough. Everything blends together, combat and sex, sex and combat. "Oh God . . . I'm dying . . . Joe . . . Joe!" This is Marion's death (489). "'Oh God . . . God . . . God . . .' she said in a dull, interminable rhythm." Nearly four hundred pages earlier, this has been the seduction of Danny Forrester (93).

As noted, however, the distinguishing feature here remains the production genre within the production genre, so to speak; and that is the representation of the United States Marine Corps in, as they say, love and war. The U.S. Marines: in legend and fact the cruelest, most sanguinary of all the military services; the most brutal and bloody-minded in training methods that have proven most like those of the totalitarian myrmidons they prepare to face; the most reckless in missions emphasizing frontal assault and economy of force, where high casualties are a standard expectation. Yet somehow, if presented with sufficient loyalty and affection, a Marine saga can still have its moments, can somehow manage to be oddly brave, manful, even *inspiring.*[75]

Here, for instance, the first thing a commander does with his unit after they have survived Guadalcanal is march them bleeding-footed into the ground *for their own good.* On several other occasions, he risks court-martial for insubordination because he is afraid that the skills of his troops will be misused if they are not included on the sharp edge of assaults. As noted, such command bravado then culminates with his actually getting them reinstated into the assault force at Saipan, where he is slaughtered along with virtually all the other members of the unit. But somehow we know that they love him; they love the pogey-bait sixth Marines; they love the corps; somewhere in marine heaven, we have to infer, not a single one of them would find fault with their colonel's working so hard to get them killed.

Meanwhile, as part of ongoing postwar battles on the part of the Marine Corps to ensure its very existence, the Hollywood effort again could not have come at a better time in myth or reality. In a time of radical post-1945 military cutbacks, interservice rivalries and scrambles for appropriations had begun at the moment of victory; they had continued through extensive defense reorganizations of the late '40s and early '50s; and they were now culminating in a jostling for new atomic-age strategic roles among the services being played out against the Cold War military spectacle of a disastrously hot, conventional war in Korea. Along the way, the marines had never ceased to be a magnet for political and administrative controversy. The army, as well as both the new air force and the marines' own parent service, the navy, rankled against the persistent depiction of the marines as the World War II glamor arm. The army, especially, resented the marines' popular reputation for somehow having won the Pacific war single-handed; indeed, in mid-1946, they had barely avoided elimination, largely by army efforts, as an unnecessary duplicate. And by midwar in Korea, they had again managed to strike a high, controversial profile in relation to larger Cold War concerns and defense policy issues. To the army's intense unhappiness, their own hero MacArthur had begged for the legendary First Marine Division as his shock troops and then had put them squarely in the spotlight during the spectacular amphibious end run at Inchon. Next came their brilliant self-extrication from the disaster at the Chosin Reservoir, described by their commander, Chesty Puller, not as retreat but — in a phrase given huge media coverage — as simply attacking in the other direction. This time it was Truman himself who felt the heat, demonstrating his concern in both immediate support and in demands for new, long-term appropriations.

Within the larger strategic scheme, the marines were never one to miss an opportunity to seize their own grand tactical initiative. *Battle Cry* appeared as a novel in 1953. Quickly it went into film development. Accordingly, precisely at a time when the Department of Defense had virtually ceased to cooperate with any film project even remotely candid about combat, let alone critical of the historical record or institutional practices of an individual service, the marines willingly let themselves be called in. Never mind that the army, the navy, and even the air force — with the latter really riding tall on the appropriations lists — not only were done taking chances with films that might make them look bad, but had decided further that it was unnecessary to cooperate on any film that risked making people think twice about war, military experience, the function of bureaucratic and administrative systems in general. For the marines, the idea that it would be a marine picture would be enough. And so it was.

As with *Sands of Iwo Jima*, the film was there when the marines needed it; and, once again, the marines were there when the film needed them. In battle scenes shot at Viequas, a small island near Puerto Rico, the director, Raoul Walsh, had full use of sizeable marine amphibious forces allegedly engaged in previously scheduled training exercises. Colonel Jim Crowe, who had assisted his fellow hero of Tarawa, General David Shoup, on *Sands of Iwo Jima*, served again here as the movie's technical advisor. For training scenes and New Zealand sequences, the company was also given full use of the Marine Recruit Training Center at San Diego and of Camp Pendleton.

Accordingly, just as they never missed a mythic step with Korea, so the marines seemed to keep up their image in popular-culture mythology through *Battle Cry* in much the same way they had done during the immediate postwar years with *Sands of Iwo Jima*. Mythic re-engineering played in with the publicization and commemoration of actual events in a degree of thoroughness and complexity beyond any public-relations officer's wildest dreams. The 1953 publication of *Battle Cry* as a novel connected the movie heroes of Guadalcanal and Saipan with the newspaper heroes of Inchon and Chosin. Its 1955 release as a film further helped seal the interwar breaches of policy and appropriations both mythologically and institutionally. Somewhere in among all the new movie ads, representations of the heroics of the big war got interfused with the headline heroics of the new war — in fact, the only heroism besides marine heroism really publicized in that dismal war of human-wave attacks, mass retreats, POWs, and interminable truce negotiations seemed to be MIG-killing fighter pilots.[76]

And in the ongoing interfusions of image and reality, art reciprocating life and vice versa in its peculiar U.S. Marine fashion, the corporate-image boost provided by *Sands of Iwo Jima* and then *Battle Cry* in its train would help fuel the marines through the next war as well, despite, as usual, their gross misuse, their high casualties, their customary supply shortages, their general sufferings.[77] By 1965, for instance, there were plenty of army troops in Vietnam. A high-ranking advisory group had been there for a decade, and the new U.S. Army Special Forces in particular were getting just the kind of glamor treatment traditionally reserved for marines. Still, no one then or ever afterward would forget the event that really made the war a war. That happened the day the U.S. Marines went ashore in 1965 at Danang. The fact that they were greeted on the beaches by city officials and flower-carrying schoolgirls in *ao dais* is no longer important. The scene was not out of Vietnam, after all. It was out of *Sands of Iwo Jima* by way of *Battle Cry*.

CHAPTER 4
THE GOOD WAR AND
THE GREAT SNAFU

s the new decade of the 1960s promised to put the war era and the immediate postwar period at an increasingly visible remove, two roughly contemporary publishing events brought the World War II classic as a popular-culture genre to a crisis of historical understanding and formal intent wherefrom it seemed to launch itself on two distinctive, even terminal vectors of evolution. The first of these was the appearance in 1959 of Cornelius Ryan's popular documentary history of the D-Day landings, *The Longest Day*, a worldwide best-seller that was followed by other successful Ryan volumes in the same vein, including *The Last Battle* and *A Bridge Too Far*. The second was the 1961 publication of Joseph Heller's outrageous novel *Catch-22*, embraced by a literary-critical following as a coruscating black-humor indictment of the war and the war-breeding system and perhaps one of the great absurdist-experimentalist masterpieces of the century. The resultant movie developments of both properties during the decade — with the film of Ryan's text appearing in 1962 and that of Heller's in 1969 — seemed to bear out this sense of final impasse. With *The Longest Day*, the World War II classic seemed to begin its long garish decline into spectacle and commemorative nostalgia, to make its inexorable departure, as Paul Fussell has aptly described it, toward the Higher Disneyfication. With *Catch-22*, the film version seemed to chart out a bleak alternative destination for the genre in radical, apocalyptic, even annihilating self-critique.

A mere listing of movie titles from the period makes clear which evolution would largely prevail. The film version of *The Longest Day* would be followed by similar docu-cameo-epics: *The Battle of the Bulge* (1965), *In Harm's Way* (1965), *Anzio* (1968), *Patton* (1970), *Tora! Tora! Tora!* (1970), *Midway* (1976), *A Bridge Too Far* (1977), and *MacArthur* (1977). These would compete for public attention with other big-war action adventures such as *The Great Escape* (1963), *Von Ryan's Express* (1965), *The Dirty Dozen* (1967), *The Devil's Brigade* (1968), and *Kelly's Heroes* (1970).[1]

If the *Catch-22* evolution, on the other hand, was supposed to write the final word on the possibility of such proliferations and commodifications, no one bothered to tell reading and viewing audiences. As book *and* film it seemed to defy its own prediction of its fate as self-consuming artifact. Maintaining steady sales as a cult favorite through the decade, it eventually achieved immense popularity as a paperback best-seller, with a large boost late in the decade from the movie version, which likewise managed to carve out its own classic niche as one of the great war films of the era. Still, as far as the ultimate extension of a genre into apocalyptic self-parody was concerned, when *Catch-22* said it was the end, there was considerable truth to the claim as far as any new "classic" genealogy was concerned. To be sure, Richard Hooker's 1969 novel *M*A*S*H*, billing itself as the *Catch-22* of Korea, quickly became the basis of the famous 1970 film and later the legendary TV series. And Kurt Vonnegut's 1970 absurdist fantasy of the big war, *Slaughterhouse Five*, similarly became a 1972 film. But of course in both cases, as with *Catch-22*, the real catch was now Vietnam. Even as the war attempted to return the favor of art as surrealist nightmare, it always turned out to be just too real for parody. A last, apocalyptic, postmodern literary gesture toward World War II would come in Thomas Pynchon's *Gravity's Rainbow*, a teeming, encyclopedic parody of all parodies, with the relationship of book and movie itself a standing intertextual joke amid Pynchon's epic scheme of demolition. In fact, at the end, the only thing *left* standing is the model of production, the empty gift of a manic syncretism.

What must remain noteworthy about this terminal bifurcation in the World War II classic is the degree to which it remains traceable, at least as far as *The Longest Day* and *Catch-22* are concerned, to two astonishingly similar variants on a single structural model which itself had become the stock of literature and film. As print narratives, for instance, they both construct a sense of the big picture as a teeming collocation of personal stories, generally distinguished by their highly individuated, human-interest quality. The first, a documentary history, is in fact intensely novelistic in its emphasis on character, plot, setting, complex interweavings of circumstance and fatality. The second, a novel, with its vast preponderance of chapter titles named for characters, seems a vast bio-biblio-documentary, with History itself presiding over all as some vast nexus of paranoiac congruencies. As film narratives, both likewise, albeit to radically different ends, become exemplars of the docu-cameo-epic. The casts of both constituted a roll call of popular-culture celebrity. Further, in the epic histories of both as legendary Hollywood projects, they seem together to have derived from some single corporate synergy.

It might have really taken a Joseph Heller to imagine, for instance, the way in which the June 1994 issue of *Reader's Digest* attempted to trump similar efforts by virtually every other American periodical or publication medium to celebrate the fiftieth anniversary of the World War II D-Day landings by the Allies in Normandy. For it did so as perhaps only that venerable, happily anachronistic repository of brisk, efficient, endlessly celebratory Americanism could have done it: with the publication of a text commemorating at once the event and the *Digest's* own institutional history as a recorder of the event. To be specific, for the condensed-book section of that month's issue, it reprinted major portions of Cornelius Ryan's *The Longest Day*, the great popular-history classic it had commissioned thirty-five years earlier to celebrate the fifteenth anniversary of the landings. As an accompanying note proudly pointed out, the project had been heavily supported in its compilation by the use of "thousands of documents and interviews with D-Day participants from both sides of the battle" gathered by "the *Digest's* staff in Paris, London, New York, and elsewhere" (183). Further, it went on to recall, "the book was a huge success when it appeared in 1959 and was made into a hit movie." It also announced that Simon and Schuster would reissue the complete original text as a fiftieth-anniversary volume.[2]

As suggested, it was all something that only so thoroughly a self-created vessel of American "tradition" as *Reader's Digest* could have even thought to do: to commemorate a great American event by commemorating its own great earlier commemoration.[3] In any event, by now the *Digest* ploy was a distinct case of the tail trying to help wag the venerable dog. For not only did Ryan's thirty-five-year-old book not need the publicity; if anything, it had now become even more widely famous than before, appearing in attractive mass paperback reissue,[4] with homage paid by commentators in a host of retrospectives and also by a new flotilla of D-Day books all acknowledging it as the urtext of history and memory.

Still, the *Digest* had a point. And the point was that without its own history of institutional support, even before a word had been committed to the page, Ryan's history would likely have never come into being. Or, to put the matter more directly, it all owed finally to the bottom-line authority of the *Digest's* founder, Dewitt Wallace, by the late 1950s the only real publishing giant left competing actively with Henry Luce for the soul of middle America and a figure known equally for his autocratic preferences. Wallace in turn had anointed the Irish-born Ryan, a former war correspondent and frequent contributor to the magazine, as one of his favorite writers;[5] and in this role, the story goes further, Ryan was simply and flatly offered one day over luncheon the providential opening every free-lance author dreams of. Choose a worthy and interesting subject to write about, he was told, and the *Digest* would commit itself to "all the money and research support he needed" (Heidenry 320).

As with any commissioned writing project involving large money, Wallace was taking a gamble. But given Ryan's experience and publishing record, it could hardly be deemed a foolish one. As a Reuters correspondent and a *London Daily Telegraph* reporter, Ryan had covered big war stories as diverse as bombing operations of U.S. Eighth and Ninth Air Force, the D-Day landings, and Patton's Third Army during its rapid advance across France and Germany. He was then sent to the Far East to cover the end of the war there, eventually becoming a *Time* stringer. Next, he moved to the United States, where he supported himself by writing several books while becoming senior editor of *Collier's*. Out of his work there, an award-winning account of the much-publicized sinking of the luxury liner *Andrea Doria* had been chosen for a *Reader's Digest* condensation entitled "Five Desperate Hours in Cabin 56" (*Collier's*, September 1956; *Reader's Digest*, November 1956); and he had also gained a reputation as a journalist with considerable gifts for literary dramatization in a comparably gripping story of disaster aboard a trans-Pacific airliner, "One Minute to Ditch" (*Collier's*, December 1956).

Surely Ryan must have felt that he had his bankroller's complete confidence. Financial support on research and writing expenses alone amounted to several hundred thousand dollars. Wallace also paid an additional $150,000 off the top to get first rights for a Reader's Digest Condensed Books version. Then there was the logistical end. From the *Digest's* in-house research division, at least fourteen people were employed in searching war records of five different countries. The department also sent out three thousand questionnaires and interviewed seven hundred participants or eyewitnesses. Also enlisted was a far-flung network of bureaus, overseas offices, and roving correspondents. Here the resources of the international edition proved especially valuable, down to telephone lines, wire and transcription services, and footwork in tracking down interviewees. Virtually all done by the *Digest*, the research enterprise for the book was a documentary historian's dream. Literally, all Ryan had to do was sit down, put it all together, and write it (Heidenry 320–21).[6]

Still, one has to give Ryan major credit for carrying it off the way he did it. For all the immense effort of research and logistical foregrounding, in retrospect, *The Longest Day* still strikes one as a tightly concentrated and even intimate book. It remains a story, that is, resolutely about individual people. To be sure, given the size and historical import of the Normandy operation, one expects the panoramic. And it is there. One gets a sense of the immensity, the sweep, the importance. But predominant in Ryan's method — perhaps itself a stamp of the *Digest* approach generally — is a real genius for close focus. Throughout, human interest prevails, as if "The Most Unforgettable Character I Ever Met" or "Life in These United States" got mixed with the occasional "Humor in Uniform" and "Laughter, the Best Medicine." Anecdotes, remembrances, testimonies, heartwarming personal accounts join with moments of grand decision and deep personal anguish. At the top of the headquarters command structures, we see Eisenhower, Rommel, von Rundstedt. At Berchtesgaden there is eventually even the overslept, overwrought Hitler — reassuringly portrayed chewing the carpet in his rage. We are present at the crucial moments in all the main combat flashpoints: the chaos of the three great paratroop-glider landings; the opening fights for the bridges, the causeways, St. Mère Eglise; the rope-climbing assault by the rangers on the cliffs at Pointe du Hoc. We accompany the armada at sea to its moorings offshore. We land at Omaha, Utah, Juno, Sword. In a crucial moment we even witness the crazy bravery of the only two Germans to get an aircraft over the beach. Meanwhile, from our own commanding perspective, the big picture remains surprisingly clear.

At the same time, by most judgments about research and documentation at the closer focus, Ryan's work also turned out to be generally scrupulous, accurate history. As important, however, by *all* publishing accounts it turned out to be a gratifying market property — if not, as according to one standard account, "a huge best-seller" (Heidenry 320)[7] — building steadily toward that status over time and then holding onto it. Obviously, it benefited from enormous *Digest* publicity. In the sections released for the June and July 1959 issues, for instance, surely it enjoyed one of the best prepublication campaigns ever devised for a forthcoming book of popular history, with two attractively produced and illustrated installments pipelined as free samples into between eleven and twelve million American homes (Heidenry 281). And all this, of course, was not to mention the various overseas editions and new publicity attending the condensed-book offering.

When the Simon and Schuster version of the complete text appeared, it certainly cleared the field of all military-history competition on the event, including David Howarth's roughly contemporary account, with which at the time Ryan's was by some reviewers unfavorably compared. It was immediately hailed both as a definitive addition to the historical record and as the locus classicus, even the original, of a whole new docu-history genre.

Whatever the claim, at the very least Ryan's book could stand as the most complete evolution of the production concept it represented. From beginning to end, it had been a total property, commissioned, bankrolled, logistically underwritten in every possible way; supported by an immense publicity apparatus and an immense distribution system; and then given the immense marketing base of a faithful readership whose respectful response was a given simply by virtue of the text's association with those fine people producing that trusty magazine out of that pretty building in that friendly town named Pleasantville.[8] It was a popular-history package, in short, that couldn't lose.

Yet even this kind of corporate effort on a book — the commitment of the whole *Digest* apparatus plus an estimated half-million-dollar capital outlay — would pale in size of effort and expense compared with the new machinery of production shortly set in motion by the movie. At the same time, here the prospects also had to be considered a gamble by anyone's reckoning. As presented to Darryl F. Zanuck, the Hollywood purchaser of the property, preproduction estimates alone boded a likely outlay of $8 million or $8.5 million for the picture. (It would actually cost the studio $10 million [Suid 162].) And this did not even begin to address questions of external support, including technical assistance, equipment, and military personnel to be requested from major participants *on both sides* — the United States, Britain, France, and Germany — on a scale of reenactment approaching the size of the invasion battles themselves. Moreover, adding to all these enormous financial, technical, and logistical anxieties was a stark warning issued by Zanuck's own son and anointed successor, presumably more in tune than his seniors on current viewing entertainment trends: after a late 1950s flurry of combat-film ventures achieving only mixed success, such an investment was likely to prove unwise, he predicted, on a subject, World War II, of diminishing interest to the 1960s.

Still, Zanuck had not been the only one in Hollywood attracted to the book's potential. Immediately upon publication, indeed, first rights had been secured for one hundred thousand dollars by a competitor, Raoul Levy. Momentary stasis followed, however: perhaps Levy felt simple paralysis over what to do next on something this size; but there was also anxiety about a script project — for which Ryan had already been paid twenty-five thousand more out of a thirty-five-thousand-dollar asking price — that seemed to be going nowhere. Zanuck, in turn, had quickly seized the opening. In late 1960, while Ryan was on assignment in Hawaii for (of course) *Reader's Digest*, he got a new offer over the phone from Zanuck, who had read the book in October and, in his own words, had gone "absolutely nuts about it" (Gussow 217).

What the enthusiastic producer did not tell Ryan, on the other hand, was that in addition he had "sat down immediately, even before he obtained the rights to the book," and "feverishly blue-lined the passages he thought should be dramatized." Further, he had produced "a continuity outline and step sheet, started mapping his war plans, and addressed a thinking out loud memo to himself" brimming with creative human-interest enthusiasm over a D-Day film not about the generals but about "the brave, funny, bewildering, human and tragic events of that day" (Gussow 217). As to the ultimate purposes of the new version according to Twentieth Century-Fox, the last paragraph was distinctly telling. "If we try to paint a rosy, star-spangled banner drawing of D-Day," Zanuck mused to himself, "we are certainly headed for disaster. . . . The only thing that will make it an enormous box-office smash is that we tell audiences *what they do not know about what happened on that day*" (Gussow 218).

Zanuck had Ryan's general intentions right — to build the big picture up out of an extraordinary collocation of individual views. On the other hand, from the moment of Ryan's acceptance of Zanuck's offer, the two were already launched on a collision course about a bigger issue of book-to-movie transition on so august a subject. And that issue would be, of course, cultural proprietorship over the mythic events depicted *as history*. To put this simply, the question would not become who "owned" *The Longest Day* so much as who finally owned D-Day.

The story of the Ryan-Zanuck struggle for "command" is variously told. In standard accounts (Gussow 218–35; Suid 148–51), Ryan, the commissioned journalist now taking quite seriously the status of the historian, is generally depicted as assuming the role of magisterial authority; the preserver and protector of the factual, relentlessly documented, "true-life" account; the monitor of accuracy, of faithfulness to the actual settings of scenes and events, of authenticity of uniforms, equipment, military custom and usage.[9] Zanuck is usually caricatured in the standard oppositional context as the Hollywood tycoon, the big creative ego, the "concept" man willing to sacrifice history for big-screen box-office spectacle.

The particulars of the conflict reveal a relationship far more complex and, in its own way, oddly creative. There was the question, for instance, of whether to interpolate into the movie war scenario various interludes of romantic love, several of which actually appeared in the book. In this case it was Zanuck who resisted, taking offense at what seemed movie stuff that would profane the faithful rendering of the great historical event. In contrast, Ryan insisted, on the grounds of historical veracity, that such things were, after all, part of the story. The upshot was a Hollywood story in itself. A subplot was written in involving a noted Resistance fighter and his fiancée, themselves shown in underground combat action. The actress chosen for the part was Zanuck's current mistress, Irina Demick. She thereby managed to garner the only featured role played by a woman in the entire film.

If script was the bottom line, Ryan, on the other hand, was no fool. He finally seems to have accepted the fact that if he knew how to write what happened so as to make it authoritative on the page, Zanuck genuinely knew how to reconcoct it so as to make it come alive on the screen (Suid 149–50). To this end, the latter turned frequently to an assistant and all-purpose right-hand production collaborator, Elmo Williams. He also brought in James Jones and Romain Gary, both novelists with experience in Hollywood re-creations of big books. Finally, as he would do with directors, Zanuck tried to bring in actual writing consultants from each of the major combatant nations. From Germany he solicited Erich Maria

Remarque.[10] From England he tried to get Noel Coward but settled for David Pursall and Jack Seddon (Gussow 223). Meanwhile, new trouble arose with likely censorship issues. Script emendations proposed by Jones in particular seemed excessive in casual GI profanity. Jones, in turn, angrily resisted official pressure for a general toning down of implications in the film that certain parts of D-Day — Omaha Beach, for instance — had been a slaughter.

Writing problems paled, however, in the face of ensuing complications of sheer movie logistics — in this case both military and political in the fullest senses of those terms. Most notably, there was the need to gain the governmental cooperation of four actual nation-states for access to historical sites and contributions of personnel and equipment — everything from uniforms and weapons to tanks, planes, and fleets of ships. Here too, at least initially, Ryan seemed somewhat imperious about the heft of his contacts, his sources, his military-political-journalistic connections. The best he could finally offer, though, was a friendship with General James Gavin. Fortunately, Zanuck on his part could call in his own roster of heavyweight friends and international political figures — veteran World War II commanders such as Lords Mountbatten and Lovat in England; Generals Mark Clark and Dwight Eisenhower in the United States; and, perhaps more important for concrete, present purposes, the current NATO commander, General Lauris Norstad of the U.S. Air Force.[11] He was also eventually able to bring in as technical advisors General Marie Pierre Koenig of France and Admiral Friedrich Ruge of Germany.

All in all, then, Zanuck, a figure with no small experience in big films and big-film logistics, may have turned out to be only slightly hyperbolic in asserting to Mountbatten, of all people, that his D-Day job had been "tougher" than Eisenhower's — "at least he had the equipment. I have to find it, rebuild it, and transport it to Normandy" (Gussow 216). Predictably, in that hands-on spirit, he started with Norstad; and, *as* predictably, his argument was cannily political in its own right. With the NATO allies, now *including Germany*, deeply threatened by the Soviet bloc as the old Allies once were in 1940 by Germany and the Axis bloc, Zanuck proposed, it would be a good thing for them to know now that they could act in cooperation and concert, especially on so worthy a historical re-creation. Norstad agreed and authorized contacts with individual governments. On the U.S. side, he was also influential in smoothing the way for Department of Defense cooperation; in turn, he indirectly facilitated the involvement of the West Germans by suggesting to American officials that a fairly reasonable, objective portrayal in the film of Germans as individual soldiers would further help cement NATO relations.

As individual governments committed to the project, the gracious, cosmopolitan Mountbatten proved helpful in getting everyone together. The British navy also undertook plans for providing a fleet. When Zanuck aborted these upon learning that fuel alone would cost three hundred thousand dollars, Mountbatten quickly managed a new arrangement. The U.S. Navy in the Mediterranean would be brought aboard with the offer that 1,600 members of the Third Battalion, Sixth Marines, would be given the opportunity to stage landings on Corsican beaches made to look "D-Day" authentic, with the use of a reenactment scenario thereby immensely enhancing their training value.[12] With a similar argument, at the actual site of the Pointe du Hoc cliff assaults, he managed to attract 1,500 U.S. Army rangers from Germany. Initially, he was also able to secure a commitment of 1,000 more U.S. troops; but because of congressional pressure over money and security issues just then being raised over the use of U.S. troops in Europe by the entertainment media, he had to settle for 250. These he somehow fleshed out with 1,000 new French military participants — despite their own bitter war going on in Algeria.[13]

The seeking of heavy military machinery and equipment involved mainly a set of straightforward cash-and-carry deals, albeit themselves not without international repercussions. Franco's Spain proved a bona fide ghost of Fascist history, leasing considerable World War II German equipment, especially tanks (Suid 152). A few Spitfires were found in Belgium; also, two Messerschmitts were duly found, again, in Spain. These were enough actual planes to get by with, D-Day itself having been too overcast for much air action. For the airborne-attack phase, however, new troop-carrying gliders had to be especially built by the piano company that had served as the original English fabricators.

As to uniforms, Allied battle dress had not become all that different in fifteen years. Old stocks of German uniforms, on the other hand, had quickly been done away with as an unfortunate reminder of Nazi past. Numerous sets of these, therefore, had to be newly tailored (Suid 151–52).

Among problems of background film logistics, producers were initially dismayed over a scarcity of documentary footage whereby they had hoped to flesh out the dramatic action, with virtually none available of the actual landings. On the other hand, in creative terms this proved a lucky spur to new awareness. Virtually all film coverage of the European war, it began to sink in, had been black and white. Thus, the thinking continued, the same effect of documentary authenticity could be achieved with great consistency by making the entire film in black and white, even without a frame of nonoriginal footage. And so it was. Veterans themselves often confessed to being fooled by the archival "realism," their assumption that the action had at the very least been spliced with atmospheric documentary.

At length, the project seemed to become possessed of its own grand spirit of military and geopolitical cooperation. Advisors appeared on the scene who had been officially deputed from the major combatants. And, while placing himself firmly in charge, Zanuck even insisted that there be American, English, French, and German *directors* involved. As normally listed, these included were Ken Annakin, Andrew Marton, and Bernhard Wicki.[14] Still, a standard estimate is that Zanuck himself directed 60 or 65 percent of the time.

Finally, there was the recruitment of an all-star international cast. From the American ranks of old war-movie reliables came John Wayne, Henry Fonda, Robert Mitchum, Eddie Albert, and Edmond O'Brien.[15] Robert Ryan was cast as the dashing boy-general of the airborne, James Gavin. (In surely one of the great production moments, Zanuck, just to irritate Ryan, recommended that the latter be replaced by Mickey Rooney.) Middle-rank performers included Red Buttons, Rod Steiger, Mel Ferrer, Robert Wagner, and George Segal. For bobby-sox appeal were added Jeffrey Hunter, Tom Tryon, Richard Beymer, and Sal Mineo, as well as teenage singing heartthrobs — Fabian, Paul Anka, and Tommy Sands.[16] In addition, from England came Peter Lawford, Richard Todd, Roddy McDowell, and Kenneth More. The glamorous Richard Burton was borrowed from *Cleopatra*. A rising British figure, Sean Connery, also worked briefly before heading to the Caribbean for a spy film, *Dr. No*. The French were represented by Jean-Louis Barrault; the Germans by Curt Jurgens and Gert Frobe; and the Czechs by, of course, Irina Demick.

The result, according to a standard film history (Langman and Borg 343), was a new genre of "semi-documentary epic" involving "over 40 major screen personalities" — not to mention a prototype for countless unhappy variations to come. Still, at the time, *The Longest Day* got generally good reviews; and it continues to be treated with a modest respect by film historians. To be sure, it does not appear in traditional prize listings; on the other hand, one might remember that its 1962 release put it directly in competition with David Lean's mighty *Lawrence of Arabia*, which swept all the glamor categories at the Academy Awards and nearly everywhere else (Garland 132).

As plausible a verdict as any was probably delivered by James Jones, himself no stranger to the travails of the big-war, big-book, big-movie business. Jones said *The Longest Day* worked as a film precisely because it wound up intractably massive and uncontrollable — something that could not be finally choreographed, directed, given conventional movie stylization. It therefore came across, he said, as somehow at once totally human *and* totally depersonalized, much in the vein of the event itself. Or, as Zanuck had claimed in midfilming, perhaps he had managed to deliver on something not so much "a war picture" as "the heartbeats on both sides" (Suid 152).

Of one formal and thematic consequence written across film history, there could be no doubt. *The Longest Day* was the great original — docu-epic, cameo-epic, bio-epic, call it what one will — that would set the pattern for a great overblown genre that continued to range back and forth across the whole media spectrum. As suggested, big-name movies relentlessly came forth as if cloned out of its example: *Tora! Tora! Tora!*, *The Battle of the Bulge*, *Midway*, and *A Bridge Too Far* — itself another tremendously successful Ryan property transferred to the screen. Massive biographical spectacles included *MacArthur* and *Patton*, with the latter perhaps redeemed only by George C. Scott's tour de force performance in the title role. TV miniepics included *The Winds of War*, *War and Remembrance*, *Eisenhower*, and a remake of *From Here to Eternity*. Heavy-budget action adventures numbered among them *The Dirty Dozen*, *Where Eagles Dare*, *The Great Escape*, *Von Ryan's Express*, *The Devil's Brigade*, *Operation Crossbow*. Eventually there were even "period" reprises — *The Big Red One*, *Memphis Belle*, *Swing Shift*, *For the Boys*.

Meanwhile, as the original of it all, *The Longest Day* generated its own nostalgia culture. It became a television favorite and later a staple in video stores. It was shown at least once on virtually every television station in America sometime in the course of D-Day fiftieth-anniversary celebrations.

Ryan's book endured and prospered similarly. And chief among its new successes was the popularity of a fiftieth-anniversary republication — accompanied, of course, by a special *Reader's Digest* condensed appearance.

Here, an additional attraction now turned out to be a special epilogue, newly written, following up some memorable figures from the original — the ranger Bill Petty, the paratrooper Dutch Schultz, the English commando Terence Otway, the German artillery major Warner Pluskat — who now reflected on their subsequent lives and careers in light of the experience.[17] But even fifty years later, no amount of updating could change that signature ending of the longest day recorded by the author, himself now long dead. If *that* hadn't really happened, it would have had to be written in a book or filmed in a movie. But there it still was. There was plain, tough-talking Norm Cota — or was it Robert Mitchum? In any event, it was no Patton, no MacArthur, no James Gavin or Maxwell Taylor, not even a Courtney Hodges or a Teddy Roosevelt Jr. It was just the stumpy, unprepossessing commander of a no-name division, at the end of a hard day's quiet bravery, spent walking up and down Omaha, getting his infantrymen up off the beach and moving inland, quite literally by personal example saving countless lives and possibly the invasion. Now he was just really tired. And, true to character, too tired to walk and willing to admit it, now he really did, the two-star general, just flag down the first passing truck and say one thing: "Run me up the hill, son." As a grand chronicle of unassuming American-ness, it all ended as it had likely begun.

As shown above, *The Longest Day* staked its success on a dogged, middlebrow belief that it could still make something big out of a popular American mythology of World War II that always skirted the edge of self-parody. The difference between *The Longest Day* and *Catch-22* was that the latter wanted to make the same mythology once and for all the self-parodic instrumentality of its own demolition. In this way, both Joseph Heller's *Catch-22* and the film made from it clearly meant themselves to be the last of the Good War's greatest hits. Their manic indictments of the war and of the war-breeding system turned on their attempts to conflate a whole genre of representation as the realization *and* reification of its own absurdist design, to bring the whole business of World War II and American remembering back on itself in apocalyptic self-critique. To put this more directly, in both its novel and its movie version, *Catch-22* sought to write the concluding chapter on the war by also writing the concluding chapter on the big-war, big-book, big-movie genre of the World War II classic, if not on the World War II production-entertainment classic itself as a cultural commodity.[18] Here was a vast, terminal compendium of all the strategies and gestures of a whole tradition of literary and popular-culture production, now self-annihilatingly turned back on themselves once and for all as black-comedy entertainment, the ultimate horrific war novel and war movie as deadly hilarious antiwar novel and antiwar movie.

Indeed, as a World War II entertainment classic in relentless self-parody, *Catch-22* never stops announcing the big cultural production number it is meant to be. From its first pages onward and at every ensuing turn, it is a truly bad war novel bidding to become the ultimate bad war movie. The text and its vision of horror become seamless versions of that single big production called World War II, the spectacle of a system making a killing on killing, in which the proudest product is death and everyone is expected to be a producer.

Some participate avidly in the big deal: power-hungry executives, all bidding to become the officer in charge; cowed, incompetent middle managers and timeservers; profiteers and cynical promoters. The vast majority of the rest — faceless, interchangeable junior officers and enlisted men — do so mainly because they are frightened not to do so. These are attended by their various consorts and sex objects, chaplains, nurses, traveling WACs. Meanwhile, the bottom becomes increasingly populated with generic victims: the Soldier in White, Lucianna, Nately's whore, Nately's whore's little sister. Amidst all the horror, Heller's protagonist-eiron, Yossarian — from the novel's first sentence to its last, a lover, not a fighter — tries to stay afloat, plays all the angles, living and running away not to fight another day but to live another day. Meanwhile, inside the war and out, the real action is on the Milo Minderbinder side, the original multinational conglomerate complete with signature logo and watered stock. A good trademark is the key; as we all know, what's good for M&M enterprises is good for America.

Ironically, it was for want of such a good trademark, that the history of *Catch-22*, itself one of the great popular-culture production sagas in our history, seems nearly to have stopped itself dead near the beginning. For Heller's initial publication had been a short story, entitled "Catch-18," with the titular catch involving the wartime duty of officers censoring the texts of letters written by enlisted men; and under that title, it had been published in *New World Writing*, an up-and-coming paperback annual (Davis 200). It had also attracted the attention of the volume's sponsor, New American Library, already the successful publishers of *The Naked and the Dead, The Young Lions,* and *From Here to Eternity.* They tried to get the novel, which by now had extended the initial catch clause into endlessly proliferating related clauses, subclauses, metaclauses. They were outbid on the book, however, by Scribner's. In turn, Scribner's now found themselves facing their own publishing catch, at least with the title. That catch had to do with Leon Uris, the popular, money-making author of *Battle Cry* — itself, among other things, exactly the kind of best-selling World War II production classic the new novel was supposed to explode. Uris had gone on to write an even bigger novel-movie blockbuster, *Exodus*, about the post-war Jewish struggle for an independent Israel. And now he had followed it with a surefire new war book, this time about the ill-fated Hungarian Revolution of 1956. Its title was *Mila 18*. Accordingly, on the advice of Heller's Simon and Schuster editor, "Catch-18" became *Catch-22*. As a title, it surely must have seemed more felicitous, with all kinds of good new attractions as well for the literary symbolmonger: the twinned twos, the double doubled, the reflection reflected. On the other hand, it also may have proved a mystifying touch to an already mystifying novel fated to be initially a slow seller. Reviews seemed similarly perplexed.[19]

It was only when a new publisher, Dell, intervened with a paperback issue, that the book would begin to acquire momentum toward a sales history that would eventually come to be called "astonishing".[20] And even here, serendipitously helping to launch it, was a new Catch-22–like production scheme itself worthy of a chapter from the inside: this time it was marketed as a straight novel. Accordingly, the editor in charge later recalled the plan:

> I remember when I sent the contract information to Bill Callahan [Dell's vice-president in charge of sales], he wrote back to me saying, "What the hell is a *Catch-22*?" I wrote back and said, "It's a World War II novel." We so-called "packaged" it so it could pass as a big important World War II novel. We had a quote from Nelson Algren that it was the best World War II novel since *The Naked and the Dead*. We had an aviator's head — not very good art — for the cover instead of the dangling man, which was the trademark of the hardcover.
>
> It would have destroyed the paperback with that on the cover. (Davis 300)

Eventually, in its various early commodifications and ad hoc promotions, the novel achieved considerable modest reputation with the literary intelligentsia. It also remained a paperback standard, a good seller but not a great one.[21] Then eventually came the war listed in the Library of Congress catalog as "Vietnamese Conflict: 1967–75." And, finally, in exactly the mechanism and moral of its own story, the book got to be what it had been all along. As Heller himself suggested, his political text had finally found its political context and vice versa. By positioning itself as a sendup of the last war, it had always been meant precisely to be always about the next, the next, and even, perhaps, failing final annihilation somewhere along the way, the next after that as well.[22]

"Virtually none of the attitudes in the book — the suspicion and distrust of officials in the government, the feelings of helplessness and victimization, the realization that most government agencies would lie — coincided with my experience as a bombardier in World War II," he wrote. "The antiwar and antigovernment feelings in the book belong to the period following World War II. The Korean War, the Cold war of the fifties. A general disintegration of belief took place then, and it affected *Catch-22* in that the form of the novel became almost disintegrated" (Davis 300–301).

That then, was just the point. This postwar production classic deriving of the war and the war-breeding system had been meant all along to trade on its own industrial-strength entropy, with the insane title phrase itself serving as the all-purpose catch and free-floating signifier. The medium itself was the madness. And here was no modernist separate peace, no putting the world back together after the end of the world, no shoring of fragments against the collective ruin — just escape. The ex-bombardier Heller, like his light-stepping survivor-hero, the ex-bombardier Yossarian, had won the war by getting away. And his book had made exactly the point both about war and about a whole history of war books and war movies as cultural cliché. Ex-PFC Wintergreen is the scariest man in the book because he keeps calling up general officers and keeps whispering a single name over the phone. The name is T. S. Eliot.[23]

Among young people, a ready-made audience existing at the nexus of the postwar baby boom with the '60s paperback production boom and the '60s boom in American higher-education access and delivery, the book gradually became a cult classic. And among their mentors, availing themselves of the same audience and the same commercial and educational venues, it increasingly became a curricular staple.[24]

Given the operative text at hand — an increasingly hot cultural property carrying the bombload of its own cultural self-destruct mechanism — it was simply a matter of time, of course, until someone would have the idea to try for a big, absurd, phony war movie, complete with aircraft, bases, equipment, uniforms, a cast of thousands. Meanwhile, however, the real war in Vietnam had turned worse than any *Catch-22* anyone could have imagined. Thus government support could be written off. In any event, it had already been years since anyone had even dreamed of getting U.S. military cooperation for a "serious" war movie. Project promoters therefore tried France, Spain, the Philippines. For a base location, they settled on Guaymas, Mexico. For a bomber fleet, on the other hand, they themselves got deadly serious, with the meticulous assembling and rerigging for authenticity of virtually every B-25 still flying. At the end, director Mike Nichols's strategic air force was variously rated, although always placing well within the top twenty in the world.

The cast likewise brought together an astonishing ensemble-like company, somehow making the film one of the great war docu-cameo-epics of all time almost in spite of itself. Yossarian was played by Alan Arkin, an actor who proved somehow born to do the role. Milo Minderbinder was acted similarly with definitive, flaxen-haired, wide-eyed menace by Jon Voight.[25] Nately was Art Garfunkel, Aarfy was Charles Grodin, Dobbs was Martin Sheen, and Orr was Bob Balaban. The unctuous Major Danby was Richard Benjamin; and Colonels Cathcart and Korn were played by Martin Balsam and Buck Henry, the latter also a writer on the film. Chaplain A. T. Tappman, Yossarian's love interest, was played by Anthony Perkins. Nurse Duckett, Yossarian's other love interest, was played with giddy perkiness by the terminal ingenue Paula Prentiss. Norman Fell was Sergeant Towser. Jack Gilford was Doc Daneeka. Bob Newhart was Major Major Major Major.[26]

General Dreedle was played by the prodigious Orson Welles, who for six years had tried to get the film for himself and now kept trying to direct. In retaliation, it is said, a number of the cast members started trying to act like Orson Welles. For the most part, however, the ensemble achieved notable success in playing out some manic impersonation of traditional character roles in a traditional war movie with something like the customary war-movie ingredients: briefings, takeoffs, bombing missions in heavy flak, shot-up landings, debriefings, base-camp hijinks by a bunch of all-American boys; wounds, illness, hospitals, nurses, chaplains; romantic leaves; visits by the general; yet with all of it *here* suspiciously accompanied, it seemed, as in the novel, by an inordinate preoccupation with death. As to absurd grotesquerie, the looping, associative plot structure of the novel proved more than sufficient for fractured, irrational counterpoint.[27] Further, in the visual symbology of which film is uniquely capable, the nightmarish scrambling of traditional narrative structure was punctuated with a set of brilliant primal scenes: Kid Sampson's torso out on the swimming raft, cut in half by a propeller and suddenly missing from the waist up after he has been buzzed by the joyriding McWatt, making its wet, pinkish, slow-motion topple over into the water; the assembled witnesses continuing to watch from the shore as McWatt silently, inexorably, almost languidly, flies the bomber into a nearby mountain; Yossarian, naked in the tree of life, looking out on the burial of Snowden, refusing Milo Mind-erbinder's insinuating pleas to eat of his newest novelty, cotton candy — or, more precisely, chocolate-covered cotton, which he is trying to unload from the Egyptian market, recently cornered by mistake; Snowden, always Snowden, lying in the back of the plane, his guts spilling from his un-zipped flight suit, God's plenty, even down to the stewed tomatoes he had at lunch — Snowden, saying over and over again, "I'm cold, I'm cold"; Yos-sarian, saying back, over and over again, "There, there; there, there."[28]

Meanwhile, the making of the film itself as a movie event *cum* produc-tion spectacle began to generate its own publicity saga. *Newsweek* picked it up as early as March 1969, as did the *New York Times Magazine*: both nat-urally paid heavy attention to numerous *Catch-22*-like anecdotes from the production company; and both made much of the immensity of the effort being made somehow to catch *Catch-22* on film and focused through the madcap role of the director, Mike Nichols, as presiding genius.[29] *Time* and *Life* followed with stories timed to herald the film's release in June 1970. In the *Time* treatment, the film even got the cover, with Nichols featured be-side an inset of Arkin as Yossarian crouching in his tree wearing boots and dogtags, and *Life* simultaneously offered an elaborate photo essay, includ-ing a specially posed vignette of the dramatis personae — with Nichols, again, naturally, in the foreground.

Most importantly included in the latter, though, was also a shooting diary by the actor-screenwriter Buck Henry; and most tellingly important there was surely his record of a culminating special-effects scene — actu-ally, the one in the film where Milo Minderbinder has paid a German bomber force in his employ to bomb his own American bomber base, not to mention Yossarian's and everyone else's. Again, even in the serious business of filming a big-budget World War II classic, intentional self-parody notwithstanding, metanarrative seemed to be firmly in command. "In the background," Henry wrote, "several thousand sticks of dynamite, a ton of black powder and a thousand gallons of gasoline are being ex-ploded by a group of haggard-looking special-effects men. In the fore-ground Arkin runs toward a burning building. Between Arkin and the ex-plosions Tallman flies a B-25 on a straight line down the runway, just high enough off the ground to slice Arkin neatly in half if something should go wrong" (46).

He then goes on to the conversation between Arkin and Nichols, just af-ter the scene has been shot: "Nichols: 'That was good terror, Alan.' Arkin:

'That was *real* terror, Mike'" (48). They were lines, of course, that could have come from the book.

Out in the world beyond the sprawling airbase in Guaymas, Mexico, *Catch-22*-like, of course, the Vietnam War, allegedly winding down, kept cranking itself up again into invasions and secret bombings. Protests continued, and the U.S. military and intelligence communities continued to work unrelentingly on the waging of ongoing secret war on American citizens. In the corporate world, the ITT and General Dynamics scandals, with revelations that U.S. and German international cartels had kept each other in business during much of the older war, recycled World War II international-business scenarios at so complex a level of conspiracy that Milo Minderbinder would have been pressed to imagine it. At home, the venality and mendacity of the Nixon White House managed to bring all of that and everything else out of the woodwork again, with undercover Watergate criminality implicating the FBI and the CIA for good measure. Apace, as the aftermath of the Vietnam nightmare started to sink in, a flood of novels and works of journalism and reportage coming out of the American and Vietnamese experience there wound up essentially once again verifying major elements of Heller's black-comedy shop of horrors. There alone, one found enough paranoiac congruencies, mused one GI protagonist, face-to-face with his own Vietnam version, to make people start thinking that the man who wrote *Catch-22* probably "wasn't crazy enough" (Durden 207).

Meanwhile, at home, the latest loop in the plot had now made Heller's book utterly canonical as at once a '60s antiwar gospel *and* a testament to the countervailing power of redemptive nuttiness in both the popular and the academic markets. Because of the immense popularity of the movie, the novel enjoyed yet another resurgence in the late 1960s and early 1970s as one of the last great iconic texts to come out of the youth culture of the era, and has maintained its popularity ever since. In Dell editions of the last twenty-five years, there have been several complete redesigns for the paperback market, including one with a preface by the author. In the academy it rarely fails to show up in college or university courses in post-1945 American literature or in a prominent position in academic discussions of the era. Secondary resources now include such somber titles as *A "Catch-22" Casebook* and *Critical Essays on Catch-22*. Most to its credit, perhaps, it also continues in the academic news to be one of the four or five most often censored books on library lists and public school curricula.

As Alfred Kazin astutely remarked a long time ago, the secret of *Catch-22*'s success was that it had always been not so much a World War II book as a novel really about modern war itself and the war-breeding system, about the twentieth-century nation-state stripped down to its real function, which is to make war. In this respect, he averred, it was never really about the last war so much as the next war. In this he was largely correct. What should be added, however, is how completely *Catch-22* had to project itself as a "big" World War II book and movie in the image of the postwar popular classic to achieve all this; and further, how thoroughly it did so in every respect by going through the old, familiar genealogy — that same basic ritual of commodification, promotion, popular consumption, and new cultural reification and institutionalization endlessly rehearsed by the World War II classic as a production genre.

In all these respects, then, *Catch-22* should have been the last of the Good War's greatest hits; but of course, it was not. For not even Joseph Heller or anyone since has proven able to reckon with the ongoing capacity of American life and popular culture at once to create and absorb what Jean Baudrillard has called images: simulacra that outstrip the possible meanings or values resident in any reality they might be taken to represent — even as they continue to construct themselves endlessly out of themselves in infinite self-parody.

As to World War II and American remembering, this, of course, had always been the problem with *Catch-22* — along with Vonnegut's *Slaughterhouse Five* and Pynchon's *Gravity's Rainbow* after it — and the attempt to render the World War II production-entertainment classic itself in annihilating self-parody: that so much of the result keeps on insistently turning out to be *true*. Still, in larger cultural understandings, this remains a revisionary view that history and memory have only recently begun to catch up to. Most notably, Paul Fussell — our greatest authority on war and modern consciousness and himself a badly wounded infantry veteran of the war in Europe — has tried to say something of this by way of cultural analysis in *Wartime* and more recently in the autobiographical *Doing Battle*.[30] And so, besides such novelists of the generation of the war as Heller and Vonnegut have historians ranging from John Keegan to John Ellis, Max Hastings, Len Deighton, and a few others.

On the other hand, it has still not been a popular message, this latest testimony, as Fussell has put it, to the curious reciprocity of art and life: that, like *The Longest Day* and *Catch-22*, the Good War and the Great

SNAFU really *were* each other, often in self-parody. Likewise, even in spite of sheer press of historical and technological change, the World War II classic, having now dominated American remembering about the event for nearly half a century, itself hardly seems to be reaching the end of the line as a production genre. Here, too, stock in the Good War remains high, with stock in the Great SNAFU largely limited to the literary-critical intelligentsia. As seen by a flourishing fiftieth anniversary market that now itself can claim nearly a decade's existence, print texts celebrating the Allied victory in World War II continue to prove endlessly produceable and salable. Likewise, the movies and television have founded a new alliance in the transition to a market heavily dependent on cable and videocassette recording. Classic-movie channels, for instance, do a boom business in World War II films; and video stores and catalogs find themselves similarly loaded with familiar titles: *Why We Fight, Victory at Sea, Crusade in Europe*. Further, as with the history-hungry way of things American in general, one may surely count on the retro-mode continuing to find its way onto the technological cutting edge, with the great hovering demon of metaphysical self-parody never any more a consideration here than elsewhere. This is, after all, the nation whose first properly political war story, as noted by John Limon, is "Rip Van Winkle," in which the titular protagonist falls asleep in an old world and wakes up in a new one and has to invent a meaning for the war that seems to have supplied the link; and it continues to be the megadollar audience venue where the relationship between history and memory replicated back precisely as entertainment technology produces a series of box office hits entitled *Back to the Future* I, II, and III. Somewhere in the Republic on any given day, as Michael Kammen has wryly observed, someone in a mayor's office or on a chamber of commerce board actually comes up with some kind of new slogan about progress being a tradition. And, given the mythic stature of the subject and the latest millennial turn of the geopolitical odometer, in the new semiological world of CD-ROM, interactivity, the World Wide Web, even hypertext, happy endings will continue to be devised for the great cultural narrative in question. If the closest analog, the Civil War, is any indication, one may suspect, indeed, that the Higher Disneyfication is likely to become if anything the increasingly regnant mode for new generations of information freaks and popular-culture hobbyists. For with the closing of the distance between information and reality, it is the technologies of remembering, the forms and processes as themselves the grounds of authority and genealogy, that will increasingly prevail. Hence, as to any actual relationship between history and memory that may be represented, the Great SNAFU will constitute the minority report at best. Heller, Vonnegut, and Fussell will have to content themselves with the forms and cultural technologies of their own last word — and perhaps just an old soldier's last, rueful, monitory laugh.

NOTES

CHAPTER I: THE GOOD WAR'S GREATEST HITS

1 The view has certainly been reinforced by news from abroad concerning historical reconsiderations of the war in Germany and Japan as both have addressed the fiftieth anniversaries of defeat and surrender. The Germans, carrying their role as historical aggressors compounded with the guilt of the Holocaust and their wartime atrocities in captured territories, seriously debated whether the anniversary should be allowed to serve as an official occasion to mourn their own war dead. The Japanese likewise were forced into reflections on their wartime atrocities — including the slaughter of civilians, medical experiments on Allied prisoners, and the enslavement of women as army prostitutes. In a series of attempts to quiet revisionary thinking about the war as the anniversary approached, the government took steps in several cases to remove from positions of public authority latter-day apologists for imperial policies. There continued to be considerable debate whether the word for *apology* in Japanese would be uttered. Finally, by no less than the prime minister himself, it was.

Indicative of general sentiment here was the controversy over a planned exhibit by the Smithsonian Institution marking the fiftieth anniversary of the U.S. atomic bombing of the Japanese cities of Hiroshima and Nagasaki. Veterans' groups and other patriotic organizations were incensed by the proposed construction of a display, in accord with current trends in scholarly fashion, emphasizing the morally questionable use of atomic weaponry to end the war, as an alternative to a costly U.S. invasion of the Japanese mainland — itself hardly a new topic of discussion. Special offense was taken in this case, however, at what seemed an attempt to depict Japanese bomb casualties, mostly civilian, as essentially innocent political victims. In response, one political cartoonist suggested that perhaps other notorious events of the war should also be renamed accordingly — the "Pearl Harbor wake-up," for instance, or the "Bataan nature walk." The official solution was to cancel the exhibit altogether.

2 This one-war view of nearly a century of mass geopolitical conflict is now accepted sufficiently to have become a historians' commonplace. Further, the dating of the "war" era has now frequently been extended to involve the whole seventy-five-year period from the onset of European hostilities in 1914 to the 1989 conclusion of the Cold War, marked by the fall of the former Soviet Union and its Iron Curtain empire. For an application of a global one-war theory to the study of strategic objectives specifically associated with major combatant nations in World War II, see Weinberg's compendious *A World at Arms*.

3 The most visible popular exponent of such a revisionary position from a perspective of American cultural attitudes and behavior has been, of course, Paul Fussell, in texts such as *Wartime* and, more recently, *Doing Battle*. For a more technically focused scholarly discussion of many of the same issues, see Adams, *The Best War Ever*. As to depictions in general military literature of various features of the Allied war effort in a less than heroic light, see also Max Hastings, Len Deighton, and a host of others.

4 In this sense of the popular-culture text as "production" classic, it should be obvious that I mean to invoke the idea of mass-cultural production used by Walter Benjamin, Theodore Adorno, Herbert Marcuse, and others, as spanning the orbits of artistic and politico-economic enterprise: in the fairly loose sense, then, used by theorists when they describe something like gender as a cultural construct or "social production"; and also in the implication of product the way a brand of automobile or deodorant is a product. At the same time, as regards the "production" of American culture specifically, I want to use the term in the sense of the frequently generative or self-reifying relationship between literary production in America from the earliest days of the Republic onward and the production of cultural myth. American mass culture has often been to this degree both a social construction and a consumer item.

5 For my purposes I also find it a useful way, in addressing issues of American democratic culture, of avoiding unwieldy distinctions such as those established by Michael Kammen, for instance, between "collective memory" on one hand — "usually a code phrase for what is remembered by a dominant civic culture" — and "popular memory" — "usually referring to ordinary folks" (10) — with the latter also recently made to embrace, as Kammen also notes, currently fashionable notions of "oral cultures" or "working-class" and "community" history (9). I use *remembering* here to address these and other ways of negotiating between history and various forms of cultural memory.

6 Engelhardt's book on the demoralizations of the postwar decades in America is entitled *The End of Victory Culture*. For broad-scale historical depictions of the quick absorption of the national consciousness into postwar doubts and uncertainties, see also Perret, *A Dream of Greatness*, and, more recently, volume 10 in the massive *Oxford History of the United States*, Patterson's *Grand Expectations*.

CHAPTER 2: MAKING A PRODUCTION OUT OF IT

1 It has been said that Vietnam was the first great American media war. World War II should surely claim that title. One might go so far as to say that the media dimension of World War II was largely responsible, for instance, for the shameful neglect or popular representation of the bitter conflict in Korea. So shortly after World War II, the Korean War was something people wanted not to think about. In this they were certainly helped by issues of scale and distance; but they could also take refuge in forms of popular remembering still being produced through retrospective depictions of the great conflict so recently crowned with total victory.

If anything, Vietnam testified to the persistence and perdurability of those same forms. The classic titles examined here, for instance, frequently appear in writings by U.S. veterans of the Vietnam War as constructions of an American mythology they carried with them into the experience. Further, one is also struck by their persistence *in* the literature of the war so frequently conceived of as the Good War's dark counterpoint, as if writing about the experience of the Vietnam War must itself acknowledge the structures of cultural remembering provided by the World War II classic. Although production forms have often attempted to set off the American experience of Vietnam as the geopolitical equivalent of the Fall, they have frequently mimicked World War II classic antecedents. We have had the big Vietnam novel, the big Vietnam movie, the big Vietnam documentary, even — in *Miss Saigon* — the big Vietnam musical.

2 For a useful outline of the formation of the official U.S. propaganda effort through such early entities as Coordinator of Information (COI) and Office of Facts and Figures (OFF) and the restructuring and consolidation of efforts by early 1942 into the more familiar configurings of Office of War Information (OWI) and Office of Strategic Services (OSS), see Buitenhuis, "Prelude to War." For an overview of wartime information control activities in the popular culture media, see Blum, *V Was for Victory*.

3 Robert McCormick's rabidly isolationist *Chicago Tribune*, as evidenced in virtually every account of prewar opinion-shaping, is the chief one that comes to mind.

4 Henry Luce's Time-Life media complex, especially, took great effort to emphasize Sino-Japanese horrors, with reports graphically documenting Japanese atrocity on one hand and on the other promoting Chiang Kai-shek's Kuomintang nationalists as the saviors of China.

5 One surprise addition to the list, in abridged English translation, was Adolf Hitler's *Mein Kampf*.

6 At the same time, as a production classic inventing its own multimedia genealogy, *Casablanca* would startlingly rehearse the composite genius of popular culture invention that would come to mark its postwar successors. Largely, of course, this was a matter of timing and production circumstance allowing for a certain sense of critical distancing from the conflict. Its setting, for instance, obviously preceded the American entry into the war; and production occurred while the fact of global American involvement was still in the process of sinking in.

Indeed, as documented in Aljean Harmetz's book-length study of the film *Round Up the Usual Suspects*, the basic artifact had origins as far back as the summer of 1940, in a stage script by a high school English teacher named Murray Bennett in collaboration with Joan Allison, a New York divorcée with theater contacts; that the original text — albeit in plot, character, and wartime North African setting very much resembling the eventual movie — was in fact Bennett's attempt to allegorize his own experiences in post-Anschluss Austria of the 1930s; that, failing to catch on with potential backers presumably on either account, it remained unproduced as a play and seems to have found movie development only in late December 1941 essentially as an available property with a war theme, purchased grudgingly by Warner Brothers amid the post–Pearl Harbor tumult of the U.S. entry into the conflict; and that, as a series of writers wrestled with a succession of scriptings and rescriptings, equally complicated casting difficulties required that Bogart and Bergman be likewise grudgingly accepted as available choices in parts originally scheduled for George Raft and Hedy Lamarr.

And then there was the song. Its strange inclusion in the mix had to be traced through an even more circuitous and eccentric textual history — across ten years, to be exact. The composition of one Herman Hupfield, *it* had made its first appearance in a 1931 Broadway show entitled *Everybody's Welcome* (despite the title, it had absolutely no connection to Bennett's project) and had simply been appropriated by Bennett as part of the atmospherics for his own nonmusical work. As to the new appearance in the spotlight that would bring it immortality as the movie's love theme, this in turn had been achieved in spite of determined efforts to the contrary by Max Steiner, the proprietary composer assigned to write the score, who had insisted to the last moment on substituting a more appropriate original melody of his own devising.

Production stretched on until August 1942. The film then waited for a New York Thanksgiving premiere. As planned — presumably in the closest connection with the war effort studio publicists thought they could drum up for the moment — this holiday event was further highlighted by a celebratory march of Free French representatives down Broadway.

But by now, historical events had also begun to play their own large hand in project development. To be exact, three weeks before the preview date in question, the Allies had cooperatively staged the successful Torch landings. These had been headlined by the capture and liberation of the city of the film's title. Further, in an almost eerie geopolitical imaging of its conclusion, much had been made of the recruitment of the North African Vichy government, headed by the morally ambiguous Admiral Jean Darlan, to the Allied cause.

In turn, this publicity windfall was compounded by new headlines at the level of Allied grand geopolitical strategy attending the national release of the film three months later. And again, the focus was on the magic name: Casablanca. This time, the city had become the scene of the first of the summit meetings of the great wartime leaders, in this case Roosevelt and Churchill. And again, the great publicity theme was their attempts to achieve Free French solidarity with the Allied cause. First there had been the shifty Darlan, attempting to work both sides of the war. He had been shot to death by a Resistance member. Now he had been replaced by the rivals Giraud and de Gaulle. In uniform, they still looked very like Claude Raines. Like Rick, someone would have to decide.

7 And thus one evidences the temptation to write a book-within-a-book on remembering in wartime. For that is what it deserves. Fortunately, interested readers may take heart in a number of generous accounts within larger cultural histories of the home front by Richard R. Lingeman, John Morton Blum, and William L. O'Neill.

8 To be sure, as the end grew near, one might sense certain openings of the model to new forms of critique. Especially from late 1944 onward, for instance, fiction began to project a distinctly postwar feel, as in John Hersey's 1944 novel A Bell for Adano, which made it to the screen by 1945. On the other hand, Harry Brown's realistic A Walk in the Sun, though published in 1945, was presumably not considered fit for movie production until 1948.

9 Further, as will be seen, in a medium not known for its social or literary prescience, the film was really a preemptive classic, first conceived of as a project by Samuel Goldwyn himself in 1944.

10 In neither case, to be sure, were the models unprecedented. The commemorative volume became a postwar staple, with texts brought forth by both major military news organizations, Yank and Stars and Stripes. Likewise, the documentary style of Victory at Sea had been rehearsed in the wartime Why We Fight series and in the postwar March of Time.

11 As will be seen, it quickly became a process fraught with its own kinds of forward and reverse production ironies. In general, because of the decline of reading in the post-

war decades and the ascendancy of nonprint media, movie developments of the properties would increasingly assume classic status. On the other hand, there was no assured timeline or pattern of necessary connection between the print and film versions. There is some irony in the fact that the first two "big" novels of the war, Norman Mailer's *The Naked and the Dead* and Irwin Shaw's *The Young Lions*, both waited a decade to appear as films. Two more, *From Here to Eternity* and *The Caine Mutiny*, publishing bestsellers of 1951, made it into film by 1953, although in both with heavy censorship exacted as a price of Department of Defense cooperation. The connection found its ideal property in *Battle Cry*, a 1953 guts-and-glory war novel written as if it *were* a guts-and-glory war movie, which it quickly became by 1955. On the other hand, as a production model it became enough of a cliché that parodic extensions of the "big" World War II novel such as Joseph Heller's *Catch-22*, Kurt Vonnegut's *Slaughterhouse Five*, and Thomas Pynchon's *Gravity's Rainbow* would make the cinematic properties of the genre a focal issue of representation. And the first two, of course, also played out the textual charade as major motion pictures.

12 These visual modes were of course important in themselves. Further, they should remind us also of the important supplementarity once existing between print and visual representations, a supplementarity now lost or at least rendered invisible by a culture of television, the movies, musical video, and new forms of virtual reality, in which the picture is increasingly photo-electronic and the word accompanying the picture is oral.

13 The August 7 story carries "The Nation" as a subject head and is subtitled "The Way Home" (15–16). The August 14 follow-up appears as the weekly "Letter from the Publisher" (15).

14 For complementary accounts of the project in these stages of initial conceptualization and script development, see Freedland (190–91) and Epstein (150–51).

15 In a moving literary homage, "Boone" is the anonymous town somewhere vaguely in mid-America where Larry Heinemann's maimed, broken Vietnam-veteran protagonist decides to get off the bus in *Paco's Story*, winner of the 1986 National Book Award.

16 Among writers praising Kantor for the attempt but expressing disappointment in the outcome was Robert E. Spiller in the December 22, 1945, *Saturday Review*. The newspaper comment on stylistic unevenness appeared in the *Springfield Republican*, December 23, 4d.

17 Basic accounts at this stage of development are again provided by Freedland (191–92) and Epstein (151–52). Detailed accounts of Wyler's involvement also appear in biographies by Anderegg and Madsen. Oddly, as regards Sherwood biography, on the other hand, the *Best Years of Our Lives* work generally rates a sentence or two. See, for instance, Meserve and Shuman.

18 The anecdote is standard in both Goldwyn and Wyler lore. For Loy's version of her work on the film with Wyler, see Kotsilibas-Davis's 1987 biography (196–201).

19 I use the term *entertainment classic* here to denote a certain kind of production artifact — as opposed, for instance, to the equally popular but more serious-minded *Best Years of Our Lives* — designed for an audience whose interests in representations of the war were already being determined by what one should call "entertainment" values. To reinforce the point, one might add that *Mister Roberts's* closest competitor for

the title was Rodgers and Hammerstein's *South Pacific,* derived from James Michener's 1948 story collection, which initially seems to have caught the producer Joshua Logan's eye as possible background material for the Broadway *Mister Roberts,* then in production. My next chapter provides a related study of *South Pacific* in this production-entertainment mode.

20 About Logan's knowledge of Fonda's service history we can be virtually certain. As members of a closely knit entertainment community comprising the elite of American stage and screen, the two had been associates and friends throughout their careers. About any corresponding knowledge of Heggen's we must speculate. Fonda's wartime service was publicized in at least three nationally syndicated wire service stories, appearing in the *New York Times,* for instance, on August 25, 1942, May 11, 1943, and August 13, 1945, and concerning his enlistment in the navy, his graduation from quartermaster training, and his receipt of the Bronze Star for service as an air intelligence officer in the Marianas. The first, which Heggen may have seen while he was in midshipman training at Evanston, Illinois, highlighted the suddenness of Fonda's enlistment as a common seaman as part of his determination to serve in a combat role. One might alternatively guess that during Heggen's collaboration with Logan, the two may have discussed the subject, thus lending the author's creative "remembering" a certain suggestibility.

21 According to a differing *Publishers Weekly* account of this false start on an earlier novel, the good advice came from another friend, who sent him a copy of Frederic Wakeman's *The Hucksters* to prove, in Heggen's words, that he had "been beaten to it" (688).

22 Decades later, in *Wartime,* his iconoclastic response to the "good war" myth of World War II, Paul Fussell would identify a contemporary word for this, *chickenshit* — petty authority, that is, arbitrarily bestowed and stupidly enforced. In a vast literature of this great war against totalitarianism, Fussell suggested, the war against chickenshit would become one of that literature's great anti-totalitarian themes.

23 Again, it is important to emphasize here the reliance of print texts of the era on what was frequently a built-in visual dimension.

24 As a demonstration of the friendship, in 1950 Logan and his wife named their adopted son Thomas Heggen Logan.

25 Here, as suggested in my conclusion, one cannot overemphasize the appeal that the hero's selfless, albeit wasted, death in combat had for the noncombatant veterans who constituted the majority of civilian returnees. Among Allied ground forces, for instance, Ellis notes, on the basis of converging statistics, that "only between a fifth and a quarter of any army's paper strength was actually involved in the shooting war" (158). The naval war would be harder to estimate, since supply ships and tankers could be blown up or sunk as readily as combat craft. On the other hand, the popularity of such navy books as *Tales of the South Pacific, Mister Roberts,* and *The Caine Mutiny* would suggest that a sense of the behind-the-lines experience was common to sailors.

26 Here too, extending the reciprocities of art and life, the production of another beloved World War II classic mentioned earlier, the musical *South Pacific* — in the process of making a similar passage from novel to stage to screen — seems to have impinged both on the remainder of Heggen's short career and on the film version of his book. Fur-

ther, major participants overlapped, including Logan, who realized, as did many of his colleagues, that the production of *Mister Roberts* as a stage comedy had largely laid the way for the new Rodgers and Hammerstein musical entertainment. In fact, according to Logan's memoir, he and his cowriter, Jo Mielzener, had come upon Michener's book while the Broadway *Mister Roberts* project was under development and, as mentioned previously, had initially considered *Tales of the South Pacific* as a source of background color for *Mister Roberts*. As Logan moved on to the new and more spectacular production of *South Pacific* that developed on its own, Heggen felt deserted by his mentor's shift of enthusiasm, and this sense of abandonment, along with a failure to move on to new work of his own, contributed to the suicidal depression eventuating in his death at thirty.

Meanwhile, as *Mister Roberts* played out its original success and took to the road, *South Pacific* enjoyed an even more extraordinary Broadway run, appearing there until 1954 and yielding millions of copies of sheet music and a best-selling original-cast LP. Then, it too went on the road. How many places did the two productions cross paths in the course of a season? How deeply, as contemporary classics of stage and, eventually, the '50s screen, were they identified in the public mind? Certainly both movies are infused with the same South Seas atmospherics and the same wide-screen, big-star, technicolor production values of the era.

27 For varying versions of the casting history and the Fonda-Ford conflict, see the Fonda biographies by Fonda and Teichmann, Roberts and Goldstein, and Thomas. On the latter, see also accounts by Bogdanovich and Gallagher.

28 This was also proved appropriate to the relatively bland screenplay, which itself had required a sanitizing of the '40s Broadway artifact for '50s audiences.

29 For listings of World War II films, see Garland, Langman and Borg, Monaco, Parish, and Wetta and Curley.

30 As *Mister Roberts* had prospered by continuing to capitalize on Fonda, this might have succeeded as a film had it capitalized on Lemmon. In fact, *Ensign Pulver* resembles its progenitor only in the look and feel of the technicolor Pacific. Besides being deprived of a Mister Roberts, Ensign Pulver, played by Robert Walker Jr., seems unable to forget that he is not Lemmon, projecting only a dreadful earnestness. The same sense of the flaccid sequel pervades the performances of Burl Ives as the captain and Walter Matthau as the slurred, wisecracking doc.

31 This really is the basic plot, like those of *Mutiny on the Bounty*, a renowned '30s antecedent, and a roughly contemporary World War II classic, *The Caine Mutiny*. Here, Roberts, the good officer, mediates between the unhappy crew and the tyrannical captain. The former, sensing his fairness and humanity, love and respect him. The latter, while knowing him to be a loyal subordinate, fears and hates him. The men feel betrayed when Roberts begins suddenly to kowtow to the captain, not knowing that he has sacrificed his virtuous independence to gain them a liberty. After he dies, his example lives on in the callow Pulver, who is transfigured in his image.

32 Or, perhaps, if twenty years earlier, *The Hurricane? Tabu? South of Pago Pago?*

33 On the other hand, not all the tradeoffs in medium are negative. Here, for instance, the film effectively represents the predawn passage of the great battle fleet imaging the magnitude of Roberts's noncombatant frustration. Thus, in contrast to the play's first

scene, when he tells the doc about seeing it go by, in the movie we too have witnessed the actual spectacle.

34 For perspective, compare *Mister Roberts* with a contemporary combat film, full of amphibious assaults and kamikaze attacks, *Away All Boats*. Again, in this 1956 Jeff Chandler–George Nader command drama set aboard an attack transport, what one mainly remembers is the intense color.

35 The history of the scene also reveals the way Hollywood values dominated the production. As shot and eventually used, it was a Ford addition, a Leroy deletion, and then a Jack Warner addition (Roberts and Goldstein 111).

36 The oddity of this, when one thinks about it, may be suggested by the only corresponding instance, to my knowledge, of such a proposition's ever being ventured about the World War II Germans. It occurs in Mel Brooks's movie *The Producers*, in which an idea man, at the end of his imaginative tether, comes up with a Nazi musical entitled *Springtime for Hitler*. One may cite, of course, such disparate aberrations as *Hogan's Heroes*, or Rodgers and Hammerstein's own eventual *Sound of Music*. These concepts, however, would rely on the notion of the "good German," an idea for which, as noted by John Dower, "no Japanese counterpart" would ever exist "in the popular consciousness of the Western allies" (8). Such a bifurcation was required for the Germans, particularly in post-Holocaust regard, probably because in their very *occidental* heinousness they remained too much like us. Indeed, the only alternative recourse in humorous depiction would lie in the black comedy, say, of a Thomas Pynchon. The Japanese, being wholly other, allowed for the ease of erasure conventionally applied to the other. One could simply make them invisible. In contrast, the Germans remained both easily other and uneasily same.

37 For a complete survey of the genre, see Dooley 205–16.

38 The two main plots were then tied together by a behind-enemy-lines reconnaissance-mission subplot involving DeBecque (who survives) and Cable (who dies), drawn, as is not generally acknowledged, from the plot of another story introducing the shadowy American operative Tony Fry, a recurrent major character in the ensuing text, and his radio mission with the brave, tragic British coastwatcher called "The Remittance Man." Further to facilitate Billis's enlarged role, one other borrowing was also made for the accidental "diversion" created by having Billis stow away and then fall into the sea en route to the DeBecque-Cable "mission" and thereby become the subject of a rescue struggle attracting most of the American and Japanese forces in the area. This, in the original, came from "The Milk Run," a story involving the pilot Bus Adams.

39 Here, as with "nigger" above, in its American usage the racist term has been culture-specific. As the former has been used to derogate Americans of African descent, the latter was, of course, one of the main racial epithets used by Americans in Vietnam. Its origins, however, go further back in American wars, perhaps including the one in question. One theory connects it with the Korean Conflict, as deriving from a word in the latter language for "foreigner." Others locate it in the pre–World War II American argot of the Pacific and even as far back as the Philippine campaigns at the turn of the century.

40 It is surely one of our supreme literary-historical ironies that Mary and Liat are identified as Tonkinese. That is, they are Indochinese, most likely brought to the islands where the play is set by migrating French colonials. To be exact, this also makes them North Vietnamese, from "Tonkin" China, the region of Hanoi and the Chinese border, as opposed to "Annam" or "Cochin" China, known to us once as South Vietnam.

41 As Paul Johnson has suggested, it may come as close to any American art form to being simply sui generis (227). The underworld stories of Damon Runyon, for instance, could become *Guys and Dolls*. A musical play about a production of *The Taming of the Shrew* could produce *Kiss Me Kate*; *Faust*, by way of a baseball story by Douglas Wallop, became *Damn Yankees*. *Romeo and Juliet* could get street-ganged into *West Side Story*. For Rodgers and Hammerstein in particular, a run of such farfetched transformations had already been effected: a minor play by Lynn Riggs called *Green Grow the Lilacs*, with a modern dance script by Agnes DeMille, had become *Oklahoma!*; a second-rate melodrama, *Liliom*, by an obscure central European, Ferenc Molnár, had become *Carousel*.

A prestigious recent consideration of the form, Gerald Bordman's, involves a highly elaborated aesthetic eventuating in one volume on American operetta and one on American musical comedy. This would seem quite beside the point. The point, rather, would seem to be exactly the wildly syncretistic nature of the form itself, a form adapted in fact, as a quite specific contextualized "vehicle" for American expression predicated on the multifarious demands of audience appeal it prepared to meet.

42 How fully this was the end of an era for Broadway was marked by a notable conjunction of big-time sports with the overnight ascendancy of television. A case in point is noted in the 1940–50 volume of the Time-Life series entitled *This Fabulous Century*: in 1947 the World Series was telecast for the first time, and Broadway theaters underwent a 50 percent decline in revenues (266).

43 It would also be the Mary Martin hairstyle seen shortly in the enormously popular Broadway production, again among the first to be seen on national TV, *Peter Pan*, when it again set off sundry reverberations in popular fashion.

44 For complete data see Murrells. In the age of Michael Jackson, it is hard to remember the significance that such figures once could claim. One might note, for instance, that the sheet music to the show at the time sold two million copies (Laufe 128).

45 Oddly, someone found it necessary to dub Juanita Hall. One further prophetic "Tonkinese" connection is also worth mentioning: the casting of France Nuyen as Liat. Nguyen is the most common of all Vietnamese names. On the other hand, one can find such racial ghosts throughout. In the Broadway original, for instance, the "Polynesian" children were played by Hispanics. One of the DeBecque servants was also played by Richard Loo, *everyone's* movie caricature of the despicable Japanese officer.

46 As a measure of the skyrocketing attention paid to the fiftieth state, in contrast to the mild interest shown in the forty-ninth, one can cite in the latter case but one movie: *North to Alaska*.

47 Thus the relocation of *South Pacific*, Michener's South Seas movie of a book, to every American tourist's possible movie dream of a South Seas isle. And thus, however, also one last other strange merging of entertainment with proximate Pacific history that

cannot go unmentioned in the Hollywood connection. And that is the relation of all this to that utter anomaly of the period, the funny movie about World War II against the Japanese. To be sure, some of these, such as *Mister Roberts,* themselves began as novels transferred to the stage. (In fact, as noted, the producer of *South Pacific,* Joshua Logan, was working on the stage version of Thomas Heggen's seriocomic book *Mister Roberts* when he first heard about Michener's book, which, turned down by MGM as a stand-alone, had been suggested as a source of background color.) Others, such as *Don't Go Near the Water,* moved from book to movie. But most seemed mainly to spin off of their own bizarre momentum. The list is staggering: *Francis, the Talking Mule; Operation Petticoat; Ensign Pulver; The Wackiest Ship in the Army; Father Goose.* If War Without Mercy had been bought for a song, it often proved worth a laugh as well.

48 It is all over the extensive liner notes that accompany the tape. James Michener himself is even invoked (though without citation) suggesting "that although neither Cable nor Nellie is originally able to overcome personal prejudice to marry Liat and De-Becque respectively, it is Nellie, the Southerner, who is better able to deal with her conflicts than Cable, the Philadelphia-born, Princeton-educated Northerner."

49 So extensive and egregious, in fact, was the particular interfusing of cultural myth and cultural commodity at hand that it eventually proved worthy of a book-length study, by Karal Ann Marling and John Wetenhall, which leaves untouched finally none of its various evolutions — the campaign for the island as a whole, the flag-raising episodes, the series of photographs in their actual evolution; the making of the film; the intertwining stories of the fates of various participants along the way, including individual soldiers such as Ira Hayes — a Pima Indian part of the second group and one of the reenactors in the film, whose story of tragic celebrity became the subject of much discussion in the press and of a Tony Curtis movie entitled *The Outsider* — and high-ranking commanders such as General Holland M. Smith; the various official enshrinements of the image through postage stamps, posters, bond drives, celebrity tours, and major public monuments; and the reverberations of the Marine Corps myth so created and preserved in far-reaching decisions being undertaken at the time on postwar military organization and defense policy. The point of my necessarily briefer treatment here will be to show how fully such an account of production as it relates to the film may be said to correspond to those of a host of contemporary analogs.

50 By March 3 Thomas was dead. Shortly, so was Hansen. Lindberg was evacuated with wounds. Michaels somehow got through untouched and eventually went home.

51 To compound reenactment ironies, as will be seen, Schrier got to play a bit part near the end of *Sands of Iwo Jima* as John Wayne's platoon leader. He is about to send a group up the hill where they will be shown raising the flag as depicted in the Rosenthal photograph. As it turns out, this is completely accurate. After the first raising and the ensuing shootout, Schrier actually presided over the second event in just this fashion.

·52 Further, as Marling and Wetenhall point out, reenactment with live participants had also by now become something of a popular fad, with re-creations of the image being made everywhere from parade floats to fraternity skits.

53 Given the corresponding eagerness of the military, in an era of postwar cutbacks, to lend their support to attractive depictions in popular-culture venues, one should not be surprised at the laudatory emphasis in all these films on *the service portrayed*. *Battleground*, albeit more problematic than wartime films in its depiction of combat, still emphasized GIs' determination and resilience in the spirit of such predecessors as *The Story of G.I. Joe*. *Twelve O'Clock High* likewise permitted new emphasis on the shocking human cost of the air war, but still within a film that emphasized the hard courage of bomber crews. As for the navy, *Task Force*, a film actually conceived during wartime but shelved after VJ Day, was brought back and rushed into production with all official blessing as a paean to carrier aviation that could also serve as a response to the challenge of the air force as the new strategic air arm (Boettcher 96, 142).

The symbiosis would be short-lived, however, especially with the '50s cycle of films arising out of major postwar novels, often written in a spirit of literary-intellectual critique. *From Here to Eternity*, *The Young Lions*, and *The Naked and the Dead* would meet with heavy resistance from the army, as would *The Caine Mutiny* from the navy. The only exception would be *Battle Cry*, a novel highly favorable to the Marine Corps, which received enthusiastic support.

54 As to glamor, the only close wartime competitors were flyers of various service branches. Especially in the Pacific, marine forces got the ground combat spotlight, although more than twenty army divisions also participated in major combat, both on their own and in campaigns mainly thought of as marine engagements such as Guadalcanal and Okinawa.

But by now one would not have exaggerated conditions at all to describe the marines as the single most endangered of all the military services in terms of such postwar defense reorganizations as those of the Thomas Act of 1946, the National Security Act of 1947, and the latter's 1949 revision (Boettcher 180). Within these developments, which created the modern Department of Defense, the navy found itself at war with both the flashy new air force and civilian budget streamliners suggesting — with encouragement from Eisenhower, the new postwar army chief of staff, and as part of rivalries that went as far back as Belleau Wood — that we no longer had need of a duplicate army (81, 83).

55 It was on this basis, according to Suid, that Grainger wrote an original forty-page treatment centering on "the story of a tough drill sergeant and the men he leads into battle." Still, his greater moment of war-related and writing-related genius may have followed shortly thereafter, when he decided to turn the project over to the novelist and screenwriter Harry Brown (94). The resultant script, notably clean and fast-moving, has much in common with Brown's screen treatment of his own novel *A Walk in the Sun*, also a realistic and insightful depiction of small-unit relationships in combat, in the latter case the concentrated, grimly matter-of-fact account of an American patrol in Italy decimating itself against a minor objective. One may in fact speculate that Brown's skill in working at this close focus may largely be the basis of the problematic realism at work in the portrayal of Stryker's relationships with his men, which psychologically dominates the film almost in spite of the heroic tenor of much of the action.

56 The production symbiosis, budgeted at $1 million by Republic, probably cost $1.5 million more in marine participation. On the other hand, beyond both parties' predictions as well surely must have been the incredible publicity windfall reaped with images of Iwo Jima, which continued to abound in the public eye even as late as 1954, the year of the much-heralded dedication of the Marine Corps monument at Arlington.

57 It is the one invariably mentioned, for instance, by Vietnam memoirists with marine service as decisive in their choices to enlist or volunteer for Vietnam, and also as an index of their postwar disillusionment. See, for example, Philip Caputo, A *Rumor of War*, and Ron Kovic, *Born on the Fourth of July.*

58 Given Republic's status as a "B" producer in search of an "A" project, Wayne seems to have been passed over because he was thought of as mainly a Western actor, and a "B" one at that. Certainly that had been part of his history. On the other hand, he had also done *Fort Apache* and *She Wore a Yellow Ribbon*, feature films that allowed for significant development of character. Further, he had also done some well-remembered wartime combat roles in *Flying Tigers, Fighting Seabees, They Were Expendable*, and *Back to Bataan* — in most cases also playing a tough, complicated, somewhat maverick character, not unlike Stryker.

  On his side, Wayne admitted to wanting the part so badly, as he later told the marine advisor, Leonard Fribourg, that "he could taste it" (Suid 96). He envisioned, he said, "the story of Mr. Chips put in the military. A man takes eight boys and has to make men out of them. Instead of four years of college, he's given eighteen weeks before they go into battle" (97).

59 Out of an extremely well documented history of production, an emblematic photograph in this respect, included among the illustrations here, is one of Felix W. De Weldon, sculptor of the Marine Corps memorial, instructing Ira Hayes, John Bradley, and Rene Gagnon, three of the flag raisers in the Rosenthal photo, in how to make their positionings in the movie scene conform to those depicted in the monument.

60 Even by marine standards, the film was regarded as too violent a depiction of training sequences.

61 Further, Garry Wills claims, Wayne also forged on the same basis here the model of all his later, "mature" roles as a fundamentally worthy, but troubled, "authority" figure (156).

62 One might protest the totalitarian dramatic and moral engineering of the scene, which pauses for a reading of an unfinished letter from Stryker expressing regret for his neglect of paternal and family responsibilities. On the other hand, in case it has been forgotten, one suddenly realizes that the proximate cause for the Agar character's position in the squad as rebellious intellectual misfit has been his resentment of his own domineering father — a marine officer.

63 To note the persistence of such perverse institutional and personal pride, see marine novels of Vietnam such as Martin Russ's *Sand in the Wind* and James Webb's *Fields of Fire*. Indeed, even so grimly surreal and harrowed a novel as Gustav Hasford's *The Short Timers* and the film for which it became the basis, Stanley Kubrick's *Full Metal Jacket*, both have the effect of bringing one to a horrified admiration for such an ethos of crazy sacrifice.

64 In itself this was hardly an original concept then or later. Competing volumes from the postwar era, for instance, included collections by the editors of *Yank* and *Stars and Stripes*. Later, a standard pictorial history would also appear in the *American Heritage* series. What the *Picture History* would always carry was a cachet of history derived from the history of a publication itself so deeply associated, as an American institution, with the experience of the war.

65 According to Robert Elson's account, the book was a "runaway" best-seller, published in October 1950 and bringing in a net profit of $1.5 million by the end of the year alone (*Time, Inc.*, 418). *Publishers Weekly* accounts validate the claim. In its January 20, 1951, issue, reporting 1950 overall sales figures, it noted 39,276 copies sold by book stores and 500,000 more by direct mail.

66 Historically, this introduction is significant in itself as an encapsulated view of the magazine's tendency to mythologize its stable of photographers, reporters, writers, and editors as a kind of alternative OWI outfitted by Henry Luce and Abercrombie and Fitch.

67 At the same time, at the height of prewar international crises, and tensions that would shortly make Roosevelt the great, indispensable war leader of the Allied chiefs, an article on Roosevelt could still be entitled "Devil or Demigod?" with a byline, "In a great crisis a great liberal has not yet unified the Republic." By G. W. Johnson, it appeared on November 24, 1941 — two weeks before the Japanese attack on Pearl Harbor.

68 While the magazine was in the planning stages, one editor had written to Luce that "a war, any sort of war, is going to be a natural promotion." This was Dan Longwell, an early associate, urging Luce to get out a first issue in time to cover Italy's military aggression in Ethiopia (Wainwright 121).

69 It was a case study, as Martin Walker has recently pointed out, in the trademark Lucean deconstruction of an earlier image and instant reconstruction for American purposes. As the war went on, Russia was actually romanticized as a valiant ally, with Stalin as a friendly giant perhaps named Uncle Joe. By 1943, for instance, *Life* had managed to make the Russians so much like us that the NKVD was said to be rather like the FBI.

In contrast, during prewar coverage Stalin had been just another dictator. After the Russo-German nonaggression pact, for instance, and the later dividing of the spoils of Poland with Hitler, he received scornful depiction as a cynical totalitarian opportunist. And even at the moment of Hitler's turn against the Soviets, *Life* restrained itself to cool matter-of-factness, describing on July 7, 1941, "Hitler's treacherous attack on his communist ally" as "a gigantic stroke of luck for hard-pressed Britain and the unprepared U.S." (28).

70 Much has been made, of course, then and now, about Luce and China: his missionary childhood and early education there; his constant publicizing of the virtues of the prewar Kuomintang government in its struggles against the Communists; his wartime promotion of Chiang Kai-shek as a wartime ally of Big Four stature (and his constant plumping for the celebrity of Madame Chiang); his dominant role as the founding father of the postwar China lobby.

On the other hand, at least in the early years of *Life*, one also needs to give credit for general coverage of the whole prewar China situation, involving Chiang, Mao, and a variety of other contending warlords and power figures. Here was China, indeed, in something of its real, and often quite brutal, political complexity. One photographic feature, for instance, involved an extremely graphic spread on Kuomintang executions of opponents — with the method of choice being a pistol shot point-blank in the back of the head. And as is well known, a young *Life* staffer named Theodore S. White also managed to scoop the world with an exclusive story on the shadowy Communists, including an extensive selection of photos from their camp.

71 Meanwhile, when it wasn't being accused of stirring up war fear, it was being indicted nearly as often for frivolity (Wainwright 117–18). Through 1941, for instance, war coverage increased substantially, and even ads became increasingly defense-oriented. On the other hand, the November 10 issue included a story entitled "Doctors Pick Prize Pickaninies at Memphis Tri-State Negro Fair." November 17 featured on its cover a photo collage of individual members of the University of Texas football team. November 24 took "How to Knit" as its cover topic and also carried inside a feature story on Veronica Lake's hair. As Pacific conditions became more menacing, December 1 duly carried an "Air Power" cover theme and a brief spread inside on the Japanese envoys Kurusu and Noruma in Washington. December 8, already on the stands by the time of the attack, serendipitously carried a cover portrait and feature on General Douglas McArthur, "Commander of Far East." December 15, on the other hand, well into production, had to carry "Junior Miss" on the cover, with a quick seven-page insert on the attack and illustrations hastily cobbled up from peacetime file photos.

Not until December 22, with a picture of Old Glory flying on the cover, did full treatment begin, including Luce's famous "Day of Wrath" essay, photos of the first American military dead, among them the legendary Colin Kelly, and also a famous photo essay on "How to Tell Japs from Chinese." December 29 provided the first actual attack photographs from Pearl Harbor; and even more familiar and now famous ones followed on February 16, 1942.

72 Indeed, out of the vast *Life* assemblage, one suddenly realizes that virtually every major photograph associated with World War II is there save one. The missing item is the Joe Rosenthal photograph of the marine flag-raising on Iwo Jima's Mount Suribachi, rejected at the time because it was considered a staged shot (Wainwright 157).

73 Luce seemed to realize as much retrospectively. "Though we did not plan *Life* as a war magazine," he admitted, "it turned out that way" (Wainwright 121).

74 On the other hand, Luce always reserved his right to be critical about shortcomings in war production or strategic policy. As to party politics, he would also support Dewey even in 1944 (Wainwright 122).

75 And one should emphasize at this point that here also was no mere promotional shilling — for it really was an epic enterprise. Indeed, after a survey of the roughly two hundred wartime issues of the magazine, one can only be stunned, in moving to any of the major postwar photo histories, to see what an infinitesimal fraction of war photography from *Life* is represented in the assembled volumes. Invariably, if an item is traced back to its original publication context, for each photograph finally selected, in the attendant story one will find as many as three or four nearly like it and in their own way nearly as memorable.

76 This, of course, was an authorial commission not without its own revisionary political ironies. In the 1920s and '30s, Dos Passos had been a classic writer on the left. By 1950,

however, he had retired into the Republican stable sufficiently for Henry Luce's satisfaction.

77 On the other hand, one hardly missed the point of a nuclear explosion depicted in accompanying full-color, double-page spread.

78 For example, coverage of the Eastern front in the "Victory in Europe" section is dominated by German images of retreat from Russia (313–16), then Russian tanks in the ruins of Berlin, and then Russians sitting at the surrender table.

79 To be exact, coverage of more than a decade of hideous Sino-Japanese hostilities has been reduced to four pages and a notation that Chinese troops "managed to tie down a million Japanese." One further page was spared to China-Burma-India, and three more to flying the Hump and building the Burma and Ledo Roads, but the chief emphasis was on Anglo-American efforts and their extraordinarily troubled working relationships with the Chinese regime.

80 The Churchill-Luce publication relationship itself proves worthy of comment as a production account. In his magazines Luce had basically become Churchill's American house organ, his favorite publisher and source of postwar publicity and celebrity. *Life* printed Churchill's previously secret parliamentary speeches from wartime, for instance, and also his *History of the English-Speaking Peoples*. Churchill enjoyed the income; Luce cherished the prestige and reveled in his intimacy with the great man.

81 The initial chapter was introduced by a painting of assembled delegates at the Versailles conference. Another color plate impressively captured Eisenhower and Montgomery aboard an armored vehicle. Original art included impressionistic renderings, the first, by a Polish survivor, of the martyrdom of the Warsaw ghetto, and the second, by an American combat artist, of a Japanese corpse moldering on the jungle floor.

82 The 1967–72 *National Union Catalogue* lists more than 120 entries for such Luce-inspired volumes — "the big acts," he called them (Elson 418) — on a virtually inexhaustible range of topics.

83 One should also mention that these in turn clearly became the model for a twenty-three-volume series on Vietnam — virtually identical in design, text, and format — published by Boston House between 1981 and 1987.

84 The role of the fledgling network NBC will receive considerable attention in the production account that follows. As to the participatory enthusiasm of the service in question, the U.S. Navy, Boettcher details vividly the desperation of navy officials at seeing their 151-year role as the nation's preeminent military arm usurped in the late '40s by the eighteen-month-old air force. Even *Reader's Digest*, according to Boettcher, had suddenly become an enemy, running a series of pro–air force articles by William Bradford Huie that seemed to have been timed to influence FY 1950 defense-budget negotiations (168).

85 As a model of early television's frequent promotional emphasis on "live" presentation as a distinguishing feature, this also became the program on which, with great ceremony, the first totally simultaneous coast-to-coast hookup was achieved.

86 For this important insight, the salience of which has been obscured by time, see the sections on early television, for instance, in Goulden's *The Best Years*.

87 On the other hand, at some point here one must also confront the issue of this same artifact's essentially sui generis status as far as ensuing large-scale attempts to depict

World War II on TV would be concerned: the issue, as noted earlier, that aside from movie reruns and other documentary re-creations devised essentially on the *Victory at Sea* model, the Big War seems to have proved unusually resistant to transfer to the small screen. Only a handful of dramatic efforts, for instance, including series such as *Combat* and *Twelve O'Clock High* or the occasional miniepic, call themselves to memory as having attracted substantial viewing interest, with the only long-running successes, ironically, being in the situation-comedy format: namely, *Hogan's Heroes* and *McHale's Navy*. And, as also suggested, one might probably ascribe the latter more to audience enthusiasm for genre than to subject matter: these are not shows about World War II but basic situation comedies, with a humor-in-the-service orientation, the first set in a World War II POW camp with some strutting costume-drama Germans occasionally in charge, and the second on a World War II Pacific island with some diminutive Japanese foes stumbling in and out as needed. At the same time, however, such caricatures certainly continued to sell vividly in more serious renderings on the big screen. For a slightly more detailed inventory of television offerings, see Barnouw, *Tube of Plenty* 374–75.

Why could World War II not accommodate itself to TV or vice versa? One simply wonders finally if the unique capacity to mediate between viewing scales was not really just the feature capitalized upon by *Victory at Sea* for its multiple successes. For war-era and immediate postwar audiences conditioned to large-screen information and entertainment, that is, *Victory at Sea* may have made a move to the small screen, but it also kept the documentary format and the standard package of wartime and immediate postwar atmospherics — film technique, narration, music. Hence, although in a new "medium," the war continued to seem remarkably wedded to the media that had rendered it familiar — the news photograph, the movie, the picture magazine, the popular book. As noted above, the initial "event" itself reinforced then all these impressions by its capitalization on the early sense of TV as a "live" medium. But at the same time, once beyond the special showings, the series could also turn around and capitalize on the virtues of segmentation, specifically of the thirteen-hour, twenty-six-installment plan's lending itself to the half-hour format that was already proving the standard for soap operas, sitcoms, and entertainment and information programming.

88 This is confirmed by a number of accounts. For one giving an inside view from NBC, see Weaver 241.

89 Salomon also repaid the trouble. Listed as naval advisor was Captain Walter Karig, primary writer on the six-volume *Battle Report* series and Morison's bitter rival, whose own history project was seen as amateur-academic competition, and who in the Morison opus, which ran ultimately to fourteen volumes of text and a fifteenth for index, had rated a footnote in volume 3. Further, Salomon surely must have reaped creative benefit from the active participation of Karig, an imaginative writer by temperament and achievement, who is remembered far less today for *Battle Report* than for more than twenty children's books and works of popular fiction in which he clearly recognized a popular audience and successfully grasped what kind of story line would appeal to them. See Pfitzer, *Morison's Historical World* 238–39.

90 In Rodgers's version, recorded in his autobiography, Weaver, identified as a "contact," described *Victory at Sea* to him initially in somewhat cloak-and-dagger terms as a navy

project, with the atmospherics of it all suggesting recruitment to some desperate paramilitary enterprise. The cryptic initial "message" he remembered running as follows: "'If you were approached to do some work for the United States Navy,' said Weaver, 'we'd like your assurance that you wouldn't refuse to consider it.'" "'Well, of course,'" replied the somewhat puzzled composer, imagining himself perhaps Emile Debecque–like in a crisis of civilian honor, "'I wouldn't refuse to consider any offer from the United States Navy.'"

Rodgers went on: "His curiously negative question, it turned out, was simply a matter of protocol. The Navy had approached NBC with the idea of presenting a television documentary series about its exploits during World War II, but before a definite offer could be made I had to give my assurance in advance that I would at least consider composing the score. One simply does not say no to the United States Navy — not out of hand, anyway" (248).

Thus, through what appears to have been Weaver's expert sandbagging, was revealed the mission. And thus was the mission also accepted, with the further patriotic stipulation by Rodgers that his work at least on the original project be not-for-profit. For Weaver's version, see also his memoir (241).

91 To judge this impact, a viewer of the era might have noted the appearance in short order of a new documentary series entitled *Air Power*, featuring Walter Cronkite, which seemed to promote a competing view of victory from the standpoint of the newly formed U.S. Air Force. (The army, as usual, had to settle for a poor third with *The Big Picture*, a syndicated public-information newsreel.)

92 It is hard to know where to begin to catalog the disappointments. On the world stage, any cheer of victory was quickly replaced by the Cold War, with faceoffs in Greece and Eastern Europe, the Berlin Blockade, the fall of China to the Communists, and full-fledged combat in Korea — and with all of this, of course, also presided over by the growing specter of final nuclear Armageddon.

At home, problems of conversion to peacetime governance and economic policy, if not sufficiently complicated by such geopolitical atmospherics, were further exacerbated by interservice rivalries and McCarthyite witch-hunting. The Arsenal of Democracy, plunged into intense military debate over defense appropriations and management policy, worried out its new strategic image amid a never-ending train of conspiracy theories, global exportation and subversion theories, containment theories, domino theories, deterrence theories, and massive-retaliation theories. In a post–Cold War world such a psychology of reception, one should hope, will prove increasingly easy for Americans to forget. On the other hand, it surely played a crucial role at the time in creating viewer response to *Victory at Sea* as a welcome reaffirmation of the grand American and Allied effort that seemed so recently crowned with worthy success.

93 The prophecy would be realized in any number of ways, some immediate and some long-term. At NBC itself, Salomon and many members of his production group moved on to the *Project XX* series, which would set the standard for television special-project documentary and put in motion patterns of similar development at the other major networks. And eventually public television, of course, would make a specialty of the documentary information-entertainment-education model, with the latter also

given further new commercial life in the age of cable, on a host of special-interest channels including Arts and Entertainment, Discovery, Nature, and History.

94 The *Time* and *Newsweek* issues were both dated November 10, 1952. The anonymous *New Yorker* column appeared on April 4, 1953, and the DeVoto assessment in the *Harper's* issue of June 1954. Further, *Victory at Sea* has continued to be so treated in historical studies. A. William Bluem, for instance, in his standard history of American TV documentary, pronounces on the groundbreaking aesthetics of an essentially new form. Without sacrificing overall effect, within each of the twenty-six segments, he observes, a "major subject was given a specific point of view around which a thematic episode could be constructed" and sustained through film, words, and music. As to sustained dramatic interest, this was likewise provided internally by a maintaining of "the distinction between the journalistic point of view and the artist's expression of theme" (147).

95 With prime later venues including, of all places, Japan, where it enjoyed a tremendous run in the late '60s.

96 The most visible of these, of course, was *Life's Picture History of World War II*, which had been followed, also in 1959, as it turns out, by a two-volume set incorporating new photo essays and text by Winston Churchill. And comparable texts availed themselves of the archives of such quasi-official wartime organs as *Yank* and *Stars and Stripes*. We may now look back at these and contemporary analogs, perhaps, as the dying gasp of photojournalism as immortalized by the great popular magazines of midcentury. On the other hand, we should also recognize again their popularity as a function of the degree to which, aside from words, classic photojournalism and newsreel production remained entrenched in people's minds as their primary means of having *seen* the war's events represented to them at the time.

97 The first, perhaps still the most familiar for those who recall the albums, printed the blow-up of a famous photograph of the carrier *Bunker Hill* in the moment of being struck by kamikaze. The movie footage had appeared in the documentary. The still had been featured in the print volume (Salomon 245). The second and third opted for vivid, impressionistic combat scenes, reminiscent of the war art of such familiar figures as Tom Lea, Jon Whitcomb, and others. Eventually the first, in new editions, recast the original photograph in an illustration style consonant with the other two jackets.

98 The jacket copy of the first volume, a standard single, for instance, began with an essay on the genesis of the project by Henry Salomon. Along the way it also managed to get in admiring commentary from *Variety* and the *New Yorker*, a specific outline of Rodgers's and Bennett's achievements, and a quote from the Peabody Award citation for series at large. On the record itself appeared new, dramatic titles with which major musical motifs and melodies came to be identified: "The Song of the High Seas," "The Pacific Boils Over," "Guadalcanal March," "D-Day," "Hard Work and Horseplay," "Theme of the Fast Carriers," "Beneath the Southern Cross," "Mare Nostrum," "Victory at Sea."

Accordingly, the second record package, enlarging on the documentary function, presents itself literally as an album, in this case a folio volume. Again, jacket text rehearsed the overall history of the project, with emphasis on Salomon's alleged recruitment of Rodgers and Rodgers's ensuing happy decision to forge a collaboration with Bennett. It then turned to matters of production continuity as well. "The present selection of themes and melodies," it claimed as "a natural sequel to the first, which it supplements without repeating. And these, duly, are then named and discussed in a sidebar — "Fire on the Waters," "Danger Down Deep" (noted as a variation of "The Song of the High Seas"), "Mediterranean Music," "The Magnetic North," "Allies on the March," "Voyage into Fate," "Peleliu," and "The Sound of Victory" — with notes credited to Richard Hanser, billed as "Co-Author of the script of 'Victory at Sea.'" Further, on the inside, the musical programming so described was also complemented with the thrill of new technologies, of sound-effect segments, strategically interspersed, creating for a given passage the appropriate documentary atmospherics. From the teeming jungle to the stormy North Atlantic, one could now hear also monkeys, screeching birds, telegraph keys, thunderous naval bombardments, signals vanishing into the winds and the silences of the cold magnetic north.

The third album, in turn, basically cycled the rest of the way through the logic of the evolutionary spinoff. Billed as a pictorial edition, in production format, it became an album *cum* narrative photodocumentary, with hard covers and actual bound pages, capturing again in text and classic photographs the feel of all the earlier artifacts. Tribute to Salomon was rendered, for instance, by the reprinting of a condensed version of the essay written for the first recording. Yet another essay then followed, by Hanser on the project's historical and aesthetic genealogy, and a new one by Bennett, identified here as conductor of the *Victory at Sea* orchestra, on musical evolutions. Accordingly, the text itself became a total package, with narrative copy, photo essays, and record tracks all integrated into a new set of motifs created by the latest efforts at dramatic retitling: "Rings Around Rabaul," "Full Fathom Five," "The Turkey Shoot," "Ships That Pass," "Two If by Sea," "The Turning Point" — and finally, in grand summation, "Symphonic Scenario (The Melodic Story)." But again, one had only to look at the cover to see that now there was even more. For blazoned beneath the title, with illustration, new notes also proclaimed this latest production model to feature "Sounds of firing of 16-inch and 8-inch guns from U.S. battleships and heavy cruisers — anti-aircraft guns and naval combat planes of World War II — submarine crash dives / and underwater torpedo launchings — produced with the cooperation of the U.S. Navy."

In sum, amid a musical fad among high-fidelity and stereo devotees for doing things like the "1812 Overture" with actual cannons, muskets, and chimes, and so forth, or recording drag racers and jet airplanes, volume 3 truly did it all. One at last could not easily tell if one was buying a coffee-table book or a glorified sound-effects record.

99 And here, especially, one may find a fitting last technological chapter in the genealogy of the artifact as defined by both its unfolding modes of production and its evolving contexts of consumption and reception. For televisions, of course, after all these years, can finally be bought with speaker systems characteristic of state-of-the-art high-fidelity and stereo equipment. To put this simply, in the particular case of *Victory at Sea*, the sound-reproduction technology has caught up with the quality of the music. One hopes Morison would have been horrified. Salomon, Rodgers, Bennett, Sarnoff,

and company, on the other hand, would surely have been pleased at the most recent commodification of the forms of American remembering they had wrought.

100 One might date a 1985 *American Heritage* survey by Geoffrey C. Ward of video editions of *Victory at Sea, The March of Time,* and *The World at War* as having caught the beginning of the buildup. But nothing might have prepared one for the array of fiftieth-anniversary articles in magazines and newspapers, wherein the title *Victory at Sea* has surely been invoked by at least one local journalist in every city in America as a particular lead-in on the sources of recollection.

101 In concluding retrospect, one might further note that the titles do represent a scrupulous and comprehensive historical collage. The Battle of the Atlantic, the Pacific, submarines, the Mediterranean, North Africa, South America, the North Atlantic, the Italian campaign, D-Day, Southeast Asia, the army, and the marines in the Pacific all get fairly equal time — although there seems pointedly nothing of the air force or the Russians. Numerically, the Pacific predominates with fifteen segments. The rest are distributed regionally, including the Atlantic, Mediterranean, South America, North Africa, Italy, and Europe. The dramatic arrangement is roughly chronological, although the division according to theater of war causes some going back or jumping ahead. The third-from-last section, "Road to Mandalay," for instance, placed after European surrender and Iwo Jima, must return to much earlier Japanese conquests in China and Southeast Asia before moving concluding installments on Okinawa and the kamikazes, and then the atomic bombing of Hiroshima and the aftermath of war.

CHAPTER 3: BIG WAR, BIG BOOK, BIG MOVIE

1 All of these novels proved to be major best-sellers, with combined hardbound and paperback sales in the millions. According to the standard Bowker survey, *The Naked and the Dead* ranked as the number two best-seller of 1948 and *The Young Lions* in the same year as number eight. Both were picked up by the New American Library in paperback, with Mailer's garnering the then-impressive sum of thirty-five thousand dollars. In 1951 *From Here to Eternity* and *The Caine Mutiny* rode the lists in an analogous configuration. *From Here to Eternity,* after becoming a Book-of-the-Month Club selection, also went under contract with New American Library for one hundred thousand dollars, a figure invariably cited as eclipsing Mailer's previous record. Then, in 1953, it went *back* on the list as a result of the movie. *The Caine Mutiny*'s appearance in a *Reader's Digest* condensed version led to pickups by the Book-of-the-Month Club and the Literary Guild. A facsimile paperback, with original jacket art, proved a steady seller. In 1953 *Battle Cry* enjoyed large sales in hardbound and then found corresponding success by working one of the first big movie tie-ins for paperback promotion (Bonn, *Heavy Traffic* 155).

Further, although Book-of-the-Month Club and Literary Guild adoptions are cited here in the context of commercial success, one should remember that during much of the period involved — especially the late '40s and early '50s — such a selection also endowed a work with a certain literary cachet. Books listed were presumed chosen for special excellence by a "selection committee," a board of "experts" including various well-known critics and literary intellectuals.

2 Individual essays will reveal the general susceptibility of filmmakers to political pressures of the era, with a tendency to downplay ideological critique and to minimize unfavorable depictions of the military services. For those versed in the political reputations of individual directors, the roster given here should already help bear out the point. Walsh was a favorite guts-and-glory military film director, having endeared himself to the marines, especially, after making the original *What Price Glory?* (Suid 24–25); and as noted by Stephen Whitfield, Dymytrk made his return to directing, in the two films cited, as one of the first emeriti of the Hollywood Ten, having achieved resuscitation by recanting earlier Communist beliefs and testifying voluntarily before the House Un-American Activities Committee (62). Only Zinnemann in *From Here to Eternity* seems to have cared much about being faithful to the spirit of the novelist's obvious love-hate relationship with the army. Some of the final script, although credited to Daniel Taradash, is also alleged to have been written by the famous blacklist figure Dalton Trumbo.

3 Actually, Mailer's *The Naked and the Dead* and Shaw's *The Young Lions* appeared almost simultaneously, albeit with Shaw by his own admission racing to finish his novel in time to compete with Mailer's, which had been the season's hottest item of literary gossip. Shaw, on the other hand, had been seeing his own work heavily touted in advance as *the* first big panoramic novel to come out of the war.

Neither figure had grounds for worry about the competition. Both novels were eagerly devoured, partly, one must believe, because they seemed so different in subject and method. Mailer's was a closely focused treatment of the jungle war in the Pacific — he was in fact said to have enlisted for the Pacific because he feared that the European war was already used up. Shaw's was a panoramic depiction of the war in North Africa and Europe, employing characters on both the Allied and Axis sides. As a GI work, much of Mailer's was devoted to profane banter and bloody combat. Shaw's, in contrast, interwove the drama of the war into a larger social tapestry of more conventional novelistic appeal, love, romance, marriage, social themes.

4 During the same years, it should be noted, two established senior figures also weighed in with "big" World War II productions, James Gould Cozzens in 1948 with *Guard of Honor* and Ernest Hemingway in 1950 with *Across the River and into the Trees*. The first quickly achieved considerable literary reputation, winning the 1948 Pulitzer Prize and continuing to be cited to this day as a neglected postwar classic. The second, on the other hand, revealed a truly great writer slipping into ridiculous mannerism and even self-parody — object evidence, if anything, that this war was going to require its own new generation of writers.

In Hemingway's case, one should add, artistic failure was also attended by a jealousy toward younger competitors that often proved virulent even by Hemingway standards. He called Mailer's *The Naked and the Dead* "poor cheese, pretentiously wrapped" (Baker 495). He scorned Jones as a combat-exhaustion case and wrote of his book, "I do not have to eat an entire bowl of scabs to know they are scabs; nor suck a boil to know it is a boil; nor swim through a river of snot to know it is snot. I hope he kills himself as soon as it does not damage your or his sales. If you give him a literary tea you might ask him to drain a bucket of snot and then suck the puss out of a dead nigger's ear" (MacShane 192). And although Mailer thought he was the target, Shaw was probably the rival Hemingway had in mind when he described to Lillian Ross "young writers from Brooklyn who think they're Tolstoy" (Shnayerson 171–72). As will be seen, in the latter case there was also Hemingway's personal jealousy of Shaw as one of Mary Welsh Hemingway's former lovers.

5 The phrase serves as the apt title of a military history of American conflicts by Geoffrey Perret.

6 To be sure, the advent of the Cold War would quickly dampen postwar happiness and optimism; but, as Engelhardt points out, even here a not infrequent or incurious response would be to seek out and enjoy representations of anti-Axis victory as a way of not having to face new Communist and possibly nuclear threat. Thus may be explained the strange cultural rhythm of what Engelhardt calls Triumphalist Despair: a concentration on remembering the victorious effort of the last war, World War II, as a way of not having to think about the next war, World War III. Further, even granting the critical function accorded the literary intelligentsia, popular sentiment was hardly about to abandon belief in the basic validity and worth of a geopolitical enterprise that had gone on so long and cost so much.

7 Part of Mailer's strategy, obviously, was backward-looking, as he sought specifically to inherit the mantle of Hemingway in the role of the novelist as culture hero and media celebrity. At the same time, in a distinctly post-1945 key, the real Mailer genius would lie in a capacity to invent Norman Mailer the literary genius as he went, making himself the creation of a whole sequence of rapidly evolving media: the new journalism; the new fiction; the self-advertising manifesto; the nonfiction novel; the careful cultivation in life, as in art, of the pose of media "personality."

8 To be precise, Mailer would return the favor of being talked up in Aldridge's influential 1958 critical study by writing an admiring preface for a 1985 paperback reissue.

9 As might be expected, Mailer's version of the story, on the other hand, emphasized a political epiphany undergone while writing, still in his senior year at Harvard, a war novella entitled "A Calculus at Heaven," for Robert Hillyer's English A5 class. He explained in *Advertisements for Myself*: "Although he assumed the great novel of the war would be set in Europe, he felt he had no choice but to focus on the Pacific theater: Americans were already at war there, and his 'progressive-liberal' bias led him to ferreting out the 'reactionary overtone' of the Asian fighting. Besides, he had far too little experience to handle 'the culture of Europe and the collision of America upon it' " (10).

10 By military regulations of the time, diary keeping itself was considered an intelligence risk, because the text might fall into enemy hands.

11 The reference is obviously to the crucial scene in *The Naked and the Dead* where the idealistic lieutenant, Hearn, makes his final break with the fascist general, Cummings, whom he has served as aide, initiating his fatal transfer to leadership of the dangerous I&R platoon. And it has all been over a cigarette butt, which Hearn, in an almost perversely adolescent act of defiance, has crushed out on Cummings's tent floor, and which Cummings now forces him to pick up. "I never thought I would crawfish to him," Hearn thinks to himself. "That was the shock," the narrator goes on, "that was the thing so awful to realize" (327).

12 Even today, it is hard to dispute the characterization of the novel as a truly well engineered book, which despite its length and discursive burden seems compact, even
small. The platoon story is well integrated into the early Hearn-Cummings material;
and the Hearn-Cummings material is well integrated into the platoon–long patrol
story, which develops, now centered on Hearn, after the crisis of authority between
the general and his aide. Hearn is then transferred more or less randomly by Cummings until he arrives at I&R. Meanwhile, he thinks the arrival is a coup on his part.
This brings the drama down to the originally intended small-unit focus.

 As to overarching structure, the book is similarly taut. Four parts, entitled "Wave,"
"Argil and Mold," "Plant and Phantom," and "Wake," define the campaign. They
move from the initial amphibious assault, the early attacks and counterattacks, down
through the platoon death-mission. As a consequence of the Hearn-Cummings plot,
the patrol is strengthened through its long foregrounding to become, with the intellectual focus on Hearn, a true existential quest, the journey into the interior darkness
of our times. And this is true despite the fact that its depiction in section 3 of the novel,
"Plant and Phantom" (entitled after the epigraph from Nietzsche), does not even begin until page 433. Meanwhile, "Time Machine" sections in the vein of Dos Passos's
early experimentalism intersperse the histories of ten more or less major characters.
These are further filled in here and there by interior monologues, conversations,
reflections, thoughts while reading or writing letters or journals, even choruses that
strike one as somewhere between *Moby-Dick* and *South Pacific*.

 There is even an economical geography, provided by the apparatus of map and
3-D topographic illustration. One always knows where everyone is: the invasion beach
and the Toyaku line; Mount Anaka and the Watamai Range, with the pass separating
them; Botoi Bay, where the battle is to be won with an Anzio/Inchon-style amphibious landing in the enemy's rear. Indeed, only with this training aid does one grasp the
full irony of the incredible, nearly bloodless overland victory that is literally blundered
into by Dalleson, the incompetent division operations officer during Cummings's
one absence from command. Perhaps Dalleson does have the right idea at the end: a
pinup poster of Betty Grable — onto which grid coordinates have been superim-
posed — as a visual aid for map-reading classes.
13 At one point, Cummings actually quotes the great fascist prophet in his journal (570).
14 At the same time, one should also invoke Alfred Kazin's more obvious notes about actual wartime experience in relation to issues of power and command. Cummings's appearance as a commander-fascist prototype was in many ways "typical of World War II
novels produced after the war — Mailer's was a generation that had gone to war rec-
ognizing it as part of the same crisis that produced Hitler" (72). On the other hand, issues of potency and aggression were hardly unambiguous for anyone involved. As
Kazin points out, even "the war of the drafted, miserable G.I." was "still the one 'big'
experience that the common man will have in his life" (77).
15 In fact, as is characteristic of other Jewish novelists in the genre such as Shaw and
Wouk, Mailer seems at pains not to make Jewish characters mouthpieces for leftist
ideology. Here, for instance, the only two Jewish characters depicted at any length
in the book, Roth and Goldstein, might be best described on one hand as suffering, alienated, and mournful, and on the other as suffering, alienated, and doggedly

upbeat. To be sure, both of them are in agreement that the world as we know it — the war and everything else, is in the hands of the *anti-Semiten* (it is Goldstein's assertion). Yet neither of them is radical in any respect. Rather, both seem to be products of Jewish culture aspiring to the American dream. Roth is college-educated and quasi-intellectual; Goldstein is still a believer in middle-class aspiration.

While Shaw, Wouk, and Uris, in contrast, have heroic Jewish figures, Wouk's lawyer Barney Greenwald is the only intellectual antifascist given a high rhetorical profile. Shaw's Noah Ackerman bravely fights army anti-Semitism, but this is also in a novel where a credible Wehrmacht hero — and an Austrian one at that — also becomes anti-Nazi. As for Uris's Two Gun Max Shapiro, the name speaks for itself.

16 In a nice touch that says as much about Mailer's liberal intellectual protagonist as about the author of *Moby-Dick,* Hearn's magna cum laude Harvard thesis has been entitled "A Study of the Comic Urge in Herman Melville" (345).

17 According to Mills, "three months before the novel's publication on May 8, 1948, reproductions of the line drawing on the book's jacket were strategically placed in bookstores and in advertisements with no mention of the book's title or the author's name and with no advertising copy whatsoever. The pen-and-ink drawing was of a soldier's face shot through with bullet holes, and as the publication date neared, the picture increased in size in successive stages" (99). Also, five hundred advance paperback editions were sent out to key figures (99); numbers of these were even sent to salesmen for other companies, just so they could talk about the book (100). It was also an unusually expensive hardback at four dollars; still, ten thousand copies were confidently sent out to bookstores (100).

18 According to Bea, Goldwyn offered Mailer five thousand dollars just to quit (Mills 119).

19 Or, as Mailer put it in longer version, "You see, after *The Naked and the Dead,* I thought I would ideally write huge collective novels about American life. One about a labor union, one about a small or medium midwestern town. But I discovered that I knew nothing about labor unions and nothing about midwestern towns and I had no characters left. I had used them all up in *The Naked and the Dead*" (Mills 115).

20 In fact, "Harold almost kissed his feet, because it was a lot of money," Knox recalls (Mills 122). And it was. The figure in question was twenty thousand dollars.

21 According to Knox, Mailer and Laughton actually "had a lot of conversations and felt they were on the right track, but whatever the problems, they couldn't solve them" (Manso 155).

22 Actually, as will be seen with *The Young Lions* or *The Victors,* the use of such garish color could be undercut by comparative implication in presumably more "authentic" films using a sober, documentary-style black and white.

23 *Maidstone,* the author's early '70s foray, with all the usual Mailer hoopla, into the domain of the great American film, has been forgotten by nearly everyone save those who forced themselves to sit through it. In the stupid, pretentious, and egregiously-boring-flop category, one might charitably describe it as the movie equivalent of *Barbary Shore.*

24 Both experiences became vital material for the Michael Whiteacre plot line in *The Young Lions.* Whiteacre, along with a Jeep-load of other Civil Affairs support troops following the progress of the U.S. forces liberating France, gets involved in a shootout

with a car full of fleeing Germans. Shortly, he also finds himself drunk and celebratory with everyone else in Paris. Here he has to undergo the boozy pontificating of Ahearn, the self-important correspondent clearly modeled on Ernest Hemingway. (To add deep psychosexual injury to insult in this case, Hemingway was already launched on decades of having to live with the fact that Shaw and Mary Welsh had already been lovers.) Also, during an artillery attack, Whiteacre's leg is broken by a speeding car that kills his patron, Colonel Pavone. This injury will result in his being hospitalized and sent to a replacement camp where he is reunited with Noah Ackerman, his comrade from boot camp. The two in turn will make their way to the old infantry unit, fighting in Bavaria, where, outside a liberated concentration camp, they will encounter Christian Diestl, the novel's third protagonist. In a pointless shootout, Diestl will kill Ackerman, and Whiteacre will hunt down and kill Diestl.

25 Indeed, an initial plan, outlined by Shaw in a *Paris Review* interview, included even more ambitiously a fourth feature in the arrangement, the manufacturing history of the bullet eventually fired in the Black Forest by Whiteacre to kill Diestl. According to Shaw, this scenario would have run the whole industrial-strength gamut: mining, smelting, manufacturing, transporting, and so on.

One can only conclude with relief that Shaw decided to leave well enough alone. The first absurd association that comes to mind here is the backward-running bomber movie concocted by Vonnegut in *Slaughterhouse Five*, where the bombs wind up getting disassembled at the end and planted back into the ground as raw materials (71–72).

26 Especially crucial here is his political cynicism. He admits, much in the spirit of the old Italian collaborator who lectures Nately in *Catch-22*, to going basically with the favoring wind. "Until last year," he confesses flippantly, "I was a Communist." But now he is prepared to be a Nazi, even if the business with the Jews is "an unlucky accident," perhaps "ridiculous." "A little injustice for a large justice. It is the one thing the Comrades have taught Europe," he concludes; "the end justifies the means" (19). Ironically, his Communist flirtation, on the other hand, recorded in a Gestapo file, will also preclude his being selected for officer training, just as, in a further novelistic connection, Michael Whiteacre's support of a socialist organization involved in the Spanish Civil War, duly recorded by the FBI, will have a similar result.

27 Most notably, again, John Aldridge, but also Peter Jones.

28 To give one simple example of what a novel can do with the carefully rendered particular in ways that film, for all its visual advantages, frequently cannot, one might consider the scene *recalled* here as depicted in the novel. Back in the Libyan desert war, the young sergeant notes that Hardenburg, his commander, is humming pleasantly while he waits for just the right time to launch an attack on a much larger but unsuspecting British unit going about their morning wake-up rituals — shaving, washing, urinating, defecating — as if he takes perverse pleasure in trying to catch the largest possible number of them, especially officers, quite literally with their pants down. All the while he waits, he hums to himself, quietly, incongruously, hums the way a person does perhaps while shelling peas or building a model ship. In fact, when the attack begins, he seems to have given the order almost unnoticed, strictly on his own time and no one else's. It is all quite mad in its way, and in the film, to be sure,

Maximilian Schell as Hardenburg gets it as nearly right as he can. On the other hand, if it transfers to film most strikingly, still it is diminished, because the film version, unlike the book, *cannot take enough time to do it all*, cannot draw it out sufficiently, can only render it as too symbolic and compressed. Further, as is characteristic of classic film of the era, in which actors become identified with roles played in movie versions of books (and in some cases, with Montgomery Clift, Henry Fonda, and others, working multiple variants on analogous roles), the feature-player or star quality of the acting actually leaves little to the imagination. Hardenburg is Schell as, in even more pronounced ways, Diestl is Brando, Whiteacre is Martin, and Ackerman is Clift.

29 The most troubling problem with the latter is the real plausibility of his motivation to wind up, as he must, getting himself into service as a front-line infantry private. On the other hand, there was the literary appeal, especially for readers who were veterans with comparable experiences, of what Heggen had mined as the Roberts syndrome. These figures responded to the need to prove to themselves — and in a way thus vicariously fulfilled the needs of countless other veterans *like* themselves — that they *could* have done it if they had gotten the chance or had been somehow cast into a position where they were required to do so.

30 Modestly, one settles later for minor just deserts: he proves a coward on the Normandy Invasion beach, cracking up when he gets his company surrounded.

31 At the same time, even here, as with Mailer and Wouk, both Jews addressing American institutional anti-Semitism, there is still the tendency to divide the problematic liberal-radical consciousness into Janus-facing WASP and Jewish versions: Hearn versus Roth and Goldstein; Whiteacre versus Ackerman; Willie Keith versus Barney Greenwald. One suspects, simply, that all three writers realized the same thing: that the mainstream novel was not ready for a Jewish liberal intellectual protagonist; or that if such a protagonist was heavily spotlighted, the text would be classified as a "Jewish" novel. Further, the latter, of course, would also have had special political consequences during the Red-baiting late '40s and early '50s.

32 In a 1956 letter Weybright added further information about the ongoing success of the books: both were selling at "beyond the million mark" (Bonn, *Heavy Traffic* 174). Of Mailer's novel, he also noted that "despite our sale of over a million and a half copies of *The Naked and the Dead*, Rinehart sales" also "rose when we released our imprint" — with sales for both companies profiting further, moreover, from the NAL opening of the Canadian market after the breaking down of censorship (174). Finally, in a telling instance of how centered the production processes of the World War II classic often turned out to be, Weybright also boasted in the same letter about the issuing of *From Here to Eternity* as a newer seventy-five-cent Signet triple. The latter, in conjunction with publicity about the Columbia picture, went on to sell three million (174).

33 He had also found controversy at home over a new novel, *The Troubled Air*, involving McCarthyite hysteria in the radio industry (Giles 6). Thanks to the intervention of David Selznick, Shaw avoided the blacklist. Still, in 1951, he began a twenty-five-year residence in Europe. There he also formed a lifelong friendship with a fellow expatriate, James Jones, the author of *From Here to Eternity*.

34 Ironically, this took place as Shaw was deciding to withdraw from a screenplay of *War and Peace*, a project he had joined at Henry Fonda's insistence, after finding that King

Vidor, the director, had inserted scenes by his wife, a devout Christian Scientist, which he felt improved on those of Shaw *and* Tolstoy (Shnayerson 239).

35 Bosley Crowther reserved special scorn for Dean Martin's performance as "a Broadway showman pulled into the army against his will as if he was lonesome for Jerry Lewis and didn't know exactly what to do" (Shnayerson 261).

36 *From Here to Eternity* was heavily invoked, for instance, in the marketing of Jones's second novel, *Some Came Running*, a sprawling book about postwar drifters attempting to accommodate themselves to middle American life; of his later novel about actual combat in the Pacific war, *The Thin Red Line;* and of an illustrated volume of wartime art, *WWII.* The last and most elaborate of such promotions would come in 1975 with the posthumous publication of *Whistle*, an almost-completed novel touted as the concluding volume in a World War II trilogy containing *From Here to Eternity* and *The Thin Red Line.* A uniform-edition book-club offering would bring substantial sales to all three texts in hardback. Meanwhile, Delacorte, the hardbound publisher of *Whistle*, also reissued in its Dell paperback line an attractive, design-coordinated edition of Jones's major fiction, including such ambitious flops as *Some Came Running* and *Go to the Widow-Maker* and an obscure military novella, itself a spinoff of *From Here to Eternity*, entitled *The Pistol.*

37 As to specific comparisons of Jones's novel with Mailer's, with which it was frequently linked, much was made of Jones's advance in the military profanity department over Mailer's celebrated "fug" compromise. As Frank MacShane points out, the latter had surely been deflated once and for all "by Tallulah Bankhead's remark that, although she liked his book, she was surprised that Mr. Mailer didn't know how to spell *fuck*" (100–101).

38 One must certainly credit Mailer and Shaw with attempting similar contextualizations. Unfortunately, Mailer is forced to compartmentalize ideological matter into intellectual dialogues between Cummings, the elitist general, and Lieutenant Hearn, his socially conscious Harvard-educated aide-de-camp, and Dos Passos–like flashbacks allowing proletarian vignettes of the lives of individual soldiers. Shaw's novel attempts to combine combat action with broad-scale social panorama, but, as with Wouk and Uris to come, one senses that its chief motives lie in the creation of romantic interest and the advancement of conventional plot.

39 For persons alive during the era, an unforgettable measure of notoriety would be the novel's and film's frequent appearance as the subject of popular spoofs, including an insane parody, starring Sid Caesar, Imogene Coca, and Howard Morris, on *Your Show of Shows.* In a staging of the surf scene, every time Caesar and Coca get ready to clinch, an unseen prop man douses them with a bucket of water. When the crucial first encounter occurs at the New Congress Hotel between Prewitt, played by Howard Morris, and the slinky Alma, played memorably by Coca, all he can do is keep blatting out notes on his bugle, which he has inexplicably brought with him.

40 For Jones, hardly a savant of publishing history, it was the Wolfe connection that mattered, since it was on discovering Wolfe in a post library, he felt, that he had first been made aware of his own urge to write.

41 In a sequel no one writing about Jones seems to want to bring up, Perkins's judgment was affirmed when, on the basis of the blockbuster success of *From Here to Eternity*,

Jones tried to resurrect large portions of the abortive draft for his second novel, *Some Came Running*, which received legendarily bad reviews. Critics and biographers remain delicate on the point. See, for instance, the attempt at tactful inversion by Giles and Lennon in their introduction to *The James Jones Reader*. "In fact," they write, "*Laughter* is, to a large degree, an early, less successful version of *Some Came Running*" (366).

42 As to Jones's work at the time or later, it is hard to evaluate Handy's status as a muse or intellectual nurturer. To be sure, there is plenty of evidence about their mutually gratifying sexual alliance, and the bankrolling of it all by her rich, acquiescent husband, even down to travel money and a trailer for Jones. This obviously made it possible for him simply to put down *They Shall Inherit the Laughter* and — in full creative energy, inspiration, and, that evanescent thing, hope — pick up the new army novel once it had Perkins's blessing and write it without impediment, interruption, or even the everyday cares of having a place to eat and sleep. As to literary-intellectual tutelage from Handy, the record must remain more speculative, although during the actual lifespan of the colony, revising and editing seemed to have been part of her self-assigned duties to her struggling artists. From what we know of Handy's own reading habits and philosophical interests, she possibly had something to do with the eclectic strain of Emersonianism inhabiting *From Here to Eternity*. If nothing else, in direct symbolic inspiration, one can note that Handy, like Karen Holmes, had been rendered sterile by an untreated case of gonorrhea given her by her alcoholic husband.

43 As part of the campaign, Jones was actually photographed with the latter.

44 For a good account of the atmosphere of yeasty notoriety, the controversiality of the reception by unhappy popular moralists on one hand and skeptical literary academics on the other, see Garrett (101–2). It was a sure recipe for success on both counts.

45 It is hard to know where to begin enumerating correspondences. Prewitt and Warden, especially, are code heroes in every sense of the term. Karen Holmes and Alma/Lorene likewise seem to have a lost-generation provenance, with the former a direct analog, for instance, to Hemingway's Lady Brett Ashley and the latter to the cynical prostitute, Georgette, whom Jake Barnes whimsically introduces around to a high-toned expatriate crowd as his fiancée. More generally, the world of the novel is itself a domain of gratuitous pain and a sexual wasteland of failed, sterile connections and/or promiscuously barren couplings. Even the military prison is here, as in e.e. cummings's *The Enormous Room*, as world-historical microcosm.

46 For a sympathetic but oversimplified discussion of the novel as a function of '50s mass culture and of Prewitt as an archetype of proletarian desire, see Leslie Fiedler's essay "The Slob as Hero." On the other hand, such contemporary readings also missed a point of the text as a military novel: that is, the stature of Warden. As one of my early readers observed, he is the book's competing hero; as a prewar military professional, that commentator rightly pointed out, Warden is "the man Queeg could have become if he had more balls." And the reader is also correct in identifying the source of Warden's heroism as "the same odd dedication to service that Prewitt emulates." For verification of Jones's admiration of the career NCO in the Warden mold, see also depictions of the analogous Welsh in *The Thin Red Line* and Winch in *Whistle*, who

similarly vie for command of the texts over such younger Prewitt-like counterparts as Witt and Prell.

47 At the same time, one is startled, even at the end, to see how the love plot with its various social and class implications keeps faith with the code of male romance. In an epilogue to the main action, Karen Holmes and Alma/Lorene actually meet on a ship they have boarded for the mainland. Karen, as it turns out, has broken with Warden over his refusal to seek an officer's commission. Alma/Lorene, meanwhile, has concocted an elaborate lie. Her fiancée, she tells Karen, was an air force officer, a bomber pilot, killed at Hickam on December 7 trying to get his plane into the air. For this he received a posthumous Silver Star. The last of an old Virginia military line, he bore the name Robert E. Lee Prewitt (798).

48 In recent obituaries for Fred Zinnemann, the blacklisted screenwriter Dalton Trumbo was credited with the script adaptation. See, for instance, *New York Times*, March 15, 1997, 35. To date, the claim remains unverified in the substantial literature on the making of the film, including Zinnemann's own detailed account.

49 The latter, Zinnemann remembers, was duly accomplished with a cut of four seconds. He also notes that theater projectionists did their own cult snipping of these now unremarkable scenes, and that Hawaiian tour guides for many years used to point out the beach area where the scene was shot (23).

50 According to Zinnemann, who does not identify Ray, Cohn explained his choice as follows: "Because he's under contract here. He hasn't worked in ten weeks, his salary's mounting up. He looks like a boxer, the girls like him. What else do you want to know?" Zinnemann objected strongly, asserting his preference for Montgomery Clift, whom he envisioned immediately by way of the first glimpse Jones gives us of the "deceptively slim young man." The producer had his own opinion of Clift. "He was no soldier and no boxer and probably a homosexual" (21). Cohn, of course, was right about Clift. Zinnemann, however, was right about the role of Prewitt as made for Clift and vice versa. "For many months after the end of filming," he later recalled, "Monty continued to be possessed by his own creation — Private Prewitt. He was quite unable to get out of that character. By his intensity he forced the other actors to come up to his standard of performance" (22).

Further evidence of Clift's involvement was his deep friendship with Jones, despite the latter's dislike for much of what had become of his book in the film. Some of the most poignant pictures of this period in Jones's life include one of his posing back to back, seated on the grass, with Clift, and another of Clift with his arm across the shoulders of Lowney Handy. All this is rendered the more stirring by a comment alleged to have been made by Jones about his willingness to "have an affair" with Clift if the latter had asked (Bosworth 254).

51 The army and the air force, on the other hand, bought the usual supply of prints for their motion picture services.

52 In the case of major Broadway properties of the late '40s and early '50s, one might add, this definition of audience went far beyond actual theatergoers to include a huge secondary constituency eager to read accounts of production, for instance, in newspaper columns or in feature stories from the great information-entertainment magazines.

53 At one point, on a matter of military detail, Fonda — having served as a naval officer for three years before playing Roberts for another five, and about to go on to become Roberts again in the movie — asked Laughton angrily, "What do you know about men, you fat, ugly faggot?" (Callow 227).

54 Differing accounts of the origins of the conflict have become the stock of theater anecdote. By one reckoning, the producer, Gregory, was said to have unwisely contracted Fonda before he had secured official rights to the play and before any coadaptation agreement had been reached by Wouk, and to have offered the actor three choices: either of the feature parts, Queeg or Greenwald, or the chance to direct. Fonda took Greenwald, he said, because he could make more of the part. The problems began to occur with Nolan's increasing visibility, in appearance and mannerism, as almost a picture-perfect Queeg. Rewriting problems with the length of the play meanwhile led to the addition of the party scene as a kind of coda after the court-martial, where even a bravura performance piece allotted to Fonda would be left hanging in the air. In resultant reshaping, cutting, focusing, according to Simon Callow's biography of Laughton, the director and the author worked successfully to fix the problem, although they still had to deal with Fonda's unhappy realization that in the new focus Nolan had been handed a star part. According to Fonda, on the other hand, the upshot of Laughton's and Wouk's rewriting had been to give Greenwald, in the banquet monologue, a scene actually equivalent to Queeg's great moment and to thereby challenge Fonda to the kind of inspired acting that would make it work (Callow 225–27; Fonda and Teichmann 243–44).

55 The importance of that issue could be measured by the comments of Admiral Lewis Parks, the navy's chief of information, who would exercise tremendous influence on the *Caine* proposals about to be offered. "I enjoyed the movie as a dramatic motion picture," he said. "The acting was magnificent. Certainly, *From Here to Eternity* reflects credit on the actors, the writers, the director, and the producer as a dramatic achievement. And it definitely is not as objectionable as the book on which it was based." On the other hand, he concluded, it surely did "not reflect any credit whatever on the Armed Forces of the United States" (Suid 129).

56 A line does seem to have been drawn at hunting up a gale for the typhoon scenes, which were left to studio special effects created by Lawrence W. Butler.

57 According to Spoto's biography of Stanley Kramer, the navy's specific demands — some of them met, some of them renegotiated through various sidesteps — included: (1) omission of *Mutiny* from the title; (2) correction of the idea that the *Caine* under Queeg's predecessor was a sloppily managed ship, whatever its combat effectiveness; (3) the upgrading of the depiction of enlisted crew; (4) in the softening of Queeg's character, the specific adjustment of the portrayal of his cowardice; (5) the recasting of the officers as "ordinary, well-trained, neat, efficient people rather than a bunch of scurvy misfits" (168).

As will be seen, the crucial rewriting focus would involve the derisive soliloquy of Barney Greenwald to the party of officers he has just helped acquit as they drunkenly celebrate the publication of the big first novel of the naval war in the Pacific by the treacherous, cowardly junior officer Tom Keefer, who has basically planted the idea of Queeg's mental incapacitation with his fellows and has later denied so doing while under oath at the ensuing court-martial. In the book and play, one purpose of Greenwald's drunken oration was to pay tribute, by way of mitigating perspective, to steadfast regulars such as Queeg who got used up on thankless duty between the wars and had nothing left when the great crisis actually came. In the movie came Greenwald's further, explicit accusation that a cabal of finicky reservists had simply resorted to old civilian prejudices in essentially turning their backs on Queeg during his solitary descent into madness.

That this may or may not have achieved the palliating effects sought by the navy remains debatable. Even with the beefed-up insistence on the wear-and-tear of Queeg's prewar service (and some allusions about prior antisubmarine service in the Atlantic), the texts aren't all that different. What made the real difference, I will suggest in conclusion, was Bogart's portrayal of Queeg, which made all the issues of combat exhaustion subservient to an inspired pathology that rendered explanations of "cause" largely irrelevant.

58 The most recent acting script bears a 1983 imprint in the Samuel French series. The hardbound printing described came in 1954 from Doubleday, publisher of the novel.

59 On the basis of personal history alone, one might have predicted the similarity between the two works. Both Shaw and Wouk had done their literary apprenticeship in the New York style. Shaw had been a short-story writer and dramatist regarded as having much promise; and Wouk had made some prewar reputation as a social novelist.

60 An explicit signature of this by allusion and gloss is a direct reference to *Billy Budd* on the part of Keefer, the novelist within the novel (268). It also testifies to what must have been the intellectual currency of such a reading. The Melville revival in America had occurred among literary intellectuals from the 1920s onward and had been spurred by rediscovery of *Billy Budd*, Melville's other "lost" classic. Since Professor Raymond Weaver had been among notable scholars participating, the excitement surely must have still been reverberating while Wouk was at Columbia.

61 Surely a more immediate set of contemporary literary connections were also being made with *Mister Roberts* as novel and play. Again, the moral center becomes the citizen-officer — the good guy in the bad situation.

62 As opposed to Melville's narrative, in which both points are left to be determined amid an infinite welter of moral and epistemological ambiguities.

63 *Aurora Dawn*, from Simon and Schuster, sold thirty thousand copies and was also a Book-of-the-Month Club selection. *City Boy*, from the same publisher, sold only six thousand. *The Caine Mutiny* had been written largely on shipboard while Wouk, a former World War II naval officer, still a reservist, served out a 1949 training cruise on the aircraft carrier *Saipan*.

64 According to Miller and Nowak (230), the role, moreover, of the postwar conservative elitist was one that Wouk would continue to cultivate and, in his fiction, to represent.

65 In a gratuitous improbability, he is placed as a native of Albuquerque, New Mexico, where he has specialized in Indian rights cases (350).

66 Particularly in the *novel* entitled *The Caine Mutiny*, this relentless depiction of the officer-novelist as villain must surely be remarked on as a distinguishing feature. The metafictional paralleling is remorseless. On the other hand, one is not sure of any particular end, political or aesthetic. The thoroughly despicable Keefer surely is, as

Greenwald says clearly, the real author of the *Caine* mutiny within the text. He is further, however, the author of a large novel, with literary pretensions astutely blended in with the formulas of best-sellerdom. Willie realizes this when he finally reads it; and Maryk has heard a similar opinion of Keefer's aspirations from a professor at Berkeley. Thus one winds up puzzling over the unappetizing depiction of the literary-popular novelist attempting to write a big navy book about World War II within a big Navy book about World War II.

To be sure, Keefer, like Mailer's Robert Hearn and Shaw's Michael Whiteacre, becomes a figure of the creative intelligentsia in a war that has no room for moral and political skeptics or aesthetic connoisseurs. It is a case of do or die. Thus it is left for Barney Greenwald, with his disfiguring burns suffered in combat and his haunted knowledge of the death camps, to testify to the mendacities and pusillanimities of the American liberal intellectual tradition.

67 This view was shared at the time, it would seem by at least one highly placed naval person, the former chief of naval operations Admiral William M. Fechteler. Upon reading the book, he was said to have remarked, "I wonder how the author collected on one boat all the screwballs I have known in my thirty years in the Navy!" (Spoto 174). And, according to Suid, his personal common-sense attitude toward the text finally proved crucial in breaking an extremely complicated eighteen-month circus of negotiation and counternegotiation between Kramer and various Pentagon and navy representatives (135). These had included Kramer's setting himself at odds with Slade Cutter, chief of the navy's public information office, who had been "ordered 'to drag the Navy's feet, so to speak, as long as possible to delay the inevitable and to get the script cleaned up as much as I could'" (132); and in turn forcing Cutter to negotiate with his initial choice to write the screenplay, Stanley Roberts, whose contempt for the military mind was paired with his association with the group of writers accused of Communist links in the Hollywood Red scares of the late '40s and early '50s (132).

On the other hand, one sees that Cutter knew he was fighting a losing battle once any negotiations were opened, with the market and book-club popularity of the novel, not to mention the prestige and additional attention accrued by the play, making the navy realize that any step short of cooperation in so well-publicized a new development would probably create more public-relations damage than anything the film could do.

Years later, it all seems much a typhoon in a teapot. In 1987, for instance, the Naval Institute Press republished the novel as part of its Classics of Naval Literature series.

68 On the other hand, as will be seen, one reserves the adjective *terminal* for Joseph Heller's *Catch-22*.

69 Details of the coveted paperback deal are provided by Kenneth C. Davis. Bantam Books, a rising new house, offered twenty-five thousand dollars for the text, a bid exactly equal to that of the industry giant, Pocket. What swung things Bantam's way was their preparation of a plan for a paperback tie-in to the movie. This, in turn, instantly became a marketing model for both industries. As Davis points out, in 1955 alone the device would produce no less than three paperback best-sellers, including *Battle Cry*, *Blackboard Jungle*, and *To Hell and Back* (253–54).

70 As noted, both, ironically, having appeared almost simultaneously as novels, would do so again as films in 1958, exactly a decade late. Along the way, Shaw would make a few vain attempts to influence matters of casting and design. Mailer, on the other hand, basically ignored the business as something no longer his to worry about.

71 In emphasizing ease of transmission, one still needs to avoid implying easiness. *Battle Cry* never, for instance, really falls into the beckoning trap of unintentional self-parody as would other novel-based big movies like *Hell Is for Heroes* or, later, *The Green Berets*.

72 Distinguishing between parody and self-parody in the World War II classic always remains a close call. In a number of scenes, culminating in a celebrated forced-march episode noted even by early critics of the novel and film as a major thematic climax, "Huxley's Whores" achieve their ultimate unit bonding. (To make things more complicated, the march itself takes place after they have already been bloodied in combat.) No wonder, then, when parody becomes itself regnant and thematic in something like *Catch-22*, the ultimate winner in the military system will be ex-Lieutenant/soon-to-be Lieutenant-General Scheisskopf — the shithead risen to become the head shit. The reason: he knows how to make men march.

73 In further testimony to Uris's genius for the composite order of cliché at hand, one should note that he is also both the book's and the movie's first-person narrator, introducing himself as a kind of salty Ishmael with stripes and hash marks ("Call me Mac," he improbably begins), but executing a quick fade into the more familiar book-movie role of friendly voice-over.

74 Further, despite the Korean War-era integration of the armed services, this would have remained largely true of both the 1943 and the 1953 marine unit in combat.

75 Indeed, we can't even expunge this quality of male romance out of something that has proven so ripe for horror and/or black-comedy as Vietnam. In large novels — Robert Roth's *Sand in the Wind* or James Webb's *Fields of Fire*; in classic autobiography — Philip Caputo's *A Rumor of War* or Ron Kovic's *Born on the Fourth of July*; in something even as agonized and hideous as Gustav Hasford's macabre fantasia *The Short-Timers*, which became the basis of *Full Metal Jacket*, one senses some kind of bizarre loyalty to the *experience of having been a marine with other marines — of having been IN THE CORPS*.

76 A recent survey of the fiction of the war by Philip Jason reveals an array of texts about army, navy, and air force units in addition to those about marines in combat. And in the popular domain, surely two of the most famous book and film combinations were *The Bridges of Toko-Ri* and *Pork Chop Hill* — the first James Michener's story of a naval aviator and the second S. L. A. Marshall's account of army heroism. On the other hand, given the carefully orchestrated newspaper and magazine legends of marine heroism — not to mention the new photojournalistic immortalization they received in David Douglas Duncan's classic volume *This Is War!*, certainly they claimed the spotlight in popular psychology. In my own experience, for instance, despite seeing the movie of *Battle Cry* several times as a teenager in the 1950s and '60s, I still tended to associate the title, given the circumstances of its appearance, with the marines in the Korean War.

77 One persistently encounters memories of seeing *Sands of Iwo Jima* in Vietnam War narratives, especially those of Marines. See, for instance, Philip Caputo's *A Rumor of War* and Ron Kovic's *Born on the Fourth of July*. Again, art and life declaim their reciprocity. During the early stages of their training, the boot-camp marines in *Battle Cry* are taken to a special inspirational screening of *To the Shores of Tripoli*.

CHAPTER 4: THE GOOD WAR AND THE GREAT SNAFU

1 In the '8os and '9os the mood would shift in turn toward nostalgic reprise: *Swing Shift, For the Boys*, and, most recently, a feelgood remake of *Memphis Belle*.

2 Presumably, in a nice bit of silent self-congratulation, the *Digest* found it unnecessary to remind the faithful that Ryan's great D-Day book — now billed in the lead-in as "the best book ever written on the subject — not just a classic of military history, but a moving, and thrilling, account of men and nations in mortal combat" (181) — had also been first published, before its appearance in hardcover, as part of special *Reader's Digest* D-Day fifteenth-anniversary issues in June and July of 1959.

3 Not that it was alone. Public dedication ceremonies specialized in the rededication of military cemeteries with attendance by heads of state, including the U.S. president. And in the spirit of the great old paratrooper movies, reunions of rapidly dwindling bands of participants included some old paratroopers making a reenactment of their legendary preinvasion jump.

4 Along with reprints of other Ryan favorites including *The Last Battle* and *A Bridge Too Far*, it actually formed part of a multivolume paperbound series.

5 Others so favored included Quentin Reynolds and James Michener. Between 1953 and 1958, roughly the time when Ryan was making a name for himself at *Collier's*, Reynolds had fourteen pieces published in the *Digest* and Michener twenty-two.

6 In the acknowledgments of the book version, Ryan made no secret of the support relationship. He thanked Wallace personally in an early paragraph for lavish funding. And in a long later one, he also outlined his research support network, mentioning "*Reader's Digest* researchers, bureau representatives and editors in the U.S., Canada, Great Britain, France and Germany" and then going on for nearly half a page further about personal indebtednesses within the organization (334). On the other hand, one finds it curious by comparison that in all the promotional copy attending the initial appearance of the text in the *Digest*, no mention was made there of the magazine's massive financial and logistical sponsorship.

7 It is not highlighted, for instance, on any of the standard annual lists from the era. To this degree, surely more accurate is Mel Gussow's description of the book as "a gradual best seller" (218).

8 In fact, the *Digest's* campuslike corporate headquarters was located in Ossining. Wallace got a special exclusion to keep Pleasantville as a postal address.

9 What is startling about both accounts is how they seem totally unaware of the Wallace-Ryan relationship and the *Digest* patronage. The image presented by these film historians, that is, props up that of Ryan as a journalist-historian who, working alone, over nearly a decade, had done a monumental job of documentary inquiry and information collection, who had assembled and assimilated on his own massive amounts of information, who had essentially taken a chance on the salability of his product to a

publisher. See Gussow's account, for instance, of the alleged financial hardships Ryan underwent as he struggled to complete the work (218).

10 According to Gussow, Remarque followed a cursory comment on the script with a bill from his agent for five thousand dollars and was not further heard from, but Gary and Jones agreed to continue without compensation. Again, the Zanuck biographer is only partly correct, at least with regard to Jones. According to the latter and several of his biographers, after being flown in as a script doctor, he was paid outrageously for services rendered in effecting a net change of one line.

11 In a further Dewitt Wallace connection, Norstad was also at the time a great *Reader's Digest* favorite.

12 The logic of simulation must have been something of a sales job, since the actual Normandy landings involved no U.S. Marine assault troops.

13 According to Suid, the precipitating cause was a TV event rather than a movie collaboration, namely, Jack Paar's attempt to capitalize on the Berlin crisis by doing live coverage of Berlin garrison activities — involving actual troop movements. This was denounced as a grave security breach in the Senate. On the other hand, as Suid notices, Zanuck had already made the news in a similar vein through itemization of support activities in a *Time* article of September 8. And nothing was helped when David Brinkley, defending Paar, made explicit comparison of the media engagements. The result — with Defense Department officials bending to renewed congressional scrutiny — was a substantial reduction in Zanuck's reinforcement count from 700 to 250. Meanwhile, according to Suid, Zanuck did manage to get the extra 1,000 French replacements, but also claimed to have paid out an additional thirty thousand dollars for the full cost of a U.S. contingent (156–58).

14 In one source, Gerd Oswald is also named, along with an executive production assistant, Elmo Williams (Garland 131).

15 Hereby, Wayne and Fonda would also relaunch their war-movie careers, so to speak, now playing senior military leaders. Wayne's role would be navy in *In Harm's Way*, but his image would also receive a final, bombastic army update in *The Green Berets*. Fonda would likewise play mainly cameo admirals, but would also show up as a cagy lieutenant colonel of army intelligence in *The Battle of the Bulge*.

16 Particularly attentive to his countrymen's appreciation for instant pop-culture celebrity, Zanuck is reported to have said he wanted audiences to get a recognition bang every time they saw someone famous coming through the door (Ambrose, "The Longest Day" 41).

17 In good *Digest* fashion, the editors zeroed in on Petty as exemplary of the men who came home from combat "steeled for success." "That's where their drive came from," Petty was quoted as saying. "The vets of World War II changed America," he went on. "They made this country what it is today" (217).

18 In terms of a title that caught on, Heller's 1961 novel surely succeeded in this broadest sense of cultural commodification — succeeded, indeed, as have few others, becoming at once a linguistic formula and an ideological commonplace, even a cliché. As a text, on the other hand, it often found itself culturally positioned — "placed" would be the better word — as itself a kind of generic curiosity, a cult piece increasingly of its own time and place, of postwar, Cold War, Korean War, eventually Vietnam War

America. Further, the latter process often seemed to be abetted by Heller's own collusion. See, for instance, the characterizations cited below.

19 The *New York Times Book Review* of October 22, 1961, was characteristic: "'Catch-22' has much passion, comic and fervent, but it gasps for want of craft and sensibility. If 'Catch-22' were intended as a commentary novel, such sideswiping of character and action might be taken care of by thematic control. It fails here because half its incidents are farcical and fantastic." An admiring critic, Norman Brustein, called it "one of the most bitterly funny books in the language" (11). Still, Norman Mailer, while speaking as a competitor, actually had a point when he described *Catch-22* as a novel that "cheats evaluation" — a manic compendium from which "one could take out a hundred pages anywhere from the middle . . . and not even the author could be certain they were gone" (*Cannibals* 117).

20 Their price, as estimated by the editor-in-chief, Donald Fine, was thirty-two or thirty-four thousand dollars.

21 For a detailed, insightful, and entertaining account of various promotion and production activities, see Eller's essay "Catching a Market."

22 Heller made his own version of this point in virtually the same words. "I wrote it during the Korean War," he said, and "aimed for the one after that" (Suid 271).

23 One might remember that Heller, who apparently could not resist a good bureaucracy joke, also puts Wintergreen in charge of the mimeograph machine and has him tell generals that their memos are prolix.

24 For a detailed discussion of popular print culture in its relation to such '60s demographics of production and consumption, see my account in *Scriptures for a Generation* (18–21). For a discussion of *Catch-22* in these contexts, see pp. 4–5.

25 The performance is so persuasive even a frequent rereader of the book has trouble remembering Heller's more overtly demonic Milo with "disunited large eyes, rusty hair, black eyebrows, and an unfortunate reddish-brown mustache" (65).

26 Less remembered but brilliant walk-ons were Susanne Benton as General Dreedle's WAC and Austin Pendleton as his son-in-law, Colonel Moodus.

27 Films are nearly always shot with scenes out of sequence, of course. Here, even this seemed a matter of intrinsic design. For a technical analysis of filming see, for instance, Thezge's article "I See Everything Twice."

28 Among these was also the kind of inspired new scene that, again, only a movie calling attention to a genre of movie could do. At one point, bomber after bomber, engines racing, pulls into position for takeoff. Aircrew after aircrew greets the tower officers with a jaunty thumbs up. Last is Yossarian, as usual, looking disgusted, silently shooting them the bird.

29 A notable collision of art and life involved a visit by John Wayne to the set. The movie hero arrived at the airstrip in a private plane, much in anticipation of a VIP greeting that did not materialize. He thence proceeded to find a local bar, get drunk, poormouth the film, break some glasses, and finish it off by falling down and breaking a couple of ribs (*Newsweek*, March 3, 1969, 55).

30 For a similarly unromantic memoir of infantry combat by a distinguished writer in his later years, see William Kotlowitz's recent *Before Their Time*.

BIBLIOGRAPHY

Adams, Michael C. C. *The Best War Ever.* Baltimore: Johns Hopkins University Press, 1994.

Aldridge, John W. *After the Lost Generation: A Critical Study of the Writers of Two Wars.* New York: McGraw-Hill, 1951. Rev. ed., New York: Arbor House, 1985. (Page citations are to first edition.)

Ambrose, Stephen S. "The Longest Day." In *Past Imperfect: History According to the Movies.* New York: Holt, 1995.

Anderegg, Michael A. *William Wyler.* Boston: Twayne, 1979.

Baker, Carlos. *Ernest Hemingway: A Life Story.* New York: Scribner's, 1969.

Barnouw, Erik T. *The Image Empire: A History of Broadcasting in the United States.* Vol. 3 (from 1953). New York: Oxford University Press, 1970.

——. *Tube of Plenty.* New York: Oxford University Press, 1990.

Basinger, Jeanine. *The World War II Combat Film.* New York: Columbia University Press, 1986.

Beidler, Philip D. *Scriptures for a Generation: What We Were Reading in the '60s.* Athens: University of Georgia Press, 1995.

Berg, A. Scott. *Goldwyn.* New York: Knopf, 1989.

Bluem, A. William. *Documentary in American Television.* New York: Hastings House, 1965.

Blum, John Morton. *V Was for Victory.* New York: Harcourt Brace Jovanovich, 1976.

Boettcher, Thomas D. *First Call: The Making of the Modern U.S. Military, 1945–53.* New York: Little, Brown, 1992.

Bogdanovich, Peter. *John Ford.* Berkeley and Los Angeles: University of California Press, 1978.

Bonn, Thomas L. *Undercover: An Illustrated History of Mass Market Paperbacks.* New York: Penguin Books, 1982.

——. *Heavy Traffic and High Culture.* Carbondale: Southern Illinois University Press, 1989.

Bordman, Gerald. *American Operetta.* New York: Oxford University Press, 1981.

——. *American Musical Comedy.* New York: Oxford University Press, 1982.

Bosworth, Patricia. *Montgomery Clift.* New York: Harcourt Brace Jovanovich, 1978.

Brustein, Norman. Review of *Catch-22. New Republic,* November 13, 1961, 11–13.

Buitenhuis, Peter. "Prelude to War: The Interventionist Propaganda of Archibald MacLeish, Robert E. Sherwood, and John Steinbeck." *Canadian Review of American Studies* 26, no. 1 (winter 1996): 1–30.

Callow, Simon. *Charles Laughton: A Difficult Actor.* London: Methuen, 1978.

Caputo, Philip. *A Rumor of War.* New York: Holt, Rinehart and Winston, 1977.

Coffin, Rachel, ed. *New York Theatre Critics' Reviews.* April 11, 1949, 312–13.

Comment on *Mister Roberts* (novel). *Publishers Weekly,* August 17, 1946, 687–88.

Crowther, Bosley. Review of *The Caine Mutiny* (film). *New York Times,* June 25, 1954, 12.

——. Review of *The Young Lions* (film). *New York Times*, April 3, 1958, 23.

Davis, Kenneth C. *Two-Bit Culture: The Paperbacking of America*. Boston: Houghton Mifflin, 1984.

Deighton, Len. *Blood, Tears and Folly: In the Darkest Hour of the Second World War*. London: Jonathan Cape, 1993.

Dempsey, David. Review of *From Here to Eternity*. *New York Times Book Review*, February 25, 1951, 5.

DeVoto, Bernard. Review of *Victory at Sea* (documentary). *Harper's*, June 1954, 8–13.

Didion, Joan. *The White Album*. New York: Simon and Schuster, 1979; New York: Pocket Books, 1979.

Dooley, Roger. *From Scarface to Scarlett: American Films in the 1930s*. New York: Harcourt Brace Jovanovich, 1979.

Dower, John. *War Without Mercy*. New York: Pantheon, 1986.

Durden, Charles. *No Bugles, No Drums*. New York: Viking, 1976.

Eller, Jonathan. "Catching a Market: The Publishing History of *Catch-22*." In *Prospects*, vol. 17. New York: Cambridge University Press, 1992.

Ellis, John. *The Sharp End: The Fighting Man in World War II*. New York: Scribner's, 1980.

Elson, Robert T. *Time, Inc.: The Intimate History of a Publishing Enterprise*. Vols. 1 (1923–41) and 2 (1941–60). New York: Atheneum, 1968.

Engelhardt, Tom. *The End of Victory Culture*. New York: Basic Books, 1995.

Epstein, Lawrence J. *Samuel Goldwyn*. Boston: Twayne, 1981.

Feingold, Michael. "Heat-Seeking Bomb." *Village Voice* 36, no. 17 (April 17–23, 1991): 91.

Ferencz, George J. *Robert Russell Bennett: A Bio-Bibliography*. New York: Greenwood Press, 1990.

Fiedler, Leslie. "Dead-End Werther: The Bum as American Culture Hero." In *Collected Essays of Leslie Fiedler*, vol. 2. New York: Stein and Day, 1971.

Fonda, Henry, and Howard Teichmann. *My Life*. New York: Signet, 1982.

Freedland, Michael. *The Goldwyn Touch*. London: Harrap, 1986.

Friedan, Betty. *The Feminine Mystique*. New York: Norton, 1963.

Fussell, Paul. *The Great War and Modern Memory*. New York: Oxford University Press, 1975.

——. *Wartime: Understanding and Behavior in the Second World War*. New York: Oxford University Press, 1989.

——. *Doing Battle: The Making of a Skeptic*. Boston: Little, Brown, 1996.

Gallagher, Tag. *John Ford: The Man and His Films*. Berkeley and Los Angeles: University of California Press, 1986.

Garland, Brock. *War Movies*. New York: Facts on File, 1987.

Garrett, George. *James Jones*. New York: Harcourt Brace Jovanovich, 1984.

Giles, James R. *Irwin Shaw*. New York: Twayne, 1983.

—— and J. Michael Lennon, eds. *The James Jones Reader*. New York: Birch Lane Press, 1991.

Goulden, Joseph C. *The Best Years: 1945–50*. New York: Atheneum, 1976.

Gussow, Mel. *Don't Say Yes Until I Finish Talking: A Biography of Darryl F. Zanuck.* Garden City, N.Y.: Doubleday, 1971.

Harmetz, Aljean. *Round Up the Usual Suspects.* New York: Hyperion, 1992.

Hasford, Gustav. *The Short-Timers.* New York: Harper and Row, 1979.

Hastings, Max. *Overlord: D-Day and the Battle for Normandy.* London: M. Joseph, 1984.

Heggen, Thomas. *Mister Roberts.* Boston: Houghton Mifflin, 1946.

―― and Joshua Logan. *Mister Roberts.* New York: Dramatists Play Service, 1948.

Heidenry, John. *Theirs Was the Kingdom: Lila and DeWitt Wallace and the Story of the "Reader's Digest."* New York: Norton, 1993.

Heller, Joseph. *Catch-22.* New York: Simon and Schuster, 1961.

Henry, Buck. "A Diary of Planes, Pilots, and Pratfalls." *Life,* June 12, 1970, 46, 48.

Jason, Philip K. "Vietnam War Themes in Korean War Fiction." *South Atlantic Review* 61, no. 1 (winter 1996): 109–21.

Johnson, Paul. *Modern Times.* New York: Harper and Row, 1983.

Jones, James. *From Here to Eternity.* New York: Scribner's, 1951.

――. *WWII.* New York: Grosset and Dunlap, 1975.

Kammen, Michael. *Mystic Chords of Memory: The Transformation of Tradition in American Culture.* New York: Knopf, 1991.

Kantor, MacKinlay. *Glory for Me.* New York: Coward-McCann, 1945.

Kazin, Alfred. *Bright Book of Life: American Novelists and Storytellers from Hemingway to Mailer.* New York: Delta, 1973.

Kotsilibas-Davis, James, and Myrna Loy. *Myrna Loy: Being and Becoming.* New York: Knopf, 1987.

Langman, Larry, and Ed Borg. *Encyclopedia of American War Films.* New York: Garland, 1989.

Laufe, Abe. *Broadway's Greatest Musicals.* New York: Funk and Wagnalls, 1973.

Leggett, John. *Ross and Tom: Two American Tragedies.* New York: Simon and Schuster, 1974.

Levy, Emanuel. *John Wayne: Prophet of the American Way of Life.* Metuchen, N.J.: Scarecrow Press, 1988.

Lingeman, Richard R. *Don't You Know There's a War On? The American Home Front, 1941–45.* New York: Putnam, 1970.

Logan, Joshua. *Josh: My Up and Down, In and Out Life.* New York: Delacorte, 1976.

MacShane, Frank. *Into Eternity: The Life of James Jones, American Writer.* Boston: Houghton-Mifflin, 1985.

Madsen, Axel. *William Wyler.* New York: Crowell, 1973.

Mailer, Norman. *The Naked and the Dead.* New York: Rinehart, 1948.

――. *Advertisements for Myself.* New York: Putnam, 1959.

――. *Cannibals and Christians.* New York: Dial Press, 1966.

Manso, Peter. *Mailer.* New York: Simon and Schuster, 1984.

Marling, Karal Ann, and John Wetenhall. *Iwo Jima: Monuments, Memories, and the American Hero.* Cambridge: Harvard University Press, 1991.

Mauldin, Bill. *Up Front.* New York: Holt, 1945.

McGhee, Richard D. *John Wayne: Actor, Artist, Hero.* Jefferson, N.C.: McFarland, 1990.

Meserve, Walter J. *Robert E. Sherwood: Reluctant Moralist.* New York: Pegasus, 1970.

Michener, James A. *Tales of the South Pacific.* New York: Macmillan, 1947.

————. *The World Is My Home.* New York: Random House, 1992.

Miller, Douglas T., and Marion Nowak. *The Fifties: The Way We Really Were.* Garden City, N.Y.: Doubleday, 1977.

Mills, Hillary. *Mailer: A Biography.* New York: Empire Books, 1982.

Mitchell, Burroughs. *The Education of an Editor.* New York: Doubleday, 1980.

Monaco, James. *The Connoisseur's Guide to the Movies.* New York: Facts on File, 1985.

Murrells, Joseph. *Million Selling Records.* London: Botsford, 1984.

O'Neill, William L. *American High: The Years of Confidence, 1945–1960.* New York: Free Press, 1986.

————. *A Democracy at War: America's Fight at Home and Abroad in World War II.* New York: Free Press, 1993.

Parish, James R. *The Great Combat Pictures: Twentieth-Century Warfare on the Screen.* Metuchen, N.J.: Scarecrow Press, 1990.

Patterson, James T. *Grand Expectations: The United States, 1945–74.* New York: Oxford University Press, 1996.

Perret, Geoffrey. *A Dream of Greatness: The American People, 1945–63.* New York: Coward, McCann, and Geoghegan, 1979.

Pfitzer, Gregory M. *Samuel Eliot Morison's Historical World.* Boston: Northeastern University Press, 1991.

Review of *Mister Roberts* (film). *Variety,* June 9, 1954.

Review of *Mister Roberts* (novel). *New Yorker,* August 24, 1946, 70.

Roberts, Allen, and Max Goldstein. *Henry Fonda: A Biography.* Jefferson, N.C.: McFarland, 1984.

Rodgers, Richard. *Musical Stages: An Autobiography.* New York: Random House, 1975.

Rollyson, Carl. *The Lives of Norman Mailer.* New York: Paragon House, 1991.

Roth, Robert. *Sand in the Wind.* Boston: Little, Brown, 1973.

Rubin, Joan Shelley. *The Making of a Middlebrow Culture.* Chapel Hill: University of North Carolina Press, 1992.

Ryan, Cornelius. *The Longest Day: June 6, 1944.* New York: Simon and Schuster, 1959. Reprint, New York: Touchstone, 1994. (Page citations are to first edition.)

————. "The Longest Day." Fiftieth anniversary condensation. *Reader's Digest,* June 1994, 180–217.

Salomon, Henry, with Richard Hanser. *Victory at Sea.* Garden City, N.Y.: Doubleday, 1959.

Sanjak, Russell. *From Print to Plastic: Publishing and Promoting America's Popular Music (1900–1980).* Brooklyn: I.S.A.M. Monographs, 1983.

Shaw, Irwin. *The Young Lions.* New York: Random House, 1948.

Shnayerson, Michael. *Irwin Shaw.* New York: Putnam, 1989.

Shuman, R. Baird. *Robert E. Sherwood.* New York: Twayne, 1964.

Spoto, Donald. *Stanley Kramer: Film Maker.* New York: Putnam's, 1978.

The Stars and Stripes Story of World War II. New York: McKay, 1960.

Stone, Robert. "'Miss Saigon' Flirts with Art and Reality." *New York Times*, April 7, 1991, sec. 2, p. 30.

Suid, Lawrence H. *Guts and Glory: Great American War Movies*. Reading, Mass.: Addison-Wesley, 1978.

Swanberg, W. A. *Luce and His Empire*. New York: Scribner's, 1972.

Tebbel, John. *Between Covers: The Rise and Transformation of Book Publishing in America*. New York: Oxford University Press, 1987.

Thezge, Chuck. "'I See Everything Twice': An Examination of *Catch-22*." *Film Quarterly* 24, no. 1 (fall 1970): 7–17.

Thomas, Tony. *The Films of Henry Fonda*. Secaucus, N.J.: Citadel Press, 1983.

Time, Inc. *This Fabulous Century: 1940–50*. Vol. 5. New York: Time-Life, 1969.

——. *Life's Picture History of World War II*. New York: Time, 1950.

Uris, Leon. *Battle Cry*. New York: Putnam, 1953.

Wainwright, Loudon. *The Great American Magazine: An Inside History of "Life."* New York: Knopf, 1986.

Walker, Martin. *The Cold War*. New York: Holt, 1994.

Ward, Geoffrey C. Review of *Victory at Sea*, *The March of Time*, and *The World at War* (video editions). *American Heritage* 36, no. 6 (October-November 1985): 14–16.

Weaver, Pat, with Thomas M. Coffey. *The Best Seat in the House: The Golden Years of Radio and Television*. New York: Knopf, 1994.

Webb, James. *Fields of Fire*. Englewood Cliffs, N.J.: Prentice-Hall, 1978.

Weiler, A. H. Review of *Mister Roberts* (film). *New York Times*, July 15, 1955, 14.

Weinberg, Gerhard L. *A World at Arms*. New York: Cambridge University Press, 1994.

Wetta, Frank J., and Stephen J. Curley. *Celluloid Wars: A Guide to Film and the American Experience of War*. New York: Greenwood Press, 1992.

Whitfield, Stephen J. *The Culture of the Cold War*. Baltimore: Johns Hopkins University Press, 1991.

Wills, Garry. *John Wayne's America: The Politics of Celebrity*. New York: Simon and Schuster, 1997.

Wouk, Herman. *The Caine Mutiny*. Garden City, N.Y.: Doubleday, 1951. Illustrated ed., Garden City, N.Y.: Doubleday, 1954. (Page numbers are to the first edition.)

Yank: The G.I. Story of the War. New York: Duell, Sloan and Pearce, 1947.

Zinnemann, Fred. "From Here to Eternity." *Sight and Sound* 51, no. 1 (winter 1987): 20–25.

INDEX

Academy Awards, 18, 29, 40, 125, 128
Adams, M. Clay, 80
Adams, Michael, 3
Adler, Buddy, 126
Agar, John, 64
Agee, James, 29
Albert, Eddie, 160
Aldridge, John, 89, 96, 107, 109, 194 (n. 8)
Allen, Fred, 134, 135
Amussen, Ted, 100
Anderegg, Michael, 27
Andrews, Dana, 18, 24
Anhalt, Edwin, 113
Anka, Paul, 160
Annakin, Ken, 160
Arkin, Alan, 4, 166, 167–68
Atlas, James, 99

Back to the Future, 170
Balaban, Bob, 166
Balsam, Martin, 166
Bankhead, Tallulah, 199 (n. 37)
Barrault, Jean-Louis, 160
Battle Cry (film), 65, 87, 93, 115, 140–41, 147–49, 177 (n. 11)
Baudrillard, Jean, 169
Bazin, Andre, 27
Bell, Raymond, 126
Bell for Adano, A (film), 90
Benjamin, Richard, 166
Bennett, Murray, and Joan Allison: Everyone Comes to Rick's, 11, 175 (n. 6)
Bennett, Robert Russell, 77, 81–82, 83, 84
Berg, Scott, 104
Best Years of Our Lives, The, 7, 14, 17–30, 177 (n. 19)
Beymer, Richard, 160
Bogart, Humphrey, 4, 87, 131, 138–39

Book-of-the-Month Club, 35, 120, 134–35, 192 (n. 1), 203 (n. 63)
Bourke-White, Margaret, 67
Bradley, John, 59, 63
Brando, Marlon, 86, 110, 113
Braunstein, Jacques, 112
Brazzi, Rossano, 44, 54
Breslow, Sy, 97–98
Britt, Mai, 86, 113–14
Brooks, Mel: The Producers, 180 (n. 36)
Brown, Harry: A Walk in the Sun, 89, 90, 100, 176 (n. 8), 183 (n. 55)
Bryant, Samuel Hanks, 36
Burton, Richard, 160
Butler, Ivan, 29
Buttons, Red, 160

Caesar, Sid, 199 (n. 39)
Cagney, James, 40
Caine Mutiny, The (film), 4, 87, 88, 93, 115, 129, 130–32, 177 (n. 11)
Capa, Robert, 70
Carmichael, Hoagy, 18, 25, 26
Carreras, Jose, 55
Casablanca, 11, 175–76 (n. 6)
Catch-22 (film), 4, 150–51, 152, 162, 165–68, 169
Cerf, Bennett, 112, 114
Churchill, Winston, 74, 187 (n. 80)
Clark, Mark, 158
Clift, Montgomery, 86, 87, 114, 198 (n. 28), 201 (n. 50)
Coca, Imogene, 199 (n. 39)
Cohn, Harry, 125–26, 127–28, 201 (n. 50)
Connery, Sean, 160
Cota, Norm, 162
Coward, Noel, 158
Cozzens, James Gould: Guard of Honor, 193 (n. 4)

Crowe, Henry ("Jim"), 63, 148
Crowther, Bosley, 131–32, 199 (n. 35)
cummings, e.e.: *The Enormous Room*, 200 (n. 45)
Cutter, Slade, 204 (n. 67)

Davis, Robert Gorham, 97
Demick, Irina, 157, 160
Dempsey, David, 102–3, 116
Devlin, Charles, 100
DeVoto, Bernard, 68, 82, 100
Didion, Joan, 128
Dmytryk, Edward, 86, 87, 113, 193 (n. 2)
Dos Passos, John, 72, 101, 186–87 (n. 76)
Douglas, Kirk, 62
Dower, John, 45, 180 (n. 36)
Dr. No, 160
Durden, Charles: *No Bugles, No Drums*, 168

Eisenhower, Dwight, 158, 183 (n. 54)
Emerson, Ralph Waldo, 101
Engelhardt, Tom, 7, 90, 174 (n. 6)
Ensign Pulver, 41, 179 (n. 30)

Fabian, 160
Fechteler, William M., 204 (n. 67)
Feingold, Michael, 56
Fell, Norman, 166
Ferrer, José, 4, 87, 138
Ferrer, Mel, 160
Fiedler, Leslie, 200 (n. 46)
Fonda, Henry, 4, 5, 31–32, 37–40, 42, 43–44, 129–30, 131, 160, 178 (n. 20), 179 (nn. 27, 30), 198 (nn. 28, 34), 202 (nn. 53, 54), 207 (n. 15)
Ford, John, 40, 179 (n. 27)
Forrestal, James, 57–58
Francis, Robert, 139
Fribourg, Leonard, 63, 184 (n. 58)
Friedan, Betty: *The Feminine Mystique*, 7
Frobe, Gert, 160
From Here to Eternity (film), 86–87, 88, 93, 115, 116, 117, 125, 130, 177 (n. 11)
Fussell, Paul, viii, 151, 169, 171; *Wartime*, 169, 173 (n. 3), 178 (n. 22); *Doing Battle*, 169, 173, (n. 3)

Gagnon, Rene, 59, 63
Garfield, John, 104
Garfunkel, Art, 166
Garrett, George, 124–25
Gary, Romain, 157, 207 (n. 10)
Gavin, James, 158, 160
Gaynor, Mitzi, 44, 54
Geismar, Maxwell, 102
Giles, James R., 108–9, 110
Gilford, Jack, 166
Goldwyn, Frances, 104
Goldwyn, Samuel, 17, 18–20, 22–23, 29, 30, 104, 176 (n. 9)
Grainger, Edmund, 61, 183 (n. 55)
Graves, Leonard, 77, 82, 83, 84
Gregory, Paul, 106
Grodin, Charles, 166
Gwaltney, Fig, 101, 105

Hall, Juanita, 52, 181 (n. 45)
Halls of Montezuma, 142
Hammerstein, Oscar, 44, 45, 48
Handy, Lowney, 118–19, 200 (n. 42), 201 (n. 50)
Hansen, Henry, 58, 182 (n. 50)
Hanser, Richard, 77, 80, 83
Hayes, Ira, 59, 63, 182 (n. 49)
Hecht, Harold, 104–6
Heflin, Van, 87, 141
Heggen, Thomas, 178 (nn. 20, 24), 178–79 (n. 26); *Mister Roberts*, 4, 31, 32–36, 89, 129, 198 (n. 29)
Heggen, Thomas, and Joshua Logan: *Mister Roberts* (play), 4, 14, 31–32, 36–37, 38–39, 129, 179 (n. 26)
Heinemann, Larry: *Paco's Story*, 177 (n. 15)
Heller, Joseph, 164–65, 171; *Catch-22*, 4, 107, 150, 151, 152, 162–65, 168–69, 176 (n. 11), 197 (n. 26), 205 (n. 72); "Catch-18," 163–64
Hellmann, Lillian, 20, 103

Hemingway, Ernest, 113, 193–94 (n. 4), 197 (n. 25); *Across the River and into the Trees*, 193 (n. 4); *The Sun Also Rises*, 200 (n. 45)

Henry, Buck, 166, 167–68

Hersey, John: *A Bell for Adano*, 89, 90, 100, 176 (n. 8)

Heyward, Leland, 31, 48

Hitler, Adolf: *Mein Kampf*, 175 (n. 5)

Hogan's Heroes, 16, 180 (n. 36), 188 (n. 87)

Hooker, Richard: *M*A*S*H*, 151

Howard, Sidney, 20

Howarth, David, 155

Hunter, Jeffrey, 160

Hunter, Tab, 87, 141

Hupfield, Herman: "As Time Goes By," 11, 175–76 (n. 6)

Johnson, Chandler, 59

Johnson, Van, 87, 131, 138–39

Jones, James, 32, 86, 88, 126, 128, 141, 157, 158, 161, 207 (n. 10); *From Here to Eternity*, 6, 15, 86, 88, 90, 92, 93, 109, 112, 115–16, 117, 118–25, 128, 132, 135, 163, 177 (n. 11), 192 (n. 1), 193–94 (n. 4); *WWII*, 30, 199 (n. 36); *They Shall Inherit the Laughter*, 118, 199–200 (n. 41), 200 (n. 42); *The Thin Red Line*, 199 (n. 36); *Whistle*, 199 (n. 36); *Go to the Widow-Maker*, 199 (n. 36); *The Pistol*, 199 (n. 36); *Some Came Running*, 199 (n. 36), 199–200 (n. 41)

Jurgens, Curt, 160

Kammen, Michael, 170, 174 (n. 5)

Kantor, McKinlay, 18–19; *Glory for Me*, 18, 19–24

Kazin, Alfred, 96–97, 169, 195 (n. 14)

Kerr, Deborah, 87, 125

Kleinerman, Isaac, 80

Knox, Mickey, 104, 105, 106

Koenig, Marie Pierre, 158

Kramer, Stanley, 138, 140, 204 (n. 67)

Kuhnhardt, Philip B., 75

Lancaster, Burt, 87, 104, 105, 125

Lange, Hope, 86, 114

Laughton, Charles, 106, 129–30, 202 (nn. 53, 54)

Lawford, Peter, 160

Lawrence of Arabia, 160

Lazar, Swifty, 112

Lean, David, 160

Leggett, John, 32, 33–35

Lehmann-Haupt, Christopher, 115

Lemmon, Jack, 40, 42–43, 179 (n. 30)

LeRoy, Mervyn, 40

Levy, Raoul, 156

Life, 66–71, 185 (nn. 67, 68), 186 (n. 71)

Life Goes to War, 67

Life's Picture History of World War II, 14, 65–76, 190 (n. 96)

Life's WWII, 75

Limon, John, 170

Lindberg, Chuck, 58, 182 (n. 50)

Literary Guild, 35, 134–35, 192 (n. 1)

Logan, Joshua, 31–32, 36–37, 38–39, 40, 48, 178 (nn. 20, 24), 178–79 (n. 26)

Longest Day, The (film), 113, 114, 150–51, 152, 155–61

Lord, Robert, 112

Lovat, Lord, 158

Lowery, Lou, 58

Loy, Myrna, 7, 18, 24, 25, 177 (n. 8)

Lubell, Adeline, 100

Luce, Henry, 66, 69, 71, 74–75, 90, 122, 153, 175 (n. 4), 185 (n. 69), 185–86 (n. 70), 186 (n. 74), 187 (n. 80)

MacMurray, Fred, 87, 131, 138–39

Mailer, Norman, 86, 87, 141, 208 (n. 19); *The Naked and the Dead*, 4, 6, 15, 86, 87, 90, 92, 93, 94–106, 107, 109, 112, 115, 119, 120, 132, 163, 177 (n. 11), 192 (n. 1), 193 (n. 3), 193–94 (n. 4), 198 (n. 31), 199 (nn. 37, 38), 204 (n. 66); *Barbary Shore*, 103, 105, 106; "The White Negro," 106; *The Deer Park*, 106; *The Armies of the Night*, 107; *An American Dream*, 107;

Mailer, Norman (cont'd.), *Why Are We in Vietnam?*, 107; *Harlot's Ghost*, 107; *Advertisements for Myself*, 194 (n. 9)
Malaquais, Jean, 104
Malone, Dorothy, 86, 87, 106, 141
Manges, Horace, 119
March, Fredric, 18, 24–25
Martin, Dean, 86, 110, 114
Martin, Mary, 44, 51–52, 181 (n. 43)
Marton, Andrew, 160
M*A*S*H, 151
Massey, Raymond, 86, 87, 106, 107
Mauldin, Bill, 9, 124
Mayo, Virginia, 18, 25
McCormick, Myron, 52
McCormick, Robert, 175 (n. 3)
McDowell, Roddy, 160
McHale's Navy, 16, 188 (n. 87)
McKenna, Kenneth, 48
Melville, Herman: *Billy Budd*, 101, 133–34, 203 (n. 60); *Moby-Dick*, 133, 135, 196 (n. 16), 203 (n. 60)
Michaels, Jim, 58, 182 (n. 50)
Michener, James, 182 (n. 48), 206 (n. 5); *Tales of the South Pacific*, 6, 44, 46–49, 55, 89, 129, 178 (n. 19), 179 (n. 26)
Mielzener, Jo, 48, 179 (n. 26)
Mills, Hillary, 97, 103, 105–6
Mineo, Sal, 160
Miss Saigon, 56, 175 (n. 1)
Mister Roberts (film), 4, 14, 31, 39–43, 131, 139, 140
Mitchell, Burroughs, 119
Mitchum, Robert, 160, 162
More, Kenneth, 160
Morison, Samuel Eliot, 77–78, 80–81
Morris, Howard, 199 (n. 39)
Mountbatten, Lord Louis, 158–59

Naked and the Dead, The (film), 4, 86, 87, 93, 94–95, 106–7, 115, 177 (n. 11), 205 (n. 70)
National Book Award, 120
New American Library, 112, 120, 163, 192 (n. 1)

Newhart, Bob, 5, 166
Nichols, Mike, 166, 167–68
Nietzsche, Friedrich, 101
Nolan, Lloyd, 4, 130, 202 (n. 54)
Norstad, Lauris, 158–59, 207 (n. 11)
Nuyen, France, 181 (n. 45)

O'Brien, Edmond, 160
O'Donnell, Cathy, 25
Office of War Information (OWI), 9, 175 (n. 2)

Parks, Lewis, 202 (n. 55)
Patinkin, Mandy, 55
Perkins, Anthony, 166
Perkins, Maxwell, 118–19, 200 (n. 42)
Pinza, Ezio, 44, 51–52
Powell, William, 25, 40
Prentiss, Paula, 166
Prescott, Orville, 102
Pulitzer Prize, 44, 135, 138, 193 (n. 4)
Puller, Chesty, 65, 147
Pursall, David, 158
Pynchon, Thomas: *Gravity's Rainbow*, 151, 169, 177 (n. 11)

Ray, Aldo, 4, 86, 87, 106, 107, 127, 141, 209 (n. 50)
Reader's Digest, 32, 35–36, 152–55, 156, 161, 187 (n. 84), 206 (n. 6), 206–7 (n. 9), 207 (n. 19)
Reader's Digest Condensed Books, 134, 154, 192 (n. 1)
Reed, Donna, 87, 125
Remarque, Erich Maria, 157–58, 207 (n. 10)
Rembar, Cy, 100, 104
Rinehart, Stanley, 100, 102
"Rip Van Winkle," 170
Roberts, Stanley, 204 (n. 67)
Robertson, Cliff, 4, 86, 106, 107
Rodgers, Richard, 44, 45, 48, 77, 81, 84, 188–89 (n. 90)
Rollyson, Karl, 98, 99, 104
Rooney, Mickey, 160

Rosenthal, Joe, 59, 61, 63, 186 (n. 72)
Rosten, Norman, 100
Ruge, Friedrich, 158
Russell, Harold, 18, 23, 24
Ryan, Cornelius, 153, 156–58; *The
    Longest Day*, 150, 152–55, 161–62;
    A Bridge Too Far, 161
Ryan, Robert, 160

Salomon, Henry, 77–78, 79–81, 83;
    Victory at Sea, 4, 14, 76–85, 140
St. Cyr, Lily, 4, 86, 106
Sands, Tommy, 160
Sands of Iwo Jima, 14, 56–65, 128, 148,
    149, 205 (n. 77)
Sarnoff, David, 80
Sarnoff, Robert, 80
Schell, Maximilian, 86, 113–14
Schoenbrun, David, 113
Schrier, Harold, 58–59, 63, 102 (n. 50)
Scott, George C., 161
Scribner, Charles, 119
Seddon, Jack, 158
Segal, George, 160
Selznick, David, 198 (n. 33)
Shaw, Irwin, 86, 88, 104, 108, 135, 141, 194
    (n. 4), 203 (n. 59); *The Young Lions*,
    6, 15, 86, 88, 90, 92, 93, 95, 104–13,
    114–15, 119, 132, 163, 177 (n. 11), 192
    (n. 1), 193 (n. 3), 195–96 (n. 15), 199
    (n. 38), 203 (n. 59), 204 (n. 66); *The
    Troubled Air*, 198 (n. 33)
Sheen, Martin, 166
Sherrod, Robert, 72
Sherwood, Robert, 18, 22–24, 177 (n. 7)
Shnayerson, Michael, 112
Shoup, David, 63, 148
Silverman, Beatrice, 98, 99, 196 (n. 18)
Sinatra, Frank, 87, 114, 125
Slaughterhouse Five (film), 151
Smith, Holland M., 57–58, 63, 182
    (n. 49)
Smith, W. Eugene, 70
Sound of Music, The, 180 (n. 36)
South Pacific (film), 14, 44, 53–55, 140

South Pacific (musical play), 14, 44, 45,
    46, 48–52, 53, 129, 178 (n. 19), 178–79
    (n. 26)
South Pacific (soundtrack recordings),
    44, 52–53, 55–56, 179 (n. 26)
Spoto, Donald, 139–40
Stegner, Wallace, 33
Steiger, Rod, 160
Steiner, Max, 176 (n. 6)
Stone, Robert, 56
Strock, George, 70
Suid, Lawrence, 140

Taradash, Daniel, 125, 126, 127, 193 (n. 2)
Te Kanawa, Kiri, 56
Terkel, Studs, 1
Thomas, Ivy, 58, 182 (n. 50)
Time, 17–19
Todd, Richard, 160
Tozzi, Giorgio, 54
Trumbo, Dalton, 193 (n. 2), 201 (n. 48)
Tryon, Tom, 160

Uris, Leon, 86, 89; *Battle Cry*, 6–7, 15, 87,
    89, 90, 92–93, 109, 115, 132, 140–47,
    163, 177 (n. 11), 192 (n. 1), 196 (n. 15);
    Exodus, 164; *Mila 18*, 164

Vaughn, Sarah, 55
Victors, The, 113, 114
Victory at Sea, 4, 82–84
Vidor, King, 198–99 (n. 34)
Voight, Jon, 166
Vonnegut, Kurt, 115, 170; *Slaughterhouse
    Five*, 151, 169, 177 (n. 11), 197 (n. 25)

Wagner, Robert, 160
Walk in the Sun, A (film), 90
Wallace, Dewitt, 153, 206 (n. 6), 207
    (n. 11)
Wallace, Lila Atcheson, 134
Walsh, Raoul, 86, 87, 148, 193 (n. 2)
Walston, Ray, 54
Wayne, David, 38
Wayne, John, 14, 56, 61, 62–65, 160

Wayne, John (*cont'd.*), 182 (n. 51), 184
    (nn. 58, 61), 207 (n. 15), 208 (n. 29)
Weaver, Pat, 78, 81, 188–89 (n. 90)
Welles, Orson, 166
Welsh, Mary, 194 (n. 4), 197 (n. 24)
Weybright, Victor, 112, 198 (n. 32)
Whitmore, James, 141
Wicki, Bernhard, 160
Widmark, Richard, 142
Williams, Elmo, 157
Wills, Garry, 61, 184 (n. 61)
Wizard of Oz (film), 10–11
Wolfe, Thomas, 118, 199 (n. 40)
World War II, 75
Wouk, Herman, 86, 88, 141; *The Caine
    Mutiny*, 4, 6–7, 15, 87, 88, 90, 92, 93,
    109, 115, 129–30, 132–38, 177 (n. 11),
192 (n. 1), 195–96 (n. 15), 198 (n. 31);
    The Caine Mutiny Court-Martial, 4,
    88–89, 129–30, 131, 132, 202 (nn. 53,
    54); *Aurora Dawn*, 134, 203 (n. 63);
    The City Boy, 134, 203 (n. 63)
Wright, Teresa, 7, 18, 24
Wyler, William, 17, 18, 22–24, 177 (n. 17)

Young Lions, The (film), 86, 88, 93, 110,
    111, 112–14, 115, 177 (n. 11), 205 (n. 70)
Your Show of Shows, 199 (n. 39)

Zanuck, Darryl F., 155–61, 207 (n. 13),
    207 (n. 16)
Zanuck, Richard, 156
Zinnemann, Fred, 86, 125, 126, 127, 128,
    193 (n. 2), 201 (nn. 48, 49, 50)